# MRS. OGG
# PLAYED
# THE HARP

## MEMORIES OF
## CHURCH AND LOVE
## IN THE HIGH DESERT

ELAINE GREENSMITH JORDAN

TWO HARBORS PRESS, MINNEAPOLIS

Two Harbors Press
212 3rd Avenue North, Suite 290
Minneapolis, MN 55401
612.455.2293
www.TwoHarborsPress.com

ISBN-13: 978-1-938690-20-4
LCCN: 2012945207

Distributed by Itasca Books

Cover Design by Kristeen Ott
Typeset by Mary Nelson

Back cover photo credit: Leota Hoover

*Printed in the United States of America*

# MRS. OGG
# PLAYED
# THE HARP

**Elaine Greensmith Jordan**
**310 Morning Glow Circle**
**Prescott, AZ 86303**
928-778-4066

egjordan@cableone.net          www.elainejordan.com

Mary Frances Ogg Plays the Harp

Excerpts from *Mrs. Ogg Played the Harp* have been published in essay form in the following:


*The Georgetown Review* (Spring, 2005 and Spring, 2008)
*Passages* (Vol. 13, 2006)
*Dreamseeker Magazine* (Vol. 6, Autumn, 2006)
*Building Bridges from Writers to Readers*, San Francisco Writers Conference Anthology (2006)
*South Loop Review* (Vol. 9, 2006)
*Underwired* (August, 2007)
*Fresh Ink* (Vol. IX, 2007)
*Apocalypse Literary Anthology* (Spring, 2007)
*Cup of Comfort Anthology* (2008, 2009)
*Alligator Juniper Literary Journal* (2008)
*Arizona Literary Magazine* (2008)
*Bayou Magazine* (Winter, 2008)
*American Journal of Nursing* (Dec. 2009)
*Damselfly Press* (Spring, 2009)
Wordworth.com (January, 2010)
*Lady Jane's Miscellany* (Summer, 2010)
FertileSource.com (February, 2011)

The author's proceeds from the sale of this book will be donated to the Prescott Area Woman's Shelter, Prescott, Arizona.

For Arizona

its land

its ghosts

its wanderers

and its gods

# TABLE OF CONTENTS

# FIRST WORDS

This memoir is an account of a stranger whom I didn't know until I began to write about her. I hid memories of being a Protestant minister because I was embarrassed by my choice to be a religious leader. A clerical image doesn't fit who I think I am, worldly and skeptical. Where did that church woman come from? Had I been taken over by a pious psyche from another dimension? Evidently not. There on my closet shelf is a box of typed sermons. Hanging beside them is a black robe. They are mine. This memoir is my way of embracing the stranger from my past.

The church members whose lives I've rendered here—without asking—deserve loads of gratitude for their love, expressed so often in laughter, kind attention, and patience. I hope they know I loved them back. While disguising and blending a few of them in order to protect the ones still living, I've tried to capture their richness and place them truthfully in our real little church. The details of church life have been altered, but our conversations ring in my head still, and I've tired to keep to the truth as I lived it. This is my myth. I anticipate arguments from some of the people I recreated or from those left out. I beg them to remember the admonition: "Condemn not, and you will not be condemned; forgive, and you will be forgiven" (Luke 6:37). It was a lesson I had to learn.

Help has come from everywhere, and I want to acknowledge the spirit of encouragement and emotional support that has flowed liberally from the hearts of Janer Eldridge, Cheryl Berry, Leslie Quenichet, Elizabeth Starling, Stuart Mattson, Barbara and John Cundiff, Naydene Eckles, Paul and Martha Strickland, Jeanette Porter, Gene Fougner, and my husband, Don Jordan. Connie and

Speed Leas read an early draft and said they liked it—a glorious inspiration.

I want to mention, too, the advice of skilled readers. My editors were Kate Robinson, Maureen VanWalleghan, Becky Byrkit, and a talented critique group of Arizona writers: Colette Ward, Ben Bakke, Carole Bolinski, Lee Reeves, Abbey Carpenter, and Vicky Young. We were led by the incomparable Leota Hoover, who snapped the photos, monitored this project for years and helped me accept the truth in my heart.

Joe Ludlow and Margaret Root, my children, have taught me forgiveness beyond measure. They never laughed at me (that I could see) and graciously accepted their school-teaching/line-dancing/play-acting/book-reading/Sunday-preaching mother. That supportive assent made it possible for me to think I could do this project.

In a note to me from Melissa Fay Greene, a fine author of nonfiction, she writes, "It seemed obvious to me that one simply writes the best and most accurately one can, in order to try to trick a bit of life into the pages." I felt that need to trick a time and place into life.

The quotations at the beginning of each chapter are from my sermons—except for the last one.

*It takes a wholly different view of God to accept a woman in the pulpit. If God is King and Lord, Father Almighty, then his minister should be a person who looks like that—a commanding male authority. But, you do things bit by bit. I followed my love of books and a need to search out meaning and mystery. So here I am—in the soup.*

## A Day of Reformation

## ONE

This story ends with a dead mouse in the bottom of a bucket of green paint, but it begins on an Arizona highway in a white Buick. I was on my way from California where I'd meet a congregation of Christians in need of a minister.

I'd heard no words from God urging me forward. No still, small voice told me I had the gifts or talent to be a Christian minister. No holy utterance from the thunder either—not much thunder in San Diego. I went because I needed to make this trip into a new life. Along the way I silently questioned whether I was qualified. A woman, for God's sake.

We moved north at moderate speed on a narrow highway. My husband, John, drove the white rental Buick while I focused on the view. Bold, confident clouds observed our car, a white dot climbing into shadowed Arizona canyonlands. In the distance, high mesas, eerie, empty. On the hillsides, six-foot saguaro cacti waved us on. No buildings. No billboards. No gas stations. Green highway signs announced, "Black Canyon City" and "Bloody Basin." This landscape was emptiness itself to California eyes. A person could get lost up here, especially me, a person often lost in unfamiliar settings.

John and I—and the Buick—headed to an Arizona settlement called Dewey and an Arizona church I'd never seen. President George Herbert Walker Bush contemplated battles in Kuwait, and the car radio blared opinions. I turned them off. We were driving away from crises, and I needed distancing. If I sound anxious, I was that, but also thrilled by possibility. At fifty-four it was time for me to go away from home. I had reasons.

"Can't believe you'd consider coming here," John growled. Aviator sunglasses made him look like a CIA operative as he gazed around taking the measure of the land. A lean man of sixty with pale blue eyes, he drove with ease, his wide shoulders relaxed beside my tense body.

I gazed out, mused, and wondered. This Arizona high country took me into childhood and Western movies with rugged heroes and happy endings—broad skies, cattle smells, and dirt roads leading to weathered ranches. This was Tom Mix country. Zane Grey had lived near this area. All of it inspired bravery. I needed a wagonload of bravery.

"You wanted to see this too," I said. "Maybe it'll be wonderful."

"Wonderful? I doubt it. Look around you." John sighed, his deep voice touching buried fear in me like a stone hitting a pond—fear of failing, of being exposed as a playacting fake who wasn't the virtuous person a minister should be. Performing was a passion of mine and now it was time to play at being a gracious church leader. How much I'd be acting, and how much I'd be authentic I had no idea.

The members of Faith United Church, somewhere ahead of us, were poised to offer me an opportunity to serve as their first full-time minister—probably because no competent male would accept their offer of a low salary without benefits. This weekend visit would give them a chance to hear me preach, and I'd take a look at them, the church, and the territory to see if I could live far from the beaches and flowers of San Diego. With firm ties there, I'm not sure why I didn't stay put in California. All I knew was I was excited to be taking a chance to lead a church in Arizona. What drove me was not a rental Buick. It was an energy some might say came from God, but I'll never know if I was led by a Great Spirit; in fact, that's what I'd spend the next years pondering. Was it a woman's thing, to struggle with motives, reasons, and purpose? The men I knew in ministry certainly didn't seem so concerned.

Though I wanted to be a religious leader, I didn't believe that God controlled my life, that God caused my pain or joy. How God involves Himself—or Herself—in human life was a question I couldn't answer. My desire to work in a church was more about learning how people interpret a holy presence in their lives. If I was missing something, I wanted to know about it.

I'd thought of going to Arizona without John. The reason wasn't complicated: he'd had an affair with his secretary. We hadn't separated, but I couldn't stop thinking about a betrayal that left me feeling vulnerable, toppled by headaches. Though I repressed anger, I felt estranged from him and nursed an abiding worry that I wasn't lovable. With this call to a church, I'd get returns from a grateful congregation, assurances that I was a warm person with the love of God in my heart. I needed those affirmations. I wasn't sure I needed my husband.

"Let's check out the church first," I said. The church should have creaky wood floors, a steeple, and a smiling congregation ready to welcome me as its first full-time minister.

Ranch country unfurled outside. A long row of mismatched fence posts leaned drunkenly along the road. *Horses Boarded* a sign read.

"Boarded horses," I muttered.

"Bored horses, did you say?"

"Just drive."

We passed a sixty-foot column standing above the remnants of a mine. "That's a phallic comment on this place," John said.

"You can't have a phallic comment. Comments can't be phallic." I sounded like a former English teacher with a headache, which I was.

"I knew that." John's mellow voice lowered my anxiety but I worried he'd offend the church people with his ironic humor. I should've come alone.

Opening the car window a crack, I felt the icy January air wash my face. Colder here than San Diego.

"We must be getting closer," I said and sneezed. Dear God, don't let me be allergic to Dewey. "Look, it says 'Prescott Twenty Miles.'"

Prescott, Arizona, up ahead, was a thriving cowboy town with a street of saloons called Whisky Row. I'd researched the storied place and had photos. Their rodeos and colorful bars suited my fantasy of the Wild West adapted from a television show, *Dr. Quinn, Medicine Woman.* I was "Reverend Elaine, Spirit Woman." I'm given to fantasies like that. As a child I once chose to dress as a nurse for Halloween, an early example of my need to be a handmaiden. The vision of my twelve-year-old self dressed in a white nurse's outfit wandering in the dark is not a bad metaphor for my venture into the unknown perils of northern Arizona.

Dressing the part of minister gave me energy and announced my credibility. The black clerical robe with stainless white collar— packed away in the backseat—represented the ideals and wisdom I'd chosen to embody. It also hid my anxiety, along with a motherly bosom.

"I can't see a bit of smog," I said. "Everything's so vacant, so untouched."

"Don't you notice the smell? I'd say that's horseshit."

"I like it, reminds me of the movies." We passed Olsen's Feed Store surrounded by pickups like horses at a trough.

"No smog. No cars. No civilization. Just horseshit." John coughed, as if choked by Western dust.

"The Mattsons said four o'clock. We've got time to see the church." A church in the wildwood, a symbol of kindness in a frontier outpost. It had to have a minister's office with a view of the Arizona mountains touched with those marvelous clouds. Dewey would be a picturesque village—though I'd have preferred a better name, like Piney Woods.

"They mentioned a country club. Would golfers be living around here?"

"Golfers live everywhere."

When I began my studies in religion, John opposed my leaving high school teaching and going to seminary. He didn't want a clergy wife. Men objected to uppity women who took men's roles back then. I went anyway. When I completed my studies, I accepted a job as associate minister in a San Diego church near our home. I assumed John had made peace with my being a minister. I had a lot to learn.

I'd taken on a typical woman's role in the church—assistant to a man—and for five years weighty church matters were left to senior clergy while I tended to the children's programs and discussion groups. If I took the Arizona pulpit waiting up ahead, I'd step up and play a major role on my own. John was not pleased, but I was excited by the risk. Besides, his love affair with his secretary meant he didn't get a vote.

A flutter of color from an American flag appeared behind some juniper trees. "Stop! I see a flag. Turn at that post office."

"A flag. A flag. God bless America." He pulled over. "Go see if the federal government knows where Dewey is."

Hugging myself in the January cold, I hurried to the modest building next to a trailer with a scrawled sign "Videos for Rent." The large woman in the two-room office told me to watch for Young's Farm up the road. The church ought to be on our left, a mile beyond the barn.

We passed the Blue Hills Market, a humble store with a fuel pump a few feet from the door. A fat man leaned against the outside wall, a Stetson pulled down over his eyes and a pistol tucked into his belt. The sight startled me. Where am I? A gun? He could be a desperado too drunk to walk.

"Something about this place I like," John said.

"Okay. Okay."

An image of the leaning man stayed with me. What had this untried minister done? She'd made a promise to a congregation to preach a sermon and ask for a position as full-time minister in the badlands. Was she crazy?

Young's Farm and Petting Zoo sat back from the road, a cluster of sleepy farm buildings in an expanse of ordered lands. The fields lay in combed patterns; the barn looked authentic, and a giant willow bent over the complex. Their sign on the highway noted that fresh corn was for sale in the summer. More pleasant than Stetson man with a gun.

We found no village called Dewey, no town hub or main street, only a green sign at an intersection. *Settlement* was the best word for it.

Then the sign appeared, "Prescott Country Club." We turned left on a wide paved street and drove into a neighborhood of homes surrounding golf links.

"I think I see the church up there," I said. "Or, I think it's a church. Doesn't look like somebody's house. It has a pyramid on top. Oh—my—God."

"Watch the language, padre."

This was not the conventional village church I'd pictured. Unlike any other building in the country club neighborhood, the square structure had wood and stone walls in red and brown earth tones and a pointed roof topped by a splash of colored-glass inserts. A single rose bush provided the landscaping.

The building and grounds looked cared for. I got an impression of solidity, originality, and a spare beauty. This church was the unique creation of an adventurous Western architect, and I wondered what it would look like inside. The church door was locked. No cars went by. No voices called out.

I pressed my face to a window. Peering through windows is a preoccupation of mine. That day I saw only darkness. Our steps around the building crunched the gravel of the parking area, disturbing the winter stillness. I wasn't disappointed with the church, so different from what I expected, but it was unsettling to have stepped onto rocky ground surrounding an enclosed mystery.

The odd-shaped, non-traditional church would work for a non-traditional ministerial candidate like this Californian. I was as unconventional as you could get—liberal, free-thinking, and female. The unusual church building, with no masculine steeple, looked like me.

You might say it was foolhardy to go to Arizona that January day. I'd traded my friends and city for self-discovery and loneliness, but the trade-off seemed easy at the time, and thrilling. When we don't know what's ahead on a rural road, we go forward. Moving on, we call it, moving on.

Faith United Church, Dewey Arizona

"Why is the golf course brown?" I asked the middle-aged couple I'll call the Mattsons who were driving us around the Prescott Country Club. The links looked thirsty. Didn't golfers require a green of some sort?

"This is winter!" answered Stan Mattson from the front seat. He glanced at Sandra, his wife, and probably rolled his eyes. "The greens come to life in early April."

John and I observed from the backseat of a gigantic Oldsmobile as we toured the pastel desert homes surrounding the bleak golf course. This neighborhood was the centerpiece of Dewey—if you don't count Olsen's Feed Store and the Blue Hills Market. We were moving through a golfing community set in a bleak landscape made for roaming wild horses.

This placid, silent district with its little church would be my territory if we moved here, and I started to imagine what it might be like to lead a church where a golf course sits at the center of its life. What would Jesus say about this place? He'd shake the dust from his sandals and proceed to Whisky Row where he'd serve the homeless and minister to the lonely.

Our host couple was full of confidence and energy. Stan had a wide smooth face, a cocky youthful air, and a bald spot that made him look monkish from the back. Sandra wore casual sports clothes and turquoise earrings I learned were favorites of the Dewey golfing women. Our travel clothes—my white wool suit and gold hoop earrings, John's gray business suit—didn't fit the rural setting. I'd have been better off in jeans.

"Elaine's been sheltered," John said. "Doesn't understand a real January winter, I'm afraid. She's never lived outside sunny California." Not since her graduate school days in Berkeley, had she lived this far away from Southern California.

John's words let me know I was far from orange trees, marinas, and bougainvillea. I felt loss—and a serious headache. At the same time, it was pleasant to be in a community with well-tended avenues of sedate homes. No reminders of divorce, of raising a difficult daughter, of teaching in a city ghetto. No reminders here in Dewey of betrayal, other than the man sitting next to me.

I couldn't wait to get inside the church building. What would that desert sanctuary look like? Would this conventional couple with their Oldsmobile accept a woman minister? They could be hiding conservative views about Christianity and female clergy. My finding any job in a Christian church had been difficult, so I suspected everyone was hiding bias against women ministers. My San Diego job as assistant minister had been available only because the former male assistant minister had seduced several women in the congregation, and he had to be replaced in a hurry.

"You need to understand," Stan said, "why we Midwesterners are living here." His voice sounded too loud, and I noticed his hearing aid. "We love the constant sunshine even on a winter day like this." He turned the car onto a street called Manzanita Trail, driving with the pace and dignity of a man who owned the place. "We get snow, but it stays only a couple of days."

"Snow," John said. "Haven't seen snow in quite a while."

I couldn't imagine how I'd take to snow covering the bristly cactus, falling in front of my window. A white-out of painful memories sounded restful. I thought of Snow White, the innocent girl fleeing wickedness into a forest.

"Do you play golf?" Sandra asked.

Did I play golf? Would that matter? "No, never learned to play."

I changed the subject to questions about the church. Did they have a committee working on problems like poverty in the area? No, but that sounded interesting. Who leads the congregation now? A retired minister, Rev. Strickland, part-time. Do they have a music program? A choir of twelve volunteers sings every Sunday, and Mrs. Mary Frances Ogg plays the electric organ. Is the Sunday attendance good? Oh yes! Our fifty-two members come every Sunday unless they have an early tee time. Is there a secretary or maintenance person? No. Volunteers do everything.

Sobered by those honest answers, I imagined myself in the Mattson's distinctive church—a building with an attitude. It could work. Yet, the members were no doubt prosperous folk who'd come to Dewey to enjoy a mild winter and golf. How would the words of Jesus matter here? Did anyone need religious comfort? I glanced over at John, his eyes behind his dark glasses, and wondered what he was thinking.

I'd come to Arizona at the end of the 1980s. Those years were considered selfish times, called the era of the "me-generation" as reflected in President and Nancy Reagan. Poet Adrienne Rich wrote of that period:

> …we lost track of the meaning of we. . .
> The great dark birds of history screamed and plunged
> into our personal weather, through the rags of fog,
> where we stood, saying *I*.

This was when the "Death of God," as *Time Magazine* put it, was a popular idea, but I'd gone into seminary intrigued by the richness of religious traditions and the rewards of church life. Death of

God? For me God had not died but was hidden, a Wizard of Oz. I'd left teaching to study sacred literature, church history, and the psychology of religion as a way to move toward that mystery. I had to put my boots on the ground, as we said about the war in the Gulf, and learn if God might be revealed in the life of a church.

Later I realized that, like Snow White, I was also hoping for safety in a time when I felt wounded. I needed to leave San Diego to recreate my life. Although that motive wasn't clear to me at the time, I know now that I put myself in Arizona because I hoped for loving acceptance. Inside my heart was a child wanting praise and affirmation.

Questions from the Mattsons in the front seat would no doubt come soon. They'd want to explore my thinking about Christianity and Jesus. While I served in Jesus' name and thought of him as a model of goodness, I rejected the idea that he was a risen son of God who walked on water. Instead, Jesus was a wise counselor like Harvey, the six-foot rabbit—a comic character in a play—who looked on and commented on the action. I'd have to make sure this little church was ready for me and Harvey. I had no intention of hiding my religious perspective, as if telling my truth was easy. It turned out not to be easy at all.

"The new Safeway center," Sandra said, "has really made shopping easy. I'm sure—"

"We've a Sprouse-Reitz dime store," Stan interrupted in his booming voice, "and a post office handy. The highway's never a problem." He drove the middle of the narrow road, John watching in amusement. "No traffic, and we're only twenty minutes from Prescott where we can get anything we need. Hospital's there too. Good one. Board-certified staff."

"Stan's a retired gynecologist," Sandra said.

I swallowed. Gynecologists practiced the black arts as far as I was concerned. "Got a pool you can use at the club," Stan bellowed.

"Great. I love to swim. When do I meet the church council?"

"Tonight!" Sandra turned around and grinned at us, her large teeth gleaming—dark eyes, age-spotted skin, a prominent nose. She could have been a member of my family. "I mean the search committee is meeting at our house for dinner to meet you. The Council *is* the search committee and vice versa. We have to double up around here. Should be a friendly interview."

That evening eight of us gathered in the Mattson's Country Club home where John and I would spend the night. Their living room was a more formal place than you'd expect in Arizona ranch country. The upholstered furniture, thick draperies, and English prints must have come from the Mattson's life in the Midwest before retirement. The jovial guests—church council members—in sport clothes looked more fit than John and me. They knew each other well and were, of course, golf partners, but they tried not to talk about golf over wine and cheese, attempting subjects that might include two Californians from the big city.

I suspected I'd invaded a nest of Republicans who might find me too liberal, but I recognized their competence and wisdom as if they'd lived, like my parents, through Depression years and now enjoyed prosperity. I felt comfortable among them. Why would these prosperous folk feel they wanted the expense of a full-time minister, I wondered. Their lives seemed easy and their needs minimal, yet they were enthusiastic about their church and wanted it to thrive. It would take some time before I could fathom the more subtle religious yearnings of this genial group.

Fragrant dishes of baked chicken, green beans, and hot rolls appeared in a spacious yellow and white kitchen. We helped ourselves at the counter and took our plates to a long table in a dining alcove with windows offering views of a street lined with leafless elms. Dr. Mattson spoke words of prayer, addressing God as if the deity were his buddy, and we ate the generous meal talking easily about church matters. Because these diners might become the focus of my new life, every face seemed larger than normal. Sandra Mattson's skinny torso leaned over her plate toward me, interrupting every chance she got.

I'd been taught that ministers should "comfort the afflicted" and "afflict the comfortable." I was sitting among the comfortable. Even though I made assumptions about their politics and their history, I didn't really know their concerns or their personal stories.

As that scene unfolds in memory, I realize how readily I profiled those strangers and their white, middle-aged faces.

Throughout dinner, no one asked about my view of Jesus Christ, a subject, one would think, might be mentioned in a ministerial interview. But religious questions didn't concern the people sitting at Sandra's table with crystal stemware on a flowered tablecloth. The council members were judging whether I was an agreeable person who could join them in creating a successful church. We knew what that meant—a happy congregation, inspiring Sunday services, generous members, chances to serve the community. Jesus didn't come into it, and I let the matter alone. The diners asked about my two adopted children, now grown to adulthood. Stan asked about my health. They also spoke fondly of their former part-time minister, the Reverend David Thomas, whom they adored: "He never used any notes when he preached." Oh dear.

A woman with a serious demeanor asked John, "Would you be able to leave employment to come here with your wife? We didn't get much information about your job status, Mr. Greensmith."

John hesitated, looking uncomfortable, and then explained that he worked for a real estate company, in advertising, but could retire in a few months. He didn't mention that he despised his job and missed his former work as a news photographer. The group listened, eager for John's news, as if they found his history riveting. My headache peaked, and I wanted to ask if he missed the woman he slept with in San Diego.

Stan of the thundering voice broke in, "Elaine—if I can call you that." I gave him a reassuring smile. "We've got the best darn church in the valley here. You'd be nuts to turn us down."

We laughed and my husband set his spoon in his dessert dish, glancing at me as if to say he approved of this friendly group. "Let me make this decision," I signaled silently. I had until after tomorrow's church service to determine whether I wanted to move to Arizona and become a full-time minister in a small church beyond the beyond.

The guests left by seven-thirty, a habit of busy retirees I learned. Sandra Mattson's voice followed me down the hall to our bedroom. "You have a good rest now, Pastor."

I couldn't wait to lie down, though my persistent headache would prevent any tranquil sleep. Instead, I worried about the distant land of Arizona, the precarious state of my marriage, my ability to lead. It didn't occur to me that it would be Jesus Christ who gave my ministry the most trouble in the days to come. And what about that sainted Reverend Thomas who didn't use notes when he preached?

The next morning—inside the church at last—I was pleased to see an interior suited to the landscape outside: natural wood, stonework, and touches of terra-cotta red, an Arizona color. In the front of the sanctuary, on rough stone, a modest wooden cross hung over a blond oak altar incised with the words "This Do In Remembrance Of Me." Plain Protestant beauty, stunning in its simplicity.

Enjoying the scent of brewing coffee from the church kitchen, I admired sunlight pouring through faceted glass set high in the walls as Mrs. Ogg, the organist, began a prelude, "Ode to Joy," with a spirited energy as if celebrating all of God's creation. This welcoming atmosphere differed from an Oregon church with a musty basement where I'd been interviewed by people eager for a new minister. I rejected Oregon. I wanted sunny Arizona. I wanted this church. My head was not so sure; it vibrated with a painful doubt I didn't understand until I began to review those days for this memoir.

Dr. Mattson and I proceeded together down a center aisle of the small sanctuary suited to a congregation of no more than a hundred people. We followed the choir of twelve singing "Holy Holy Holy," a familiar hymn about the "Lord God Almighty." I joined in the singing. Hymns have power over me. They anchor me emotionally to the church whether the music is tender or bombastic. Forget the prayers and pronouncements and give me choirs, bells, and a pipe organ. Let me sing until I find the feelings that send me into hope.

Sacred places have always fascinated me, though when I was a child my immigrant parents had no use for churches. They came to America with families who wanted to escape heavy-handed European Catholicism, so I was protected from the tentacles of religion. The attitude of my parents let me know that religious folk were a bit dotty, so my fascination with churches had to be kept quiet. My Austrian mother preferred to gather the neighbor children on Sundays and tell us fables of a princess with virtues she hoped my sister and I would emulate. Then Mother would give us candy as a reward. I liked the stories and the candy, but both were presented in an uninspired setting, our living room.

In the attractive Dewey church of wood and stone, seated in the raised area under the cross, I wore the black robe with white collar I'd brought along. The congregation of sixty expectant people looked familiar, like neighbors from my childhood. They resembled their matching houses: tidy, white, middle-aged, hair permed and combed, voices respectful. Some were dressed in golfing outfits, others in Sunday suits and dresses. They'd been informed about my qualifications—and my gender—and I appreciated their friendly smiles. I wanted this church.

Suddenly I was surprised to spot a familiar face, all red beard and freckles. A minister I'd studied with in seminary grinned from the front row. He'd been raised in a small town nearby and somehow learned of my candidacy in Dewey. Reverend Gil Bisjak brought a comforting face into this Arizona church as if he'd been sent as escort. My headache faded.

As I think now about that headache, I was not so much under stress about open country and golfers as I feared assuming the role of a virtuous person capable of unconditional love. I wanted to be such a person but felt selfish and inadequate. My feelings of unworthiness manifested in that headache. I could pretend to be virtuous for a while, but I really hoped that within the shelter of the church I'd become worthy.

Dr. Mattson, standing at the lectern, began the service with, "We are pleased to have with us this morning our candidate for our first full-time minister here at Faith United Church. We of the search committee have been working for a year and we're confident we have the right person." I felt like an astronaut with the right stuff, having landed on the moon. "No cause for alarm," Mattson added, "but in a previous life, she was an English teacher." I smiled. Laughter. Reverend Bisjak winked.

After a meditative hymn and a prayer from Mattson, I stepped into the pulpit—wishing I could speak without a manuscript like the Reverend Thomas before me—and began a sermon:

There are so many ways to see Jesus, so many ways to interpret the gospel accounts of his life. For the orthodox Christian, Jesus was born of the Virgin Mary and is the Son of God. For them, Jesus' baptism—when the dove appeared in the heavens and God spoke of his beloved son—is proof of Jesus' divinity. . .

But there are Christians of *other kinds*, and I want to explore with you this morning some other ways Christians interpret the greatest life ever lived. . .

Elaine at pulpit
If I'd been reciting the Mad Hatter's "Twinkle Twinkle Little Bat"

few would have noticed. Their focus was on the sight of a woman instead of a man in the pulpit—a rare sight in 1989 when many were horrified at the idea of women leading churches. They must have thought the real quarterback had gone missing and a female was passing the football.

> Those who differ from the orthodox say that Jesus was *not* the Son of God but a Nazarene carpenter chosen to be God's man. The book and film *The Last Temptation of Christ* presented that interpretation and caused an enormous fuss among church-going Christians…

A woman I'd met at dinner, whom I'll call Janet Godfrey, turned to her husband and registered disapproval of that Temptation movie. With her firm mouth, wavy gray hair brushed back from her face, and plain dress, she looked dedicated to simplicity and hard work. Would she accept Snow White as her minister? I made a silent pledge to charm her.

> This *carpenter* Jesus is like a prophet come to teach us how to live in new ways. He's not divine…
>
> I'll bet we find both kinds of believers here today. On the one hand are those who take as fact the divinity of Jesus who now sits at the right hand of God the Father…
>
> On the other hand some believers belong to the Carpenter Camp: those who believe that Jesus stood a man among men, chosen by God to change the world. This Jesus is not God, but God's man…

On stage and having fun, I felt confident I could reach the congregation. The sermon was truthful. If it was rejected, I'd know I didn't fit in Arizona. Sandra Mattson gave a toothy smile that animated me even more. The final words went to her:

> Both kinds of believers agree that Jesus came to make the "crooked straight and the rough places plain…"
>
> However you see Jesus, in the last analysis,

people have been profoundly changed by the
forgiveness he taught—for ourselves, for others,
and for the world.

Forgiveness. Speaking that word didn't help me forgive John for a
love affair that hurt so much. My pain was a firm part of me and
I clutched self-pity to my breast like a frightened child holding a
security blanket. It was easier to preach about forgiving than to
make it real in my life. The gentle, wise minister I personified was
a creation separate from the fallible human being who stood at the
pulpit wrapped in clerical robes.

Mrs. Ogg's confident music ended the service with a hymn
of upbeat assurances: "Joyful, joyful we adore thee, God of glory,
Lord of love." The music seemed to settle my spirit. I soon learned
that the tiny robed figure at the organ, Mary Frances Ogg, was the
church angel who could work transforming magic every Sunday.

Then, standing next to the minimal church kitchen—revealed
behind a sliding screen at the back—I shook hands with the
congregation, watching them watch me as we drank decaf coffee,
a disappointing beverage to a preacher with a headache.

Afterward, John and I waited outside while the congregation
held a meeting and took a vote on new leadership. In minutes they
presented a *call*—the term used to mean job offer—and I accepted,
letting myself be dropped like a potato—live lobster?—into a hot
Arizona soup. Being chosen by a people's vote delighted me. I
wanted this church and now believed they wanted me too.

We said our thanks and good-byes, climbed into the neutral
comforts of the rental Buick and began the drive down to the
desert floor and Sky Harbor Airport in Phoenix to return to San
Diego. Three months later my ministry in Arizona would begin. It
would be April and green.


I've been fascinated by churches since I was a youngster. Other
kids were intrigued by derelict houses, wanting to peek in their
windows and see something frightening, but I longed to peek into
churches where I might see something holy. The Mission Archangel,
an eighteenth century landmark in our California neighborhood,

enchanted me.

I pressed my eight-year-old nose to the window of our black Ford as we drove to the market one summer afternoon. "What's going on in there? Is it a hotel for church people?" I asked Mother as I stared at the mission and outbuildings dominating a large part of San Gabriel, the Los Angeles suburb where we lived. You couldn't see much of the mission buildings from the street because of the high walls.

"No. It's a church and an old farm," Mother answered. "The Indians made the mission for the priests when they came here a long time ago. You've asked me this before, you know."

"Why did the priests come here?" I persisted, ignoring Mother's dismissal of my question. Her rimless eyeglasses and short dark hair gave her a no-nonsense appearance that made you think carefully before bothering her with questions. She preferred my younger sister, Connie, who sat silently in the backseat.

"Well, the priests came from Spain to, let's see, give the Indians religion." Mother's hands gripped the steering wheel, and she concentrated on the road. "I'm told they have a baptismal font from the King of Spain," she added. I thought about that mysterious font but didn't have the courage to ask for more explanations.

A curved high wall, featuring niches for six bells of different sizes, rose above the massive doors of the mission church. You had to look up to see the bells. I wished I could go through the doors to see the king's font. Inside you'd be protected from the guns and bombs of the World War thundering in Europe. Our family talked of war all the time because Mother's sister and my young cousin Uta were trapped in an Austrian basement on the enemy side. Bombs were destroying their city. Thoughts of World War frightened me, and I had frequent asthma attacks, fighting to breathe like a child hiding in a suffocating bomb shelter.

One summer Saturday, Mother took our troop of Brownie Scouts into the mission precincts, stopping at the gift shop where she paid a fee. I was the tallest in a group of seven wearing brown uniform dresses falling above scabby knees. Stitched above the right-hand pocket was the name we chose for our troop, "Butterflies." On the way inside, I posed in front of the window glass, admiring my long brown hair that Mother kept curled.

The mission gift shop sparkled like a Christmas place. A smell of rotting flowers made my nose itch, but no one mentioned the odor. The shop visitors were respectful and murmured like guests at a funeral. Two candles in frosted glasses decorated with saintly pictures burned on the long glass counter next to a small plastic crucifix. A pale Jesus hung on the cross, dead. Blood drained in lovely streaks over his face. I reached for him but a clerk in a gray hairnet frowned at me and I pulled back my hand. She took a cloth and rubbed where I'd touched the cold glass surface.

When we heard the warm sound of a tolling bell, we moved outdoors where our feet echoed on the stone floor as we passed a courtyard of dusty weeds and a central well made of stone. Indians drank from that well.

Inside the cavernous candle-lit mission church I stared at Jesus hanging on the cross and the painted statue of Mary with her blue drape. A pulpit stood high above my head, and to the side was a baptismal font. I'd never visited such a place before. The captivating mission with its statues, smells, and echoes was better than any movie I'd ever seen.

You could forget the war, the bombs, and submarines hiding in the Pacific while you stood in that mission because God was in that old church redolent of candles and toiling Indians. I could almost hear voices intoning chants like those I'd heard at the Episcopal Church when I'd gone to services with our neighbors. "I believe," they intoned. "I believe in God, the Father Almighty, maker of heaven and earth and of all things visible and invisible." The strange words made no sense to me, but I repeated with everyone "Born of the Virgin Mary…crucified, dead, and buried" and felt comforted by the sounds, which seemed to bring absolution for being a child Mother criticized for flaws in my character.

Back in Arizona, we settled ourselves on the plane taking us to San Diego. I asked John, "Did you notice the coffee tasted a little weak? They love their decaf. I need caffeine. Helps the headache."

Cramped by the minimal space of the cabin, John tried to get comfortable in his seat. "Maybe they don't need stimulation. Maybe they need soothing. Suits me today. How's the head?"

"You'll excuse me if I throw up." The ache across my scalp felt permanent. "Thanks for supporting me in the process. Those people liked you."

"I liked them too," he said and tilted his head in a compliant way, as if wanting my affection and sympathy, but I couldn't reach out to him. If I hugged anything it was my own wounded self.

I nursed my headache thinking of the hypocrisy built into the task of leading churches—all the words I couldn't speak, all the insincere smiles needed from God's minister. I'd worked churches long enough to know that people expected ministers to be exceptional, kindly, and virtuous. It would be like being on stage constantly. I thought of a note I'd received from Nancy Hernandez, a Sunday school youngster in San Diego: "Dear Mrs. Greensmith, you are the best priest I ever met! Keep on doing good deeds!" How could I back away after encouragement like that? Nancy was my nine-year-old personal angel. Her support reminded me of my grandmother's kindly words. Grandma held me in her lap, called me pretty, and marveled at my accomplishments. She'd have applauded my first Arizona sermon.

Three years of study in a seminary didn't make me a conventional Christian. My studies helped me search for a spiritual center, but I'd not emerged a true believer, more like a true questioner. The Brownie Scout who longed to take hold of bloody Jesus on the cross was alive inside me, but I couldn't accept a theology built around a risen Jesus—a resurrected savior god. Such a narrative never could be true as I understood the world and the history I'd studied. How a life in the church could work for a questioner like me would have to be revealed as I made my way far from civilization.

"Do your think you want to move with me to Arizona?" I said to John and took off my glasses. "I should leave San Diego by early April." I felt competent saying that, making plans, moving ahead.

"I can't make April, but I can be there by May, I think. You know I've always hankered to photograph rodeos." John's photos of horses won honors, and he showed them in a Del Mar gallery near the race track. "Prescott claims to have the world's oldest rodeo."

"You'll have to give me time to, well, work on how I feel," I said in a soft voice. I imagined a month alone in Arizona, time to experience what it felt like to be separated from him.

John tilted his backrest and closed his eyes.

The plane ascended into the skies over Phoenix, and I raised the plastic window cover. I caught my reflection in the window glass: a dark-eyed woman with short brown hair—resembling my grandmother—looked back at me, curious, as if she wandered the skies searching for something.

Down below were shiny puddles of swimming pools and green patches of golf links. Arizona felt so small compared to the infinite land of California. I'd just promised to put myself into a miniature community where I'd know every face and be known. The Mattsons' good will, the mood of acceptance around their dining table, and Mrs. Ogg's confident touch at the organ in a unique sanctuary inspired courage for the journey. It pleased me to be away from hurtful memories in a place where I could close my hands around what I needed.

It wasn't necessary, I hoped, to have perfect Christian beliefs in order to preach a message of forgiveness, love, and morality. I'd grow into deeper Christian faith beside the believers in the congregation. We'd sing and pray together until I caught up. They were not a group with unified belief, of course, though they called themselves "Faith United." What mattered to them was a congenial, trouble-free church life. I could give them that. We Brownies have the innocence of butterflies.

Next spring I'd see Whisky Row, absorb the atmosphere of ranch country and taste the fresh corn at Young's Farm. This Western-movie adventure was moving me closer to a dream I'd had since childhood—to get inside a church and stay there. My headache reminded me it might not be that easy.

Taking two aspirin out of the tiny bottle in my purse, I swallowed them without benefit of water, wondering if I could be a priest to busy golfers who drink decaf. In snow? Near a menacing man with a gun? I wanted to try. Standing with me, I hoped, was a six-foot imaginary rabbit ready to lend a paw.

*Perhaps we are not as much in command of the way things go as we like to think....It's really a world of mystery. Can we even prepare for big surprises? "It's like the rake, the old rake in the grass, the one you step on, foot to forehead," writes one of my favorite poets.*

## A Parable of Lonely Silences

## TWO

"Here's our new pastor!" Sandra Mattson said in a piercing voice that could vibrate the cross on the church wall. "We're having a potluck dinner. Come join us!" When I stepped inside the church, she dashed to my side, took me by her cold bony hand, and seated me at a table. "Have some of Martha's marinated carrots!"

People smiled and continued eating. Marinated carrots? Wasn't there supposed to be a fanfare for the arrival of a new minister, a Spirit Woman at that?

I'd left San Diego and everything I knew, including my husband—who'd join me in a month—and driven by myself to Dewey, arriving at the Prescott Country Club as the sun set in an April sky, all pink and turquoise. No one was home at the assigned residence where I'd gone first, hoping to rest, but a note on the door directed me to a potluck at the church and into the hands of Sandra Mattson.

After the eight-hour drive in a car stacked with luggage, my brown hair hung straight from the dry air, my bones hurt, and my glasses were smudged—though I'd no sign of a headache. Pearl ear studs provided the only jolly touch to my appearance. I didn't feel like an astronaut or a quarterback. I was a weary traveler in a yellow shirt and gray slacks who felt like a foster child set down among strangers who expected her to be good. She was pleased with herself for her daring and wanted a little applause, damnit!

Curious faces at the tables watched me. Someone said, "I wish she'd known Reverend Thomas. Never used any notes." Saint Thomas again. The comment made me all too aware that I was not a man and would need to prove myself. I felt assaulted and in a sour mood but pretended to be pleased with food, church, and the pot-luck diners. Experience in acting had its benefits.

Later that week the Mattsons helped me carry my boxes into a sliver of an office at the church. Studying the small room with a more discriminating eye than before, I noted that though it had a desk, bookcase, and window, the only high-tech machine was a telephone. Part of me thrilled to the challenge. The other part worried. How did the sainted Reverend Thomas manage to produce printed programs for Sunday services? Elves?

Determined to make this work, I decided to turn the empty office into a comfortable nest worthy of a warm-hearted minister. I placed photos of my children and a small glass bluebird on the big clumsy desk. In the top drawer I tucked a wine-colored notebook of previous sermons and a vintage fountain pen my son had given me. I shelved four books I'd brought with me: a revised translation of the Bible, *Women in the Life of Jesus, What the Bible Really Says,* and the recently published *All I Really Need to Know I Learned in Kindergarten.* John would bring the rest of my collection with him next month, including a treasured book of children's literature. My clerical robe and stoles—long liturgical scarves—went in the closet. At last, pleased with the assortment of decorative crosses on the wall, I decided I could work in what I now called a snug office.

In the following weeks, the church members offered smiles and support, but they were also scrutinizing. Trying not to put a curse on Reverend Thomas's head, I preached from prepared manuscripts, using a biblical text and unpacking it until it led me into an idea. I preached about the Christian gift of love in the face of pain, loss, and heartache, about forgiveness and hope, using stories from my life as mother and teacher as well as episodes from children's stories, movies, and my favorite books.

My thinking was influenced by my membership in the liberal United Church of Christ denomination that had grown since the seventeenth century in the American colonies. Those pilgrim churches had evolved into a progressive organization of people who'd marched for the abolition of slavery, for the rights of women, justice for minorities. I preached from that perspective, though I had to be guarded or I'd hear criticism like the recent comment that I loved God more than the American flag. I had to hold back on matters like the pacifism of Jesus or welcoming people into the church regardless of sexual orientation. I thought I could become more forthcoming over time if I used my talent as a speaker. Looking back, I find that innocence amazing.

The music of Mary Frances Ogg—the fine church organist I'd admired in January—worked a soothing magic on all of us, and only occasionally did I get unwanted tips on how to do my work. The feeling of being a forsaken child in a foreign place fell away.

On Sunday mornings we sang old familiar hymns, including "Onward Christian Soldiers" or, rather, the congregation belted out the hymn and I choked on the words "Marching as to war / With the cross of Jesus going on before." Hymns matter, and this militant piece needed to be retired. That would be my first innovation at the church: to eliminate sexist, militaristic music. With that change would come new thinking. We'd retire the songs of judgment and punishment and bring in justice and mercy.

As I think back on those early days in Arizona, I'm amused by how sure I was that I could change people's opinions and tastes. Why not enlighten the church members as I'd dictated to high school students? Spirit Woman had a lot to learn.

John joined me in the spring. I liked being on my own, but when he arrived I welcomed him to Arizona, glad to have his protective, funny spirit with me. John and I would attempt to love each other in our new world, but our relationship was as awkward as if we'd just met. I was too hurt to understand the discomfort he must have felt standing behind his minister wife—like Sarah Palin's husband standing in the shadows behind her while she takes the spotlight.

We bought a house on a hillside in the country club with lots of windows overlooking the golf course. Some called our home a "Halloween House" because of its orange shutters, unlike the understated houses around the golf course. Being set apart worked for me. Church congregations felt they owned their ministers and could call on them at any time, so a bit of distance was essential.

After enough time passed agreeably, the congregation held a formal afternoon service to install me as their minister. Members crowded into the church to witness my answers to a litany of questions asked by denominational leaders and I vowed to serve the congregation as pastor and teacher. I couldn't know much about the journey I'd begun that afternoon as I pledged to regard "all people with equal love and concern, exercise pastoral care and undertake to minister to the needs of all," but I was willing to accept the challenge.

The reception after the installation was held in our Halloween house. Older church members were driven up our steep driveway in a golf cart, four at a time, by a proud golfer. Everyone crowded our outside deck where we could see the links—now turned to flowing green—and admire its scattering of apple trees from days past when the area was an orchard. Having come from Southern California, I'd never seen flowering apple trees before. All things were made new, as the Bible says.

The church women wore pastels, a cluster of flowers as they served sweet desserts and poured pink punch floating with pink sherbet. Mrs. Ogg, church organist, brought a golden harp to the party, but noisy conversation and laughter overwhelmed the heavenly music she played in front of the fireplace. It seemed only I could hear it.

The usual decaf coffee was offered too. By now the constant presence of decaf amused me. It streamed in copious floods from "fountains of great waters," as the Bible says. In my opinion, it represented decaf attitudes in the church members. They spoke mostly of weather and gardens, golf scores or family, but they ignored more serious matters like battles over civil rights, a terrible war in Vietnam and the struggle for women's rights. Like lotus-eaters they avoided speaking of anything that seemed un-American. I felt that Christianity couldn't offer a response to the world's needs if we hid in a complacent decaf retreat. I wanted to be a minister who changed lotus-eaters into firebrands. As I look back on those ideals, I can see that I was more qualified to bring caffeine into the coffee than change people into my version of Christian.

It took some months for me to understand that the marches and protests of the recent past must have rocked the lives of these gray-haired church members. Just as they'd left cold winters, they chose to leave these struggles behind when they came to Arizona. Some had left difficult adult children who made radical choices. They needed retreat, and I had to meet them in their retirement away from chaos. They came to this quiet neighborhood to live in peace. Decaf worked for them.

John took photographs of the guests at the reception eating and talking and roaming the house and deck. His photos show people bending over the punchbowl, a tiny golf cart approaching up the drive, and Mrs. Ogg with her golden harp framed by the stones of the fireplace. He was comfortable at the party, and I wondered at the end of festivities—as people filed down our outside stairs—if I'd hear sarcasm from him about these mild-mannered decaf folk and their pink punch. But John made no cynical remarks.

I was installed, serenaded, and toasted; now I had to be a real full-time minister in a Christian church. No turning back after pledging in front of people. Fortified by marinated carrots and a golden harp, I embarked on a quest to find a path through this land of golf and decaf—without a copy machine—while turning over the question of my imperfect soul and my fitness for ministry as if fingering a chain of worry beads.

She came unannounced. A woman I'll call Bernice Miller climbed the stairs to our front door. She moved slowly, carrying a package. I was glad to see her and hoped she and I could talk, get to know each other. Bernice enjoyed the shocking sight of a woman in the pulpit while some women saw me as a witch woman in a Halloween house—though they politely smiled, deferring to their husband's decisions.

Bernice appeared that day in a flowered skirt and appliquéd jacket, different from what you saw on the local women with their sweat suits and golfing outfits. When she stepped inside, she handed John—recovering from illness—a tan box tied with a raffia bow. "I found these," she said in a soft voice, "in a shop in Prescott. Fred and I like to explore the antique stores from time to time."

We admired the unusual gift, a peculiar wooden chess set nestled in white tissue. Bitter looking knights and pawns. The moment was awkward.

"Thanks for thinking of me," John said, glancing down at our guest, a short woman. "Gets a little boring around here." He handed me the chess set. "I keep myself entertained watching the birds and following the mess in the Gulf on TV, but it'll be nice to have a try at chess—if I can teach Elaine."

Bernice smiled, silent.

John added, "Let me show you my photos of Fain Ranch. Caught some good ones of the antelope."

Bernice and John examined an open book of photos on the dining table. They talked in low voices, a tall balding man next to a short, round matron. Despite the contrast, they had similar artistic temperaments, except you'd never catch John wearing bright colors like Bernice. He preferred neutral shades that blend into the desert. Like her, though, he was taken by the look of things, the textures of the land and its shifting colors provided by clouds, winds, and storm.

While John and Bernice talked, I carried the chess pieces to the sofa near the fireplace at the other end of the living room, an open space with a speckled brown carpet that matched everyone's in the country club, yards of serviceable floor covering that seemed to unite us neighbors together.

I turned the chess queen over in my hand, feeling her complex angles and trying not to see a metaphor for a woman minister in this crabby chess piece. Did Bernice think the sharp-edged pieces represented the congregation? Even though I'd been properly installed and was accepted by the congregation with smiles, mostly, my foster child sense of not belonging returned often. In those early nineties, a woman minister was an oddity in the Wild West and I knew it.

Bernice backed away from John and bumped the kitchen counter. She looked over at me and laughed nervously. "Fred's waiting for me," she said. "Time to put the roast in." Glancing out of the window, she added, "You've got a great view up here," and hurried out. I followed her into the afternoon glow and we stopped on the deck to admire the sunset. A piney smell tickled my nose.

"How've you been?" I asked, hoping to learn more.

"Oh, we're fine, Reverend. Fred's been landscaping new property on Cinch Ring Road and I've been teaching watercolor in Prescott."

"I'll have to get over to their community theater," I said. "Prescott fascinates me. You're keeping busy, sounds like." I sneezed, surprised by the pungency in the air. Our heavy wind chime clanged bong-bong like a ship's bell, reminding me of the Pacific Ocean, far from Arizona high country.

"See you Sunday." Bernice started down the stairs, her floral skirt billowing around her. She'd keep her private thoughts concealed, "pondering them in her heart," like Mary, the mother of Jesus.

"Will you be at Council on Monday?" I called to her as she approached her car.

"No. Fred and I stay away from that part of things." Her answer felt like rejection, and I tried to ignore the feeling as I watched her drive away, the wheels of her maroon Cadillac snapping the gravel drive.

A penetrating smell of skunk now joined the pine, an Arizona perfume. Reluctant to return to my husband and the chess set, I stayed on the deck waiting for something—courage or faith, I suppose.

Why wouldn't Bernice confide in me? I had an easier time winning the confidence of alienated high school students than the church-going adults in Arizona. I wanted to feel of use to them but it was hard to wait for their trust. I wasn't pious enough, I thought, feeling a self-doubt that stayed with me like the skunk smell in the desert air.

In the earth below the deck were broken shards and hand-worked stones, tokens of former dwellings of native peoples who disappeared from their pueblos in the fourteenth century. We lived on borrowed—or stolen—property, and I felt an Arizona guilt we recent settlers shared. Those past inhabitants disclosed none of their private stories, like the reserved church people around me; all I could gather from them were shards dropped accidentally into my hands.

One evening John and I decided on dinner at the Riata Pass Steak House, a smoky restaurant with rough plank paneling that reeked of stale beer. Sounds of upbeat country music greeted us. The fat man with a gun we saw back in January leaning against the Blue Hills Market belonged at the Riata Pass but we didn't venture into the bar where he might be lurking.

My son, Joe, had enjoyed the Riata Pass when he visited. He liked the barbequed beans, the flirty waitresses in tight jeans, the cowboy hats tipping and turning around us. Joe, twenty-two and living in California, worked with computer programs and, of course, laughed at my low-tech office.

Finding our way to a table, I felt myself moving to the beat of the music and imagined being swept into the arms of some handsome cowboy and running away with him, a familiar fantasy of leaving husband and church and all the unknowns in Arizona.

We noticed Bernice and her husband, Fred, seated in a booth along the far wall. They faced each other over a red vinyl-topped table, their hands around cocktail glasses. Fred, thin-faced and tanned, waved us over. "Sit for a minute."

"Fred, you look healthy," I said, sitting next to Bernice. "Doesn't working outside in this weather wear you out?"

"It's nothing," he answered, making room for John. "I like our spring weather. Some days it snows. Some days I get a burn." He drank the last of his drink.

John leaned forward, his bald head picking up the light. "I think I was outdoors too much during the war. Look at this." He pointed to his fair skin mottled with big freckles. "I've got spots on my spots." While I'd been a fearful youngster during World War II, John, nine years older, had been on a warship in the Pacific acquiring spots.

"We missed you at church last Sunday," Fred said, referring to John's illness. Fred and the other church people enjoyed John. His unease endeared him to the congregation who liked his Buster Keaton sorrowful face and his deadpan sense of humor. I wanted to be the beloved one, not this unfaithful bald guy. After all, John wasn't calling on the sick, teaching Bible class, preparing wonderful sermons and trudging the streets to duplicate Sunday bulletins at the local school district office.

Bernice spread her fingers on the table top, her rings and red nails making her hands colorful pointed stars. Sparkling silver bracelets gave her a gypsy look until her face suddenly crumpled into a silent weeping and she became Bernice in tears. Drawings of geezers on the wall-panels gaped at us with obscene interest. Fred, John, and I waited, unable to speak. Perhaps the presence of her minister released Bernice's tears, as if she felt the protection of God and could express her vulnerability.

At last John and I settled into a table nearby and I asked, "Do you think I should do something about Bernice's, um, her sadness?" Like some wand-waving fairy godmother—a Spirit Woman, for God's sake—I should have understood Bernice's pain, I thought, as if spiritual insights came by magic to ministers.

"Sadness can't be fixed," he said, the words coming straight from his troubled soul. Taking his arm as we left the noisy restaurant, I felt his body warm and protective beside me.

Hoping for more information about Bernice, I sought out Reverend Paul Strickland, a handsome gray-haired gentleman with a kindly manner who'd served Faith United Church as interim minister after the sainted Reverend Thomas left. Strickland advocated for my candidacy as minister reminding the congregation of an Arizona woman, Sandra Day O'Conner, recently appointed Supreme Court Justice. I was grateful to him for preparing people to accept a woman quarterback and wished my pastoral manner was more like his. He reminded me of Jesus, though he looked nothing like Harvey the rabbit.

Strickland disclosed that Bernice and Fred had suffered the death of their daughter last year, but he didn't explain the details of the tragedy. He let me know I was supposed to do my work at Faith Church knowing only the agreeable news. Changing the subject, he encouraged me to get a word processor, an idea out of keeping in a rural setting where I felt notes should be sent by pony express. Besides, I was still working on getting a copy machine.

The mention of Bernice's daughter made me think of my adopted daughter, Margaret. A powerful presence in my life, she spent her teenage years skipping school and in rehab programs. I missed her wild spirit and remembered every detail of a pivotal day, years ago, when I made a crucial decision.

Margaret stood in my bedroom doorway glaring at me. Dark-haired and fully developed at thirteen, she looked formidable in her nightshirt—with its motorcycle logo—and high-top sneakers.

"I hate your motherfucking car."

"What are you talking about?" I asked, surprised by her outburst so early in the morning. "My car?" I finished making the bed, knowing Margaret wasn't finished.

"That car sucks. I wish I lived with Daddy," she declared, her dark hair an uncombed mass around her face. "He's got a good car. I hate living here." She stomped away with a final declaration: "You're ugly. This place is stupid."

Sitting on the side of the bed, I tried to ignore the familiar insults. I knew what upset her. Margaret had voiced our dread about starting the school year—middle school for her and high school teaching for me.

I put on flat shoes that felt like the heavy boots of a mountain climber—so unlike oxfords I'd worn as a girl during World War II when we replaced the soles of our leather shoes with a piece of cardboard as they wore out. I was helping out the soldiers on the front back then, a simple sacrifice compared to another year of teaching and struggling with an uncooperative daughter.

In the mirror I saw a forty-four-year-old single mother. Could I face another year of managing high school students and directing theater productions? I enjoyed my students but felt a pull toward graduate school, a pull toward something new. I wanted to leave everything, including my daughter's curses, including John, whom I'd been dating. His dark moods did nothing to make me want to stay in San Diego. I admitted to the lady in the mirror I wanted to go to graduate school to study religion.

Daisy, our golden spaniel, greeted me with a wag of her tail as I headed for the kitchen to make tea. Her sad eyes reflected back my mood. "Cheer up, old girl," I said, speaking to both of us. "Take care of Margaret." A burst of noise came from upstairs. Was she shoving furniture?

Steve, a teenage neighbor, appeared in the doorway ready for his ride to school. After seeing that Margaret got on her bus, we set off in my car, an Ambassador, a name too grand for its rusted, tired appearance—as my daughter had so colorfully pointed out.

When I pulled off the ramp onto the freeway, the car stalled.

"O God," I said as we rolled on to a shoulder. "I'm so sorry, Steve."

"Doesn't matter," he grinned. Steve had the sandy-haired look and easy-going nature of a bespectacled Huck Finn. He stretched his arms above his head and leaned back. "A good excuse to be late."

"I take this as a sign from God," I sighed.

"You been mentioning God a lot."

Margaret's insults, the dog's face, and the breakdown of the car. The telling signs had appeared. It was time to slip out of teaching shoes and into the sneakers of a graduate student at Pacific School of Religion in Berkeley—a non-denominational seminary I'd learned about from a woman minister I knew.

John would object to my going, but the separation from him felt right. Margaret must come along, of course. She might grow out of her defiance in a college town, away from her friends and the temptations of San Diego urban life. In Berkeley? Maybe not.

Margaret grew more difficult in Berkeley where she found a friend, Diana, who could match her in daring and mischief. They adored the university town and traveled its streets like two coyotes on the prowl. In the first semester, they learned to panhandle, smoked behind the trees in the schoolyard, and made friends with shady characters. Their exploits gave me headaches.

Now, far from those days, I sat across from a dignified minister, Paul Strickland, who kept church secrets close. He smiled and left me to my thoughts in a snug office with artistic crosses on the wall, books in a tall bookcase, and a window to the sunny stretch of desert highway outdoors.

I couldn't let go of worries about my daughter who, at twenty, had disappeared into Oregon with a man she hastily married. The telephone refused to bring me word from her and the room felt as empty as the Berkeley apartment on the day we'd arrived there—me, the dog, and a feisty teen.

Daisy bounded out of the car and peed on the parking strip while Margaret crawled out warily and grabbed her duffle. I followed her up the stairs of the apartment building. Margaret quickened her pace, taken over by curiosity. I was slower, carrying anxieties like extra luggage. Cautious School Teacher follows Fearless Teenager. She'd protested taking this trip into the north, pouted and complained, yet here she was breathing it in. She dumped her possessions onto the twin bed.

"I've never lived in an apartment before! Pretty neat!"

The narrow bed was the only furniture in the bare rooms, and I tried not to take the emptiness as a sign that I was too spiritually empty to study religion. I'd go to the seminary offices and see about the furnishings that should have been provided.

"Do you want to come with me to check on things we need?"

"No. I'll stay here and look around. Wonder if there are any kids in this place."

Daisy and I hurried out and began explorations, lingering at the shops that served the University of California that loomed over the Northside District of Berkeley. Students of all ages—a collection of hippies and grunge—moved around me and my dog. Vintage apartment buildings, tall eucalyptus trees, and unkempt streets brought back college scenes from my past. All of it looked wonderful.

Daisy liked the area too and sniffed the new smells while we headed uphill toward the seminary buildings dominated by a gothic chapel—enough imposing righteousness to make you stand straighter. Enough religious symbolism to make me wonder about the mysteries of Christianity: How are compassion and hope fostered? Why did some people of the first century leave Judaism to follow Jesus? Who wrote the Bible? Where did the strange Trinitarian ideas come from?

In a few days our one-bedroom apartment on the second floor was furnished with an overstuffed couch, wood table, and a green well-worn rug. The fireplace, full of messy ashes, gave off a smoky smell like old churches. From the window I watched Berkeley life below. I could spy into the patio of the Dominican monks' residence where a mariachi band played tunes at top volume for their parties. Monks making merry. It was fun to pick out other seminarians with their serene faces walking the sidewalks. Some had angelic children attached front or back. I envied their certainties as they paced themselves to inner music I couldn't hear. They came from a place of faith while I watched from a window hoping to some day understand what they already believed.

In my office in Arizona, I gazed out of the wide window to view the expanse of desert dotted with yellow wildflowers. I still felt sad about Bernice's sorrows and wished I'd known how to comfort her. Living with a sense of not having done enough was hard. I thought of the chess set and wondered if the dour pieces were unhappy people who carried their pain behind Protestant good manners. Bernice did seem as confined in her private pain as a queen behind the walls of her castle.

I began staring out of windows when I was a child, and the practice became constant when I was a California teenager longing to be secluded in a convent where I'd be worthy of my mother's respect and love. In a convent you didn't have to be afraid. It protected you from war planes and a frightening high school.

On a pre-dawn Monday morning, in my fourteenth year, I waited at the kitchen window for Suzy Kohler's father to drive us, two ninth graders, to our first day of high school. Staring at the driveway and a low white fence dividing us from the neighbor's yard dotted with orange trees, I knew I looked stupid, especially my face, too long, too plain. My brown hair was parted on the side and fixed in a clip like a baby's. Gone were those pretty curls Mother fixed years before. My clothes were awful—a skirt and blouse Mother made and an old sweater from the dark ages. The shoe situation was worse. Mine were plain oxfords. I should have Spaulding saddle shoes like every other high school girl.

Boys would be in that high school watching me, boys who had fights and smoked cigarettes. I wished I could go to a convent for girls like the one in *The Bells of Saint Mary's* with Ingrid Bergman. Boys were not allowed in convents.

A pitiless overhead light illuminated Mother's Austrian plates on the wall. Their cheery designs of dancing peasants mocked me on this black day. I didn't want to go to high school. How did a person act in a high school?

Mother was at the stove stirring a smelly pot of oatmeal. Every Monday she served oatmeal. I hated that mush. I hated my fat mother. She paid no attention to a person's suffering. She'd never even been to high school and reminded me of that fact every chance she got. I chewed on a pinky fingernail while my younger sister Connie, the perfect seventh grader, blond and tanned from her summer outside, sat at the table eating her oatmeal. Another reason to hate my life.

My father, dressed for work in suit and tie, smiled at me and smoothed his moustache. After a few minutes, his gray Chevrolet backed out of the driveway and the strength of my life disappeared. At the same time, Mr. Kohler's black Ford came around the corner. I considered throwing up, but Mother knew I could vomit at will, so there was nothing to do but get in the car beside Suzy.

The school was like a prison with its long halls painted ugly green. Every door looked the same, and it was hard to find the right classroom. Kids were already seated at almost every desk when I entered English class, so I had to walk to the front while everyone stared. I wished Suzy was with me. No one was as miserable as I was. No other girl was as tall as I was. The teacher's name was on the blackboard. She was an old lady and she didn't smile. All you could hear were shuffling feet. One pretty teen with a blond ponytail tied with a pink ribbon, grinned at everyone. She reminded me of a photo I kept of the movie star Betty Grable in a bathing suit, smiling over her shoulder and showing off her round bottom.

At the end of the school day, Suzy and I waited on the sidewalk for the bus. Hot rod cars came roaring toward us—growling monsters from the underworld with greased heads of boys inside. Suzy wasn't worried. She had the advantage of being short with cute bangs, store-bought clothes, Spaulding saddle shoes, and a little red purse that matched her lipstick. I hated standing there watching those boys approach. What if they laughed at me?

The lure of a holy safe convent was like the attraction of the old Mission church. In those cloistered places you wouldn't be exposed to any of the risky edges of popular culture—like hot rods, and gorgeous movie stars. My imaginings of those religious havens provided as much escape for me as retreat into wilderness or alcohol did for others.

A year after that first day of high school, I followed Suzy to our seats in a church assembly room in South Pasadena where a large group of teens chatted quietly. She'd brought me to "Pilgrim Fellowship" at Oneonta Congregational Church, a large modern structure presiding over emerald lawns and towering trees. To a self-conscious girl of fifteen, whose discomfort centered on her imitation Spaulding saddle shoes, the church felt intimidating.

I studied the crowd, glad they were different from the untamed bunch at the high school. No one could have arrived in a low-slung hot rod. A tall young man, smiling and self-assured, began the proceedings with capable ease, speaking as if to grown-up members of an important club. His baritone voice, his height, and competence reminded me of my father. He led us in the song "Jacob's Ladder" about the climb to freedom, and we sang "Every rung goes higher, higher."

"His name's Carl Ludlow," Suzy said. "He's seventeen and he's a great dancer." She glanced around the room looking for George, her boyfriend.

"I wasn't paying attention."

"You were too!"

I stared at Carl's mature, compelling figure and could imagine what kind of boyfriend he'd be, taking me dancing or on dates to movies. He'd buy me hamburgers at a diner I adored called "Hamburger Heaven."

"I heard he wants to be a minister some day," Suzy said, and I mused about that astounding fact. If you married a minister you could stay in this beautiful church forever.

I soon joined the Pilgrim Fellowship and the youth choir. We girls sang in the choir loft at the early service on Sunday mornings wearing white choir robes and facing the boys. I could watch Carl Ludlow, a frequent soloist and future minister. His sexual appeal in that holy setting added lively energy to the attraction of religion and church.

One Sunday morning, our minister, Doctor Henry David Gray, quoted from a poem in his sermon:

> Little faces looking up
> Holding wonder like a cup.

Holding wonder. The sanctuary, the poetry, and the organ music made me feel like that, holding wonder. Doctor Gray talked about caring for others and the ethical life. He found answers in Christianity, and his message flashed with dazzling language. He seemed in command of us young people, the church, and the universe, striding the galaxies like a caesar, convinced of his righteousness and that of the Protestant ethos. As imposing as the sanctuary, Gray persuaded me that the Protestant church mattered profoundly in America and the world.

Gray was one of a line of powerful Protestant ministers in the fifties whose sermons combined Christianity with post-war patriotic values. "Under God" had just been added to our Pledge of Allegiance, and an American flag stood by the church altar. To us young people, the church was fundamental to American life.

During my senior year, Gray approached me in the choir room. "Elaine, I'd like you to speak at the chapel one Sunday next month." Up close he wasn't so dramatic a figure as he was in the pulpit, and he was shorter than my secret love, Carl Ludlow. "I'd like you to take the third Sunday," he said, referring to the evening chapel service for teenagers held at the end of our Pilgrim Fellowship meeting.

I turned my back, cowed by Gray's dark eyes behind heavy black-rimmed glasses, and put the silky white choir-robe in the closet. "Are you sure? I don't think—"

"Time to get over your shyness," he interrupted in a raspy voice. "You've had a good experience here. Just tell what Pilgrim Fellowship means to you."

He walked away, not waiting for an answer. "Have you taken leave of your senses?" I whispered to Doctor Gray's back. I'd read the remark in *Gone with the Wind*, my favorite novel. The idea of speaking to the group frightened me, but it was a chance to say out loud all that I'd been thinking about the youth fellowship. Gray was right about my enjoying the group. I edited the group's newsletter and won praise. I went to their parties where Carl Ludlow taught me to jitterbug. I made friends among teenagers who lived in beautiful Pasadena homes and went to college. I chose their lives: respectable, American, and Christian.

Of course I gave that talk Doctor Gray asked of me. I can't remember what I said, but no doubt I affirmed the clear directions Christian teachings gave me, instructions on how to be a good person. I must have spoken of the activities I enjoyed, the parties and planning meetings. What I do remember is that before my chapel speech the popular seniors ditched the chapel service for their cars and Hamburger Heaven.

Not long after—thanks to the sponsorship of a family in the Pasadena church—I was admitted to Pomona College, a small liberal arts school nestled in the orange groves of Southern California. A bosomy friendly girl by then, I'd become a practiced listener with a suntan, lipstick that matched my clothes from Sears, and a head of curled hair, thanks to a home permanent. A number of young men sought my company, and I dated the Christian youth leader, Carl Ludlow, who took me dancing and bought me gifts. He thrilled me with deep kisses and escorted me to night clubs in Los Angeles where we danced to orchestras with singers like Frank Sinatra. Carl Ludlow was "Someone to Watch Over Me," as we sang in those days. His religious intentions were arousing too, as if he had a magical potency.

Standing at my Arizona window, I conjured Carl and his

irresistible self-assurance. Everything about him was seductive—a golden singing voice, strong sexy legs, a powerful self-confidence. He was going to be a minister. He had the approval of God. Carl's image, in a religious glow, obscured part of him that he hid from me—*The old rake in the grass.*

I wonder now what my Pilgrim Fellowship friends would say if they knew the truth about Carl, my first husband, father of my children. I didn't notice anything wrong when we were dating except that other young men didn't choose him for the best fraternity. And there was an incident at college when, at the dean's request, he left for a term. I kept doubts buried below consciousness and couldn't, or wouldn't, process anyone's concerns about him. Even when the college chaplain spoke with me about postponing our wedding, I didn't listen to his misgivings. I was twenty years old and in love. In the photos I've kept, I'm wearing corsages and white gloves—a poster girl for virgin bride, virgin everything. In the fifties, women like me behaved themselves, especially virgins.

I'd been captivated in a beautiful church by two powerful men, one in a pulpit with a PhD, and a sexy one with idealistic religious pretensions. It seemed right to follow them into a clerical life of icons, love, good works, and tolling bells.

*When we look into scripture at the stories of love and sexuality, we find mixed messages. On the one hand we have praise of love, and a delight in sensuality, like the "Song of Solomon." On the other hand, we have David's lust for Bathsheba, a good example of sensuality gone too far...*

## Sex and the Moral Life

## THREE

I turned the car onto Old Chisholm Trail—a street name at the country club that made me smile—and headed for a council meeting at Faith United Church. The wide sky showed streaks of high clouds. The warm air weighed heavily even at 8:30 in the morning. Moisture in the atmosphere left wet drops on the windshield. A rumored monsoon rain seemed impossible here in the high desert; I knew as little about the summer weather in Arizona high country as I did about the whereabouts of God.

The wood and stone church, its peaked roof gleaming with sunlight bouncing off the abstractions of colored glass, presided over a respectable, quiet neighborhood. No one could do harm in this attractive place below forested mountains where pointed pines gave rest to songbirds. The only indication that trouble might erupt that summer morning was the oppressive humidity.

Carrying my tote bag, I stepped out of the car and noticed the church rosebush sprouting a new bundle of coral buds, a "rose e'er blooming" as the song goes. I found a mega-symbol in that bloom—of a thriving church, of a rejuvenated marriage, of God's approval of my work.

The church members were more at ease with me now that I'd been their minister for four months. My foster child status had changed, and murmurs about Reverend Thomas speaking without notes stopped. I married and buried, baptized and presided, managed study groups and organized committees. We still sang "Onward Christian Soldiers," but I planned to raise our awareness of inappropriate music soon—once I figured out how to do it.

Inside the church, under two turning overhead fans, several members of the church council sat at a square of tables at the end of the sanctuary near the kitchen. They could be a gathering of grandparents chatting amiably and eating muffins set out on cocktail napkins. Smells of decaf and nutty bread—touched with the odor of bleach—created an atmosphere of home, a very clean home. Cheerful light shone through the faceted glass as if our meeting was blessed from above.

I placed a small notebook on the table, thinking I made a professional impression with my silver cross set with turquoise stones—a surprise ordination gift from Mother—on a chain over a white shirt. My gold hoop earrings remained at home since I wasn't ready to appear bejeweled at church meetings.

So far my ministry in Dewey had gone well and much of it was fun. The drama of each worship service lifted my spirits, thanks in part to the good music from Mrs. Ogg at the organ. Youngsters now attended on Sundays, and people tried to care for each other, contributing generously to the church and setting aside funds to support struggles for justice in the world. I convinced myself I was an effective minister. So said the rose bush. Still, I constantly wondered if I needed to do more to move us more intentionally toward God—but the whispering in my ear wasn't coherent enough to explain what that might be.

Marjorie McLellan, representative of the music committee, came in wearing shorts. A skinny woman with the keen eye of a bird, Marjorie's lighthearted manner kept the meetings from dragging. A man I'll call Cal Appleton sat next to her. He appreciated Marjorie's sassiness and was partial to blondes. His oxygen tank rested next to him on the floor but his exhausted lungs didn't slow him down.

The chairperson, whom I'll call Sarah Howard, appeared at ease that morning, her pale eyes reassuring. A devoted woodworker, she had the lean poise of a sculptor. Sarah would keep order. She'd suppress Sandra Mattson's talking and move the business along. Next to her, our records clerk, a frontier type, was ready to take notes. Her face looked tired, though she was younger than the retired folk at the tables.

Lew McLachlan, a favorite of mine, represented the volunteer crew who did the maintenance. His faithful attentions made the cross glow, kept the plumbing repaired, and the blessed overhead fans spinning. The predominance of women on the council didn't bother Lew. He took church work as his calling and would have served our needs if we'd been a gaggle of gangsters.

The council meeting should perk along like our faithful coffee maker, source of all decaf, but just as Sarah stood to begin the meeting, Jim Godfrey—not a member of the council—appeared in the doorway. He strode into the room and glared at us, like the formidable chess king. Dressed in a gray sweatshirt and workpants, Jim looked like a janitor, but he was a tithing member of the church and an accomplished Christian complainer.

Hoping Jim would disappear and leave us to our business for the morning, I centered my attention on my blueberry muffin, food prepared by a woman I'll call Ardith who'd come early and prepared the tables and made the coffee. With sparse red hair brushed away from her freckled face, she set a tone of competence and caring. She could be Mother in a Norman Rockwell print, and her muffins completed the picture.

When I looked up, Jim hadn't moved. I sipped the decaf wondering what was troubling this agitated visitor.

With a nod from Sarah, I began an opening prayer. Jim bowed his head. A good sign. "Be with us this morning, O God," I prayed, "as we plan the work of this church and try to respond to the needs around us..."

As soon as I said the Amen, Jim bellowed, "I'd like to address the council." We stared at him, shocked at the intrusion. "We've gone off the rails around here. I have a list of problems that can't wait!" He waved a clipboard, his dark eyes blazing behind shining eyeglasses.

The people around the table turned to me. Did they want me to send Jim away? Box his ears? I didn't respond. My role was to offer prayer and give a report—not to maintain order and discipline as I had in high school classrooms. Sarah, the elected leader, had full responsibility.

"We've no time for new agenda items, Jim. Our minister is giving her monthly report this morning," Sarah said, taking charge. *Thank you, Jesus.* "If you'd like to give me your lists…" She held out her hand and kept her voice at a quiet level in contrast with the shout from Jim. I noticed her gold wristwatch, similar to the one I'd been given at high school graduation, a dated timepiece ticking the hours of distant days.

"The Lord is not being served here!" Jim's cry felt like a speeding baseball hurled past our heads, and we flinched.

The Lord. Oh dear. Once you take up with The Lord you have right on your side. Jim was going to shout criticism of me, a woman in the pulpit defying the laws of God and nature. My sermons weren't serious enough, and I preached from prepared notes, or—I couldn't think, but Jim was here with a list of my faults.

The ball was Sarah's to catch, and she did. "There is no time today, Jim," she pronounced a second time, raising her voice. "Does anyone want to take time for this?" I prepared to defend myself. Resign? Run?

Sandra Mattson, usually an outspoken woman, bent her head as if to protect her face from flying baseballs. She'd have much to say about this interruption, but now she was silent.

"Um…let him speak," said a woman I'll call Millie. Chairperson of the Diaconate, a committee charged with assisting at worship services, she was new to the council. The flowered scarf over her shoulders gave her a fragile feminine appearance, and I thought she might soften Jim, but he didn't glance at her.

Like a clean-shaven Jeremiah bent on reform of the Israelites, Jim seized his chance, speaking as if a life was at risk. "Last Sunday the service was a disaster! There was no coordinator and—"

So it wasn't about me.

"Now just a minute, Jim," Lew interrupted, rising to his feet. "I was there for set up and—"

"You might have been there, but no one worked the fans," Jim said, raising his voice. "The mikes picked up a CB radio going down the street!"

I wanted to defend Lew, who took responsibility for Sunday morning preparations, but this skinny gentleman stood his ground without my help. The two retirees faced each other like two gladiators. We sat riveted, the crowd at the contest anticipating the final battle, while overhead fans churned the humid air around us.

"Jim, you're taking us away from the agenda items we must cover this morning," Sarah said. "Give—me—your—lists!" She was angry. Lew sat down, but Jim didn't hand over his clipboard. Was something seriously wrong?

"The council must take care of these matters before our services fall apart!" Jim said. "The lighting and the fans have to be on and ready by 8:00 in the summer. Why is there no roster for volunteers?" Glancing at his clipboard, he started up again: "The minister's voice could not be heard over the crackling from the sound system! The speakers were not properly adjusted!"

Jim's display of righteousness made me think of the sermon I was working on, "Sex and The Moral Life." Jim had the moral life in his sights. He took a breath and made his final pronouncement: "The candle lighters were wearing ugly shoes!"

Ugly shoes? *Shoes* were the objects of Jim's anger? He referred to the hightop sneakers of the neighborhood youngsters, Becky and Dana, who paraded down the aisle to light the candles during Mrs. Ogg's organ preludes before the Sunday services began. Did other churches deal with these subjects?

No one spoke or nibbled or swallowed. The hot air felt even more oppressive. Marjorie crossed her naked legs and stifled a giggle. John wasn't with us, thank God. He'd not be able to resist a funny remark.

Millie pulled her scarf around her shoulders, tears in her eyes.

Suddenly our bellowing Jeremiah left, rushing to the next emergency. Millie hurried after him, and I followed them both. Jim got into his white pickup, as gleaming and immaculate as his Christian heart, and drove away. I put my arm around Millie and we went inside, the dance of colors less charming now.

Sarah urged us to ignore the interruption and continue with the planned agenda. I gave a report—clearing my throat more than usual—and mentioned the families who'd joined the congregation. I told the council I wanted to find a used copy machine and a professional choir director, though I kept quiet about my hopes for modern hymns. The group also needed to know of my appointment with the courts as an advocate for a foster child. One day a month I'd serve the juvenile justice system to give back to a system that helped my daughter when she was a teenager. Last, I reminded the council that Becky and Dana, with the offensive sneakers, were going to bring other young people to church and we should encourage them.

After more reports, including the treasurer's concerns about our finances—a perpetual story—we adjourned and cleared the cups and napkins. No one mentioned Jim's outburst. Millie, running water in the kitchen sink, smiled as Sandra Mattson talked softly with her. I thanked Sarah for her strong leadership and went home to have lunch.

Trudging up our front stairs at home, I considered Jim's minor tantrum. His use of the term *The Lord* gave me clues about his religious background. He believed his Sunday School God—the demanding Jehovah who flooded the world to rid it of evil—must be served by complying with rules of orderly conduct, everything in perfect repair, and proper dress. Without those standards, we lose our bearings and the ship goes under. Jim longed for a safe place. So did I. Should I try to revise Jim's beliefs about his god? How does anyone do that? I'd assumed everyone was polite in churches, never hitting people with baseballs. Evidently church life was not removed from wounded egos and troubled personalities. My honeymoon period had ended.

Inside, where John sat in front of the television, the heavy air added to my weariness. "Hot in here," I said. Our evaporative cooler worked well in dry air, but on a muggy day like this it only added to the humidity.

The house vibrated with television coverage of the congressional debates about whether to stop the incursion of Iraqi troops into Kuwait. Like our church council, the United States Congress had to make important decisions. Our Christian deliberations, however, had just centered on children's shoes. Jesus was probably more worried about wars and rumors of war, as the Bible says.

After John muted the sound, I told him what happened at our council meeting. Without taking his eyes from the television he said, "I should have been there. The guy gives new meaning to 'holy terror.'"

"It wasn't funny." I turned up the cooler to max, knowing it wouldn't help. "It was more high tragedy, if you ask me. Jim's a real problem. I'm going over there to visit tomorrow."

. John snapped off the set. "Tell Jim to buzz off, stop coming to your meetings." He stretched his lanky body in a wide easy chair of dark green leather. "Does he golf?"

"Of course not," I said from the kitchen. "He's more a retiree with lots of mechanical skills. I wish he did play golf." Contemplating the contents of the refrigerator, I added, "His wife, Janet, is a straight-backed critic too. I'd like to send him to Sally. She'd fix him."

Sally was the church secretary in San Diego where I'd been assistant minister before coming to Dewey. A cynical woman in a tame church office, she had a dramatic past of many men and serious health crises, and she was as direct and truthful as a wise prophet— even though she was ten years younger than I and as blonde as the pinup girl Betty Grable. One time she gave me excellent advice when I was mystified about John's critical attitude.

Sally and I headed toward a Mexican restaurant on the main street of our pleasant San Diego neighborhood. We walked slowly—because of Sally's spinal problems that impaired her movements—talking of Scott Turow's new mystery novel *Presumed Innocent*. Murder provided a necessary tonic when you worked in a church.

"I love it that his wife was the killer," Sally said. "I can relate." We laughed. "Let's go in here and buy something." She turned into a small jewelry store.

"Hey, I can't buy jewelry just like I was buying a cabbage." I'd never gone into a jewelry store before except to buy a wedding ring.

"Yes you can. It's easy. Lighten up." She viewed the array of rings and bracelets with the eye of an expert. Sally loved jewelry, especially the pieces she inherited from her mother.

"Lighten up? Am I boring? I don't want to be boring."

"Then buy those earrings." Sally pointed to a pair of gold hoops with intricate designs on the curve, stylish and sexy.

"You have cunning persuasive powers. In a former life you were probably a courtesan."

"Whatever that is. Anyway, you need a poverty-stricken former doper to get you going. Buy the earrings."

I gave the matter serious thought. I'd survived a shattering divorce from Carl Ludlow, the rake in the grass; now, newly married to John—a difficult man—and working full time as an assistant minister and raising an uncontrollable daughter, I could jolly well wear gold earrings. So I bought the dazzling hoops and took a step toward a carefree personality.

Over lunch that day I complained in low tones about John. "He's getting to me with silences, doesn't give any hints about what's going on with him. Won't talk." I tried to enjoy my spinach enchilada but felt myself frowning at the plate. "He's got these constant aches and pains, and he, well, makes remarks about me." I never imagined he was having an affair at the time—which he was—but did consider he might be sinking into mental illness that caused his hurtful remarks and passive silences.

"Criticizes? Give—me—a—break. I say leave him." She scooped up salsa with an ample tortilla chip. "Or just back off and let him be miserable." The expression in her flecked blue-green eyes made my self-pity ridiculous. "Some people get off on misery," she said, taking a bite.

Leave him? After the end of my first marriage and its painful revelations, the idea of once again ending a marriage was too terrible to consider. I had to fix things, I thought, though at times I wanted to run. If only I was as worldly as Sally, not to mention blonde.

That evening on the way home, I stopped at Lucky's Supermarket wearing earrings that felt like the bangles of a belly dancer. "Walk humbly with thy God"—Micah's words from the Old Testament— did not include flashing about in gold, and I felt guilty for such a frivolous display.

Sally and Elaine

Guilt had been with me like a coin in my pocket for as long as I could remember, starting with Mother's judgments when I was a child. She called me selfish and ungrateful. Those words had power. She scorned my singing and storytelling, leaving me with feelings that I was the weak link in our hard-working family. I carried the guilt everywhere, worried that there was something basically wrong with me. It didn't occur to me then that my father's affection for me, and our singing together, might have caused her glare.

"I miss Sally too," John said as we worked in the kitchen where he created a ham sandwich and I thought about leftover vegetable soup. "She could see how funny churches are."

I heated the soup, staring into the pot as if studying the entrails of a goat. "Maybe I could've defused the situation with Jim."

"It's not your fault. Everything can't be your fault."

I took my bowl to the table and sipped the soup, thinking about how I'd deal with Jim and his stoic wife, Janet, when I visited their home. I'd need compassion for a man who disturbed our peace at the council meeting. I'd need to respect the faith that sustained the Godfreys—and leave my golden earrings behind.

The following Sunday morning, as we entered the church, teams of motorcycles zoomed by, screaming over the expanse of our open landscape with the siren-song of rural freedom. Only God could keep our church rosebush protected from the billows of dust.

People scurried to their chairs—with padded blue seats—talking and whispering during Mrs. Ogg's prelude, a medley of familiar old hymns: "In the Garden" blended with "Bringing in the Sheaves." Motorcycle roars added a counterpoint.

Attendance was up from last week. The summer numbers were increased by folks up from the Valley of the Sun hoping to find some respite in our cooler climate. Some spent the hotter months in a nearby mobile-home park, shaded by big old apple trees, and drifted across the street to the country club and our church when the spirit took them.

Sandra Mattson moved like the Holy Ghost among the chairs, appearing everywhere you looked. As she nodded her greetings, silver earrings swayed in the soft light. Fred and Bernice sat in the back next to John. Mrs. Johnie Fain, the grand lady of the congregation, was seated as usual in an aisle seat, her cane propped at her side.

Standing in the back of the church, I silently asked for God's guidance and then followed the choir down the center aisle. Led by a woman I'll call Virginia Regan, the choir sang "O Worship the King, All Glorious Above" as if they longed for dictatorship, a very undemocratic notion in my opinion. That hymn would have to go too. The singers looked too warm in their silky gold robes, and as soon as they sat they fanned themselves.

Virginia had been the volunteer choir leader at Faith United for several years. She never complained about her responsibilities, but now she hoped to pass the baton to a new director so she could play more golf. She deserved her freedom as much as those noisy motorcyclists.

My crusade to bring in enlightened music was ignored. That Sunday morning the words of the hymn about a royal male God made me cringe. Suffering humanity didn't require a ruler; we needed assurances and love—modern ideas about Jesus, God, and all things theological. We should raise the music standards at the church so it felt like a place removed from archaic old ideas about bowing to kings. I'd made timid suggestions, but so far my campaign had no followers.

When I asked other ministers about how to retire outdated music they told me they had more important matters to worry about. Their opinions made me feel like a nattering nabob. They didn't realize how music influences people. I'd wait and suffer the old traditional stuff until I could alter people's tastes with shrewd maneuvers. Changes in institutional life take time—and political charm. I'd have to build my base.

The truth is I'm moved by all sacred music, even the sexist, militaristic songs. "The Battle Hymn of the Republic" is a war hymn that can move me to tears. A shift occurs in the spirit of the room when the music is beautiful. Gentle songs like "Breathe on Me Breath of God" touch memories of comfort like those I felt while staring at the Virgin Mary's bowed head in the safe enclosure of the Mission Archangel.

Seated in the front that morning were the youngsters-of-the-terrible-shoes, two black-haired sisters of ten and twelve. Becky, the younger, still looked babyish. I loved her perpetual grin. Dana, tall and slender, had a reticence older than her years and smiled less often than her animated sister. Both girls had the brown skin of the outdoors. They lived across the street and had been curious about the church. They told us they'd never been in a church before and the cookies were good, so they joined us most Sundays, invading our middle-aged church like a pair of native pranksters, two Kokopelli.

I called the girls forward to pass the collection plates, and they took the brass trays grinning as if presented with passports to glory. With their clumpy sneakers and noisy energy, they reminded me of seminary days when Margaret and her friend Diana would clatter up and down the hallway of our apartment building.

While I waited for the offering ritual to finish, I studied the décor of the sanctuary. A portrait of Jesus hung on a side wall, his white Anglo face like a movie star's—unrealistic on a Jewish man of the Middle East. *The Last Supper*, a small print of the daVinci painting, dangled crookedly under the clock. A bunch of dusty plastic flowers stood on the organ. Those meager decorations would have to be replaced along with the music. Bernice, with her flair for the artistic, could make a real difference, I thought. Her creative designs might move even Jeremiah Jim to consider a gentle God who welcomes children with clumpy shoes.

Parading down the aisle, Becky and Dana moved with a solemnity suited to their task and handed me the brimming offering plates. I said a sentence prayer of thanks, set the plates under the cross and stepped into the golden-oak pulpit enclosure. A week of hot weather and the throbbing of motorcycles brought me to biblical accounts with sexual implications.

> When we look into scripture at the stories of love and sexuality, we find mixed messages. On the one hand we have praise of love, and a delight in sensuality, the "Song of Solomon." On the other hand, we have David's lust for Bathsheba, a good example of sensuality gone too far…
>
> It's a fact of human relations that people lose good sense, moderation, and sanity in order to be sexually satisfied. I'm talking about plain old lust— for your neighbor's husband, for the girl in history class, for the waitress at the diner. Acting on the temptations of sexual feelings can result in terrible pain for us and others. I name it as did the early church—sin…

No one passed out when I said that old word *sin*. Jim and Janet

Godfrey looked pleased. I'd visited the Godfrey's home last Tuesday—about Jim's interruption at Council—and they'd been friendly. I noted his complaints about laxity in service preparation, and he showed me his shop where he restored clocks, pieces of which lay in ordered ranks on a high workbench. The presence of a minister in their home seemed to answer the Godfrey's need for respect and attention, and I felt less annoyed with Jim afterward, as if I too had been visited by a spirit of reconciliation.

Standing under a spotlight wearing a white summer robe and my turquoise cross, I continued the sermon, taking the occasional drink of cold water Lew McLachlan had set on a pulpit shelf. The polished wood sides of the enclosure surrounded me with an embrace of revered traditions. I felt cared for.

> In no way would we want to adopt capital punishment for broken marriage vows, a rule we find in the Old Testament, nor would we want to revert to the Puritan standards from early Protestantism...But we are vulnerable to temptation, so I think we need an inner compass, moral convictions on sexual matters. The challenge is one of the hardest we face in life...

Someone coughed, and only Jack was napping, his usual posture. Sandra smiled, and I heard myself preaching to her as before. John's pale eyes watched me, and I hoped he didn't think I was attacking him with this sermon. No intention to hurt him occurred to me when I'd written it. He appeared content, and I smiled, trying on a face that showed affection.

> What happens if we fail to stay true to our partners? For one thing, we can offer apology, confession to those we've hurt. I've found that most people can understand and forgive even if they've been wronged. To humble ourselves before another is hard, but it is, I believe, the way to return to the heart of God whose mercy is wide and flows generously when we are sorry for having been cruel or selfish or stupid...

Attending to my words about humility could have been a way for me to overcome guilt for being an imperfect daughter, mother, and wife, but it's hard to accept God's mercy into your heart, even for a religious leader. Giving up long-cherished guilt would be like pouring a pocketful of treasured coins into an open drain. I left such spiritual disciplines to my listeners and wished them well.

We sang the rousing hymn—"Come, ye joyful, raise the strain of triumphant gladness..."—and I spoke the benediction, sending the congregation outside to the roar of motorcycles: "May you live a life abundant with joy, careful to do no harm to others." Most of the congregation adjourned to the back of the church to greet me and enjoy a cup of decaf, but like the teens who avoided my talk at chapel when I was in high school, others rushed to their cars and Sunday brunch.

My sermon about love and faithfulness sent me into memory, or it does as I reread its words. I see a lady minister retreat to her office with a mug of decaf, feeling despondent about love and sex and married life. The oppressive summer heat adds to her discomfort. Preoccupied with regret, she straightens the desktop, making orderly what's already tidy while a portable fan sends a breeze toward her legs.

After we'd married, my first husband, Carl, didn't become a minister. His plans changed when he took a low-paying job as a church youth director and then got poor grades during one semester in ministerial studies at the Southern California School of Theology. I helped him with his assignments, fascinated by the reading, but he rarely attended classes, preferring a bridge game in the college coffee shop. Soon after, he abandoned seminary and took singing lessons while I taught at the high school. He hoped to break into the music business and become a nightclub singer or appear on television, a foolish dream. I felt like a hard-working parent to a child. I wonder, as I revisit those days, if Carl sensed those feelings. I regret that.

I ought to go home, I thought, and be with John, fix lunch, rest, but I didn't move. The summer silence and heat was enveloping, and I was still preoccupied by my sermon on love. My marriage to John Greensmith, eight years after the divorce from Carl, felt like rescue from the hard life of teaching and being a single mother, but

I didn't need rescue, not by a man of dark moods and a penchant for cheating. Actually, I rescued *him* from loneliness and grief over the loss of his marriage and the end of his exciting job as a news photographer. For a time we had a good life—until I went off to seminary and became a minister. After that, John seemed to despise me, and his attitude was enough like my mother's critical manner to send me into worry, blaming myself for his attitude.

I worked in San Diego as an assistant minister then, and we lived in my home with my children. John contributed little to expenses and worked at a job he disliked. I didn't think he was envious of me or felt diminished by my status, but he began to torment me with words and silences I didn't understand. I finally decided to ask him—thanks to Sally's encouragement—and find out why he was calling me an obstacle.

I waited in the kitchen, planning a confrontation. Pacing helped. Mumbling about his hurtful remarks helped. I had to know what my husband was hiding from me. What had made him so angry? Was he melting down? My daughter Margaret played loud stereo music upstairs, a fitting accompaniment to a showdown.

At last John walked in the back door of our San Diego home wearing a tweed cap and his CIA sunglasses. He'd been at the racetrack in Tijuana—across the Mexican border—where he photographed racehorses for their owners.

"Wait a minute," I said. "I've something to say before you go upstairs." He placed his camera on a shelf and threw his cap and glasses on the kitchen table as if disgusted by my request. The gesture made me want to toss down something too.

"I can tell you're angry with me." He looked up, surprised at my statement. I rushed on, afraid I'd lose momentum. "What's going on? You seem miserable here. Do you want to leave? Yesterday you called me an obstacle." The afternoon paused. I'd shocked both of us. "What does that mean, *obstacle*?"

"Nothing. I don't remember saying it. Forget it." He cleared his throat loudly, emphasizing his health problems, and took off his jacket and placed it on the back of a yellow kitchen chair.

"It sure feels like you want me out of your life," I said. "I can't take your silences, your critical words. If you want to go—"

He turned to me, his eyes frightened. "No! I don't. I don't want to leave!"

Aware of the pounding from upstairs, where my daughter walked with her heavy step, I asked in a tone more forceful than usual, "Then what's going on? You didn't say one word to my friends at my birthday dinner." John dropped his head, a familiar submissive pose. "You didn't even look at us. You act like you'd prefer to be out of here."

"It's that I've been mixed up." His deep voice lowered to a rumble. "My job is so boring. I can't stand it." He referred to his job in advertising at a real estate office.

"Your job? I'm not sure..." Heavy-metal music crashed through the house.

"No! Can't you see? It's Lois—at work."

"What? Lois and you? Your secretary? You've been sleeping with Lois?" So that was it. I'd been an obstacle to John's love affair with a woman I've called Lois. I'd have preferred a confession of racketeering.

"Yes—but it's over. I'm sorry. It didn't mean anything. I'm sorry." He leaned over and steadied himself on the back of the yellow chair, turning his face away from me.

Everything stopped while I tried to breathe. The kitchen— scratched white cabinets, window over the sink, orange floor tiles— became miniature and John a huge Gulliver leaning over a tiny universe.

"I don't care if it *meant anything*!" I said. "I don't even know what that means!"

I marched upstairs crying. How could I be so stupid? Margaret's explosive music got louder. How could I be so stupid! I hated him. First Carl—youth group charmer—rejected me for a young man, and now John was sleeping with his secretary. I was in a bad movie. Crap. I didn't want to see John's face again, ever. Collapsing onto the side of the bed, I leaned over, my head in my hands, fighting nausea.

John's feet hit the stairs in time with Margaret's music. As soon as he came into the room I blew my nose and told him to leave—

right now, the house, forever. An arc of pain gripped my skull. I started for the bathroom.

"I'm sorry," he said. "Don't send me away. It's over." He began to cry, his pale eyes watery. "I don't want to leave. It's over. I love you."

I felt like John's mother and fought the urge to comfort him, but at the same time I felt sorry for him—those tearing eyes, the look of hurt, declarations of love. Barely able to keep my balance, I went to him and wrapped my arms around his shaking frame. "Okay, okay. Right now I need to go to the bathroom."

I knew Lois, a dark-haired young woman, tall and shy. She'd come to my ordination ceremony. What brought her there? To witness the competition? At an ordination? In a church? John told me he'd taken her on two overnight assignments out of town. The news hurt me, but he made excuses, denying any affection for her, so I tried to believe him. Could I stay with a man who'd done this?

Again and again, John said it wasn't my fault, that he loved me. I tried to believe him. Nothing was said about my choice to become a minister as a reason for John's love affair, and we never explored the matter. We did go to a marriage counselor who ignored that question and asked me what would keep me in the marriage. Without hesitating, I replied that I wanted John to pay more into our joint bank account—financial matters I never had the courage to bring up before. I look back on that response surprised by my concern over money. The new financial agreement must have represented a capitulation to me, and I needed that.

After a counseling session, I insisted that John get Lois transferred from his office. He agreed and I dialed his office to talk with Lois before she left, hoping to ruin her day, maybe her life. It was easier to blame Lois than to explore more problems with John, so I transferred my anger to her as if my innocent husband had been seduced by Salome in seven veils.

She picked up. "Coldwell Banker," she said in a cheerful voice. How dare she be so happy!

"It's Elaine, Lois. I've something to say. Please don't speak until I've finished."

"I can't talk to you. No. Don't—"

"What you've done has damn near ruined my life. How could you? Didn't you know this would cause hurt? You've wounded me, and—" I wanted to attack her, to take revenge, but didn't have enough bitter language. Back then, we women were not used to expressing anger and had no vocabulary for confrontation and righteous indignation, at least I didn't.

"I'm sorry. I—"

"I want you to know I'm devastated." The only word I could think of. "You've destroyed everything important to me."

No response. Maybe choking.

I repeated that she should know I was *devastated*. Her stuttering sounded hurt and confused. That helped.

In the Dewey church three years later, I wandered from my stuffy office into the cool empty sanctuary with pulpit, altar, and cross. The room murmured, except I couldn't make out words. Afternoon light, tinged with sepia, gave the sanctuary an evening feel, a peaceful retreat containing my stories without judgment.

*On Easter evening Jesus appeared, stood among them, and said, "Peace be with you." When he had said this, he showed them his hands and his side. He breathed on them and said, "Receive the holy spirit" and told them to forgive one another, and he left.*

## A People Remembered

## FOUR

I followed the edge of the golf course on my morning fitness walk and pondered the Easter story about an empty tomb and resurrected god: "On the third day Jesus rose from the dead." Who could believe that? Jesus walked away from his tomb fully restored after being murdered by the Romans? That magical thinking required to accept the resurrection of Jesus was too much for me. The leap of faith into acceptance of the Easter story was a leap I was not able to make.

A year had passed. It was April again and time to preach a sermon to believers on my first Easter Sunday in Arizona.

My feet on the pavement made no sound. No cars came by. The setting felt newly born, as if Arizona hadn't accepted the wheel yet. Here in the wide silence I felt in contact with otherness, with transcendence, you could call it. Prayers came easily—"Guide me. Help me. Teach me."

A roadrunner darted across my path with a young snake in its beak. Poor snake. Dangerous around here. This was not the flowery springtime of Hallmark Easters. The cold wind whipped at me, and the only signs of new life were tips of green spears that emerged from desiccated earth.

No ideas for an Easter sermon struck me. All I got was the bite of cholla cactus that snagged my skin with invisible needles when I passed too close. Arizona was a place to try on prickly ideas, to study scripture and tell the truth rather than perpetuate the old biblical legends, I thought, but I was still wary about disclosing what I knew about the Easter accounts in the Bible.

When I'd studied biblical texts in a Berkeley classroom with a professor who could read the New Testament in the original Greek, I learned to be a biblical skeptic. Maybe it was springtime then too.

"Notice the different biblical versions of the resurrection and the discovery of the empty tomb," said Dr. W, a man too short for the high table. Eight students waited, pens poised. The professor explained the contradictions in the accounts of Jesus' death and afterward. The chapters telling of the empty tomb, he said, were additions to the Jesus stories that scholars call "imaginative elaboration." I readily accepted that the resurrection stories were fabrications written to reinforce faith in Jesus as a divine messiah, but some in the class were astounded by the professor's information. They'd been raised in Bible-believing homes. Two dropped out.

I got advice from other ministers: "Keep it under your hat." "You'll lose your job if you talk about this." So here I was, in the trenches, as they say, caught by the needles of a dilemma: tell what I know about the Bible stories or preach the party line and secure my job. Could I keep my knowledge of biblical scholarship and archeological findings secret so I wouldn't upset Christian parishioners? I sneezed in protest. New information about Jesus would undermine people's long-held beliefs. Couldn't we trust our churchgoers? Some of them, I suspected, already knew the results of recent biblical studies and imaginative elaborations in them. The charade was humiliating, and I felt the needles again.

It would have helped if I'd heard a godly voice in the desert wind speaking assurances that my hypocrisy was necessary, that Christians longed to believe in a risen god, that I was on the right path. No show. No supportive affirmations from seraphim flitting over the golf course either, and I couldn't find a sign in a ravenous roadrunner. The only heavenly apparition that appeared was a red-tailed hawk swooping above my head searching the earth. I was marching through his property.

In the distance, a kidney-shaped pool gleamed on the emerald golf links, a rare sight in the desert—like me, a free thinker in a conservative land. The sight reminded me that everything in Arizona is about water. One of the family dynasties in the state is named Goldwater. Water *is* gold here, a healing element we yearn for, the liquid of survival, renewal. We crave it. We require its cooling, restoring life. Because it's so necessary, the ceremony of baptism in an Arizona church seems more meaningful.

Arizona is a special place, and I was growing to understand and appreciate its beauty and history. Many of the green plants were imports, I learned, and so was their infuriating pollen. Everything had been brought in, carried by us outlanders who wanted to make Arizona into a copy of home. I'd read that the state could die from too much artificial change. Like the *USS Arizona,* drowned at the bottom of Pearl Harbor, Arizona could be sinking beneath overpopulation and development. The resistance to change I'd seen in the church members was not unlike the resistance from Arizona to invasion and plunder. I didn't want to plunder faithful Christians.

On the bright side, as Mother would say, springtime rebirth sprouted at the church. I now had a new salary and benefits package that was fair. We'd created a "Roadrunner" newsletter born with the help of our new copy machine. We replaced the old religious pictures with hand-stitched bright banners, and Bernice prepared the altar every Sunday with fresh flowers or art pieces that said "this is sacred space." She used liturgical colors to mark the proper mood for the season—like purple for the meditative period of Lent. Last week her display of palms fanned out under the cross for Palm Sunday.

Today, over in the fields past the greens, pronghorn antelope grazed. The sleek animals chomped the grasses or lifted their heads to stare at my pilgrim's progress. The atmosphere changed, smelled earthy. A handsome buck, proud of his magnificent horns, turned his mighty head to regard my long-legged stride. Being observed with disinterest made me uncomfortable. I wondered if I belonged among the Easter folk in Arizona. I was a first-class doubter who sometimes thought of Jesus as Harvey the rabbit. Guilt jangled in my pocket. I wanted to sit down and watch the antelope but I walked on, hoping to get somewhere.

The note I kept under the glass on my desk, a quotation from W.H. Auden the British poet, helped me deal with doubt. Auden, a gay man, had accepted Christianity and decided to live with its contradictions: "Christianity is a way, not a state; a Christian is never something one is, only something one can pray to become."

The graceful antelope reminded me of two quiet characters of the church, a man I'll call Andy Follette and Mary Frances Ogg. She served us with music that created a unifying spirit in the congregation and transformed the empty building into a place of worship. I remember few conversations with her, but I recall clearly the devotion in her music, a love that gave me strength.

Faithful Andy Follette, a born-again Christian, came to our congregation with his wife, Pearl, because we were the only church in their neighborhood. They were believers who knew that everything that happened was God's doing. If people cheated him or hurt others, Andy never wavered from faith in their redemption, and his own, through Christ. Every word of the Bible was the truth. His instincts for forgiveness and generosity were enough to raise everyone's spirits and teach us what it meant to live a faithful life. Such people were as necessary as the water of life to a church of Jesus Christ. He and Pearl cheerfully accepted me, a woman minister privately questioning the Christian dogma they cherished.

"You been washed in the blood of the lamb, Pastor?" Andy asked one day, as if it was the most natural of questions.

"That's a hard one, Andy. You catch me off guard," I answered, grateful for a ride to the car repair shop.

"It's changed my life since I found Jesus." Andy's age showed in his shaking hands and the droop of his eyelids, but I thought he was adorable.

"I know. I can tell you're a man at peace with God." The

afternoon had a rosy glow through my sunglasses. Cottonwood trees along the river bed moved in leafy vibrations as if responding to silent music.

"Jesus found me, you could say. I was a sorry man before that. Down in the dumps—Pearl bein' sick so much and all." Andy was a master of tools and machinery. He could haul a tree stump or pack down the church parking lot, but nothing he did could change the vague sickness in his wife.

"I'm glad you're doing better. You always seem cheerful to me, like a happy man." I sneezed.

We passed a shop selling spas and sewing services. Dewey didn't seem like a place where people frolicked in spas, but maybe more was going on here than I suspected.

"I am a happy man, a saved man, you could say, Pastor. Found my personal savior, like the Bible says." He slowed the truck and glanced at me. "Wish Pearl could look up. She's a believer, you know, but it don't seem to fix her much."

"I'm sorry about Pearl. I worry about John's illnesses too." Pearl didn't come to church often enough for me to get to know her. When I'd visited their home, she provided a tasty meal with dumplings, but like Bernice she wouldn't talk about herself. Wishing I could do more for the Follettes, I blew my nose into one of John's soft handkerchiefs.

One afternoon, Andy came to our door carrying a paper sack. Like a clean-shaven Santa, he stepped into the living room, took off his baseball cap, and grunted, "You got some view up here."

John got up from his green easy chair and snapped off CNN's coverage of the struggles in the Gulf. Fires blazed across the Middle East, and Saddam Hussein was stonewalling. Tensions were rising.

"Good to see you, Andy," John said.

"Sorry you been sick." Andy referred to John's latest illness, a blood disorder. He handed me a jar from his paper sack. "Brought you some of Pearl's peach jam."

"Thanks!" I said. "Tell her we appreciate this."

Our visitor—in blue jeans, a white shirt, and black suspenders—rested his heavy body in our bentwood rocking chair, stretched his legs, and peered into the open beams of the ceiling.

"Pretty cold spring so far," he said. "The apricots'll freeze if it snows after Easter."

I withdrew to the kitchen, preoccupied with rumblings about the Middle East I'd been hearing from the television. Sometimes I caught hateful words from Christian preachers speaking of our superior Christian culture under attack from evil Muslims as if Jesus ordered us to assault a godless enemy. Thank God for Andy Follette in the rocking chair. He reminded me of redemptive love in the hearts of many Christians. Andy was the real thing.

"Hear you're feeling real weak," Andy said to John.

"Yes. It might be something related to my work. Probably from the toxins I used in developing photos at the paper."

"Has to be hard…Pearl's not doing so good."

"What's the matter?"

"Oh, some sore muscles in her neck. Back too, I think. She's been in that recliner two days."

"Elaine likes a chiropractor. Have you thought of that?"

"Pearl, she won't try anything. She gets up to cook, but I know she's hurting."

Andy mentioned his wife's back a second time and John recommended a neck vibrator he used to relieve tight muscles. He brought the oval device from the cabinet next to the couch, snapped off the lid and pressed the button while Andy studied the process as if he'd never seen such technology. Persuaded to borrow the vibrator for Pearl, he put the instrument in his sack, shook John's hand, and said, "You take care now," and left.

After a few days, Andy came to see me at the church. He stood in the office doorway holding a tired hat in his hands. "Charlie chewed it up, Pastor," he said. "That vibrator. Maybe the humming thing sounded like a critter." His head bowed and his hands—and hat—went into his pockets.

I suppressed a laugh and told him not to worry. "Charlie didn't mean it."

"I was raised to return what I borrowed in better condition than when I borrowed it," he said, studying the floor.

I stood and smiled, reassuring this gentleman with the authority of my height and status. "We don't need that vibrator, Andy. Don't worry about it." My smile was benign, pastoral.

"I'll find one for you. Be a little time," he told the floor.

So much for my pastoral smiles.

Andy dropped by the church office periodically to say he'd not been able to find a vibrator in the hardware store or the beauty shops of Prescott. Then he decided to search in Phoenix. I begged him not to bother to make that four-hour trip, but I was arguing with a believer and his Christian ethic.

I didn't anticipate that Andy would go to a sex shop, and I have trouble envisioning that scene—an overweight kindly man in suspenders and clean work pants walking into a store selling pornography: "You got any vibrators?" Andy returned pleased, with a different kind of vibrator. While he demonstrated for John how the new one fit over the neck and gave a fine massage, I left the room.

Now, as I walked beside a green golf course, the budding trees and noisy birdsong reminded me again that the sermon for Easter Sunday loomed. The people in the blue chairs expected a proclamation: "On the third day, Jesus rose from the dead." To say, "Maybe not," would mean I'd have to step away from the Dewey pulpit. I'd not been called to question biblical accounts; I'd been called to reinforce faith, and that's what I had to do, or leave. That alternative felt awful. I liked being a minister. I liked Dewey and Arizona and the little Faith United Church. I couldn't give them up.

I decided not to preach the resurrection of Jesus as fact. Whether or not my sermon matched everyone's Easter story, I decided, I could count on the good will in the congregation and Mrs. Ogg's music. *Thank you, Jesus.*

At the halfway point in my walk, I turned at the usual signpost and headed back to my house and its steep driveway. This morning pattern, a simple routine, brought clarity out of confusion and made the rough places plain, as the Bible says.

When I arrived at the church early on Easter morning, everything was ready for a celebration. Lew had placed extra chairs for the extra people who'd be coming to the service. Bernice had banked white lilies in front of the altar, and they burst forth in a glorious array that made me sneeze. Hanging from the pulpit was a white cloth with the letters IHS—the first three letters in Greek for *Jesus*—stitched in gold. The wooden cross on the rough stone wall looked proud under a spotlight, and spring radiance poured through the colorful windows. On the side wall was a white Easter banner: "He is Risen." It felt as if God arranged it all, but I knew that God's people, Lew and Bernice, had taken care of everything.

Cars crunched across the gravel parking lot. The voices of three women soon echoed from the kitchen as they prepared decaf and set out the Easter cake. Mrs. Ogg came early too. She brought her harp for this special occasion and began practicing a soft meditative prelude. In my office the portable heater warmed my back as I started to practice my sermon out loud to the collection of crosses on the wall, including a driftwood cross from a California beach and an Arizona art piece in wood and copper.

I turned the manuscript pages—speaking softly, making corrections—until I smelled a chemical odor and felt a hot sting on my legs. The entire back half of my white pleated skirt had melted away! Unhurt, I took off what was left of the skirt, dropped it on the closet floor and put on a white clerical robe, disguising the catastrophe. Was my Christian commitment melting away? The question was never far from my mind, but this was not the time to find a metaphor in a melted skirt.

Minutes later, conscious of a warm nylon underslip touching the back of my legs, I walked down the center aisle of the church following the choir, a group of sixteen in gold robes with white Easter stoles. Every seat in the church was filled, and the atmosphere felt charged. A few women were wearing Easter hats. We sang "Christ the Lord is Risen Today" with the fervent hope that the Easter service symbolizes—hope for peace, for protection from evil, for a long life on a nurturing planet. A trumpeter played a triumphal phrase between verses of the hymn to stir the hearts of everyone who'd come to church on Easter Sunday to be moved by the sight of lilies, the words of Christian liturgy, and Halleluiahs.

After announcements and the hearty singing of another Easter hymn, "The Day of Resurrection," I stepped into the pulpit and asked for concerns from the congregation to include in a community prayer. Andy mentioned Pearl's health; Becky said someone hurt the school hamster; and a visitor asked for prayers for rape victims, a matter often left out of church prayers. I added words for those suffering from AIDS, for the military marshaled in the Middle East, and for Arizona under assault from us trespassers.

Creating my presentation for Easter had been a tough discipline, given my doubts, so I preached a message that spoke of an earthbound Jesus who changed lives. I began with some background:

> Spring has become the season to remember the miracle of the empty tomb, but we who are enlightened know that April nineteenth is not really the day Jesus rose from the dead. I like to put it this way: some believed that Christ reappeared, like a tulip, after they had seen him killed, so spring is the proper time to celebrate that miracle...
>
> The real Easter day is shrouded in mystery, and we must live with that. No matter the date. In this flashing Easter moment our faith is centered. A murdered man appears to his followers, to his disciples and to the church ever after...

As I look back, I see a tall woman in middle years standing in the pulpit, a woman whom God never called. She feels uneasy. All she has for assurance that she belongs in Arizona preaching in a church is a gesture from a strange woman in her backyard one afternoon years ago.

> On Easter we celebrate both the reappearance of Jesus and spring coming into our colder, darker winter. Halleluiahs, bunnies, and chickies are quite right for this celebration—and so are those gorgeous hats!

The face of Andy Follette down in front looked content with his risen Jesus, son of the very God. These words were for him:

> "Christ is risen." That affirmation is wonderful.

It means no more fear of the unknown, no more
absence of love. Death is not the end. Our Easter
egg is full of sweetness to nourish us the rest of our
lives, and springtime is perfect for re-awakening...

I finished the sermon and we sang the offertory hymn while I
wondered whether I'd hear complaints that I'd edited out some
Easter details. The faces in front of me let me know that most in the
congregation assumed I preached a risen god. Jim Godfrey wasn't
frowning. He and the others heard the version of the story they
needed. How that happened was an Easter miracle.

The Easter cross

I'd learned the art of sounding Christian by using theological language that accommodated the orthodox without proclaiming ideas too hard for me to accept, but my disquiet over how little of the Christian message I could accept increased as the months went by. When I considered the Christians I knew in seminary, and the fine clergy I met in Arizona, I knew I was not really in their camp. They believed in the Father, Son, and Holy Ghost, or it seemed so. They believed we Christians are favored by God. After death those who had given their lives over—been reborn they say—will reside in bliss with God. None of that squared with my thinking. I'd come to Arizona to preach and teach what I learned from the beautiful sacred stories, and I loved the church, but I couldn't go where St. Augustine and St. Paul had led Christendom. That doubt I kept to myself.

"Crown him with many crowns" we sang at the end of the service, and the choir recessed to the rear of the church followed by their leader, a proud Virginia. I followed them and greeted the crowd eager to taste the Easter sweets.

During the reception after the Easter service—featuring decaf and a sheetcake as big as a bedspread—it occurred to me we should have a ceremony to bless the neighborhood animals like Andy's dog Charley and the wild creatures living in secret around us. Inspired by Becky's plea for the school hamster, I thought of the animals in the desert. They came into my consciousness often. The minute you stepped outdoors, you noticed movement, heard whispers of scurrying. We lived alongside javelinas, bobcats, deer, rabbits, and songbirds. I wanted especially to bless the antelope and the red-tailed hawks. Honoring the spirit within all creatures seemed an Easter thing to do.

When I suggested the idea of having a ceremony to bless the animals, the council members looked as if I'd suggested giving up decaf for rum. They rejected such a blessing ritual, they said, because it was what the Catholics did. I sipped my decaf, wanting to leave the conference table and walk away.

Now, remembering that first Easter in Arizona, I sense that disappointment again and see a burned white skirt lying in a heap in the closet.

On a glorious May morning that year, I drove to the church and opened the empty building, letting myself in and turning on the heat to take off a chill. Wandering through the cold church with the lights off, I thought about how odd it was that I was in such a place. What had brought me to a career in ministry? Maybe the spring season, the coming of the light, inspired thoughts about what started my transformation from sarcastic, even cynical, English teacher to Christian minister.

I blamed the breakdown of my car and my dog's sad face, but the truth is, I'd been thinking about religious studies for months, even years, and my interest had spiked after an odd encounter one afternoon: I saw an otherworldly figure standing in my backyard—a strange woman who reminded me of my grandmother. The ghostly woman beckoned to me. I somehow knew she was indicating that I act on my desire to leave teaching and go to seminary.

After seeing that apparition, I visited the Reverend Carole Keim, a minister who worked as an assistant at the Congregational Church across from my home where I lived with John and my daughter. (My son, Joe, didn't live with us then; he'd gone to live with his father.) I needed to tell Carole about the ghost.

I seated myself in Reverend Carole's office at the church, a converted closet with pale pink walls adorned with a beach watercolor painting. I told her about my grandmother, Aurelia, an artist and loving figure in my childhood. "I saw her standing in the backyard after she died. This is hard to talk about."

"That name is so beautiful. Aurelia," Carole said. "Has a mystical sound."

"Yes," I said in a low voice. "I'm not sure what I really saw but it made me curious." I tried not to stare at Carole in her clerical collar, a trim pretty blond. Minister Barbie. "Grandma Aurelia was dressed in long robes. Her hair was flying around in the wind. I don't think it was windy. She waved. Or, I think, spoke to me. This sounds crazy."

"Tell me more about what the vision means to you." Barbie leaned her arms on her desk.

Vision? I've had a vision? "Grandma loved me unconditionally."

My voice faded. "She never mislead me. And, truth is, teaching's no longer what I want to do." I cleared my throat. "Things have changed in schools, left me behind maybe."

"You don't seem old-fashioned, Elaine."

"Well, under the current regulations there's no classroom time for serious discussion and writing." I stared at a large curved shell on Carole's bookcase and sensed my rising anger. "The emphasis on passing state-mandated tests makes me crazy! The bureaucracy is gaining on me."

"I can imagine. And then this vision?"

"Yes. It was in the late afternoon, my favorite time of day. I was reading on the backyard lawn swing and must have fallen asleep or moved into an altered state." I stopped and managed a smile. "Grandma didn't look like she used to before her death. She seemed like a character from an old book. 'Come away,' she said, or 'Come here.' Or not really saying words. I can't..."

Carole nodded. "I think I understand. Are you considering a religious vocation?"

"Oh dear. That sounds too...It's just that I feel drawn to religion—have since high school. Sacred music seems to, well, send me somewhere, and I want...I don't know what I want." Carole waited. "I do have time and some money—thanks to the divorce from Carl—and I could, maybe, go to graduate school, I guess, and...John thinks it's crazy."

"Then I'm as crazy as you are."

"But, I'm not a pious person. I feel angry sometimes. I've not been super-mom, and I'm divorced, for heaven's sake."

"Nothing else?"

"Well, yes. I'm full of self-doubt, and..." The tiny closet-office felt stuffy. I wanted to push my chair back, but there was no room to move. "The worst part is I can't buy into the Christian stuff about Jesus dying for our sins. I need to study it all."

"You qualify," Carole said, smiling. "Perfect people can't understand anything. And Jesus will keep you going for a long time."

I breathed out tension. "How'd you get the courage to leave your real life and go to seminary?"

"Let's see," she said as if it was hard to remember. Glancing away from my face, she said, "I raised the children alone after my husband died. (pause) I was active in church. (pause) Then I took leadership training and met rare women who were in ministry. That did it. I took a chance and followed the longings of my spirit."

The longings of my spirit? How could she say that with a straight face? I didn't have spiritual feelings—whatever that meant—and envied them in her. My urge to study religion came from unknown territory that I wanted to enter, a hidden place beneath a trapdoor under a rug you explored with quiet steps and watchful glances.

Absorbing the meaning of our conversation would take some doing, not to mention dealing with the contrast between the two of us. When she was in high school, Carole probably twinkled like the girl with the pink ribbon while I skulked along ugly hallways. Unlike her, I'd not spent much time volunteering, let alone working, in a church. Though I directed a children's play there once and attended the Sunday services—and had my children baptized—mostly I sat in a back pew captivated by the music and watching Carole in her robe.

"I think you'd love Berkeley and the Pacific School of Religion," Carole said. "The place has character and attracts excellent theologians. They offer courses in the arts I know you would like." She took a glossy booklet from the shelf and handed it to me. On the cover was a photo of a gothic chapel with three pointed stained glass windows. Pacific School of Religion.

"I just want to read more about it. Don't ask me to do anything." I hid the booklet in my purse.

"I know. You can see the Golden Gate Bridge from the seminary lawn."

"You're not helping." I got up to leave, thinking of the remarkable fact that I had enough money from the divorce settlement to quit teaching and go to graduate school.

The decision to resign from my teaching job and go off to study took only a few days and felt like conversion. Every task felt lighter and my students seemed funnier. Hassles with Margaret were less devastating. Within days of talking with Carole, the dog pulled a sad face, the car broke down, and I was sure that next fall I'd drive up Highway Five on my way to the Golden Gate Bridge and Pacific School of Religion.

Silence and peace in the Arizona sanctuary brought back the vision of my grandmother whose unconditional love reassured me that I could be a minister. Her validation was reinforced by women friends who supported me through a divorce and my choice to go to Berkeley. I was riding a new wave of women's liberation, one in which we encouraged each other to take chances and intrude into men's territory carrying the flag of equality.

John, of course, had an interest in keeping me in San Diego where he enjoyed living in my home at low cost. I told him of my plans to go to seminary as we cleared the table after dinner one evening.

"I can't believe you'd leave," he said with a whine. We hadn't married then, and he must have felt unsure about our relationship.

"It's just an experiment." I carried the messy plates to the sink talking amiably and avoiding John's face. "I want to look into…It's hard to explain. I'm not sure where it'll take me." I tried to sound positive, though I had a list of worries: about leaving him in San Diego, taking my daughter where she didn't want to go, abandoning my son to Carl—a man not altogether trustworthy—and uprooting my dog. "You'll visit when you can. We'll be home at all the breaks."

"You aren't thinking of becoming a minister, are you? It's Carole's influence, I know. I don't trust her." He blew out the flames of two green candles on the table, his bald head shining in their fluttering light.

"Hey! No one needs blaming here. This is my idea. And yes, I am thinking of ministry. Why not?"

The wine bottle and butter dish made an unnecessary clatter in John's hands. "Women ministers aren't normal. I mean, they seem like…"

Not normal? I took a breath before saying "I'm just responding to, well, something, an appealing idea." My pile of dishes banged on the tile counter. "Besides, I'll probably hate it and miss you terribly."

Knowing I wouldn't hate leaving him or hate going away to study, I opened the dishwasher and noticed the birdfeeder—illuminated by the kitchen light—outside the window. The feeder moved in the night breeze, a silent bell. Twelve-year-old Joey had placed it there before he left our house to live with his father.

The reality of my son's leaving home at age ten hit me again while I sat in the quiet church thinking of my children. Joe was as deliberate as Margaret was chaotic. He delighted in school, had many friends, and was a creative child with ideas that continually surprised. He sang and questioned and pondered. I had him pegged as a future symphony conductor or Nobel scientist. Because he was small, he loved the Stuart Little stories, and I loved reading them to him— until one day he took all that energy and went to live with his father.

I heard again his shout the day he announced he was leaving.

"Mom, I'm home!"

Joey had spent the weekend with Carl who lived in a small ocean-front hotel in La Jolla where he sold art—paintings, sculpture, and antiques—and played backgammon for money. Carl was bitter toward me and refused to pay child support, but he took Joey on weekends and occasionally included Margaret. Both children adored Carl's company and loved his hotel penthouse above the Pacific.

"How'd it go, Joey?" I expected the usual account of adventures with Daddy.

He dropped his backpack on the round table in the kitchen. "Can I talk to you?" He sat in the yellow chair, his eyes watching me.

"Sure. What's on your mind?" I turned from the sink where I'd been peeling an avocado and faced my son, a small-boned boy in a fringed leather vest, the one he'd worn since he was five.

"Mom, could I go live with Dad?"

I'd probably ignored Joey's earlier hints about this plan, but now the words were out, lying on the table like dirty socks. "This is quite a surprise."

"I've been thinking about it a long time." He was unsmiling. A child of mixed heritage, his Chinese features altered as he'd grown older, and he now looked more like his Portuguese forebears, the olive-skinned explorer. "I don't like the new school, and Margaret bugs me all the time. I want to go."

"Does your father want you to live with him?"

"Yeah! I'd have a room in the hotel, and there's good schools in La Jolla."

"I know." I marvel now that I didn't worry that Carl's lifestyle could get in the way of his parenting. It never occurred to me. I knew my ex-husband well enough to feel confident that he loved Joey and would never hurt him.

I opened the refrigerator, feeling Joey's green eyes staring at me as I lingered in front of the lighted interior, facing into the cool. I turned back to him. "You've had a hard time ever since you were bused to Lincoln. I'm sorry."

Random chance had selected Joey to move to the all-black school across town to increase the racial mix in our local elementary school. No excuses were allowed. What had I done?

"It'd be so much better with Dad," Joey said softly. "I could help out at the hotel. I want to learn to surf. I already do some of the cooking for Dad and me."

"Surf? Of course." I sat at the table without any wonderful food, my hands clasped together as I'd been taught in second grade. I couldn't think of a reason that might persuade Joey to stay. He looked so appealing in his western vest, his wide eyes blinking.

"Joey, I had no idea. Are you sure this is what you want?"

"It's just that I want to go."

On the birdfeeder outside, a blue jay sat on the perch, hanging on despite a strong breeze. To force Joey to stay with me felt cruel. He had a volatile sister and an embattled school. I waited for inspiration. Alone with Margaret, I could give her more attention and calm her spirit, help with school problems. I wouldn't have the expense of two children.

I wish I'd refused my son's request and kept him with me. At the time I couldn't face his disappointment, his tears, or his anger.

Carl's Mercedes convertible appeared within days at the curb and we carried Joey's things out, including the leather vest. By the time I walked the few feet back into the house, my nose ran, my head ached, and I saw a failure of a mother in the mirror. I retreated to bed early and dreamed my father died.

Elaine with children Margaret and Joe at her wedding

Sitting in a blue chair facing the cross in the darkened Arizona church, I felt again the sorrow of the day Joey left, but it helped my spirits to remember the strength it took to leave San Diego with Margaret and drive into Northern California headed for Pacific School of Religion in a dubious car with only an agreeable dog for support. The Holy Spirit must have been involved.

*I hope you will go along with my definition of what I've called a "spiritual life," an inner life where we find resources for growing and coping with troubles that come our way. Our spiritual life affects our values, our ability to love, and our strength in times of crisis. When we have it, we have "presence," when we don't, we are shallow, empty, and easily led.*

## Two Models for the Spiritual Life

### FIVE

"You do a good job at the church, Reverend," the handsome man I'll call Grant Barringer said in a Western drawl. "Hard to find open minds here in the provinces." He stood behind the bar of his downtown Prescott cafe wearing a bistro apron.

Pleased by the compliment, I watched Grant from a seat at a table in the small, empty restaurant cooled by merciful air-conditioning. Another Arizona summer had arrived with some muggy days, and the drive over from Dewey left me too warm. Grant looked like a flashy Hollywood phony with his tan skin, open shirt showing a gold chain on dark chest hair, and luminous eyes made for seduction. I was in the mood for Hollywood at the moment.

Grant and his wife, Rosemary, had landed in Arizona—and on our church—from a faraway planet called California. He'd been a self-styled minister. Rosemary, an aging blonde beauty on her third marriage, was a psychotherapist and frequent guest on Los Angeles television. Now she managed their home in Prescott and Grant managed their café. Nothing could be more captivating to a restless minister than these two aliens.

I'd been in Dewey over a year and had forgotten about pampered and polished Californians like the Barringers. My first impression was that they represented the Me generation of the high-flying eighties. They came to church each Sunday dressed as if for cocktail parties, and they preferred ballroom dancing to golf. Second impressions come later.

"Don't you feel bored in quiet Arizona?" I asked Grant. I'd come to the café to meet him because he and Rosemary had been attending our church for several weeks, and it was my job to get to know them. Usually I brought a small loaf of homemade bread with me as a token of good will from the church members. Today I came empty-handed, assuming the Barringers wouldn't be receptive to anything home baked, a faulty conclusion.

"I don't get bored here," he said. "I come from a Western background, y'know." He tried to sound like a John Wayne cowpoke while he polished a stack of ashtrays one by one and replaced them in a row on a bar of polished wood.

"Funny. I thought you were from the big city, from greater Los Angeles." I missed Southern California, especially the beaches and masses of flowers in San Diego.

"Not at first." He wiped the clean surface and grinned. "I come from the Res."

"Oh? You mean the Reservation?"

"Yep. Mom was an Indian prostitute, carried me on her back." Grant was having fun with his account of himself, though he may have actually returned to his roots. Prescott is close to the Navajo Reservation, and the Yavapai tribe prospers in the county.

As he placed a 7Up in front of me, complete with cherry, I pondered Grant's story and watched cars move by on the street outside the window facing Prescott's courthouse square. A propped sign on the sidewalk welcomed everyone to The Gurley Street Café and Bar. The potted tree near the door waved at passing cars.

I smiled and said, "You've come a long way. My sources tell me you've done some preaching."

"Sure have, ma'am. Had a church in LA with quite a following. They were hungry for a progressive approach to religion. I never said much about Jesus—don't know much about him in fact." He smiled, showing off his George Hamilton white teeth. "Like to help people get along."

No Jesus? Grant left the Nazarene out of his ministry? I shouldn't have been surprised. The idea of eliminating Jesus from Christian churches was a new trend in religion, gaining ground with people who wanted the fresh bread of a spirituality that spoke of living the good life rather than bloody bodies hanging on crosses. Some were calling it "New Age," and Grant was evidently a disciple. He liked to help people get along? John would enjoy that.

My own Christianity was not so far from Grant's, but I saw Jesus as necessary to spiritual growth. He was, I believed, a moral teacher, a radical spirit that changed history. Jesus needed to be part of our study and prayer because I believed he was in touch with the spirit of God, but I didn't explore the matter that afternoon in the Barringer bistro.

"Got tired of ministry," Grant said, "and Rosemary wanted to leave Hollywood." His comment rang with honesty though I suspected a scandal had sent them to us.

"How come you've decided to drive all the way from Prescott to our little church in Dewey?" I asked, taking my drink to his counter. "There's a big Congregational Church right here that would probably suit you."

"Rosemary likes the idea of a woman minister. We talked to a few people who said you were from California and gave a good sermon." A heart-stirring smile. "Drove out to Dewey, and the people were nice. Your message pleased both of us. So we stayed."

"Thanks. I'm glad." I was more than glad. I was thrilled by the compliment. "I think you two bring a new energy to our church." I sipped the sweet drink, pleased that our golfing and gardening congregation accepted this unusual couple. "I'm sure we'll get along just fine," I assured him, hoping that was true. "I've some books about Jesus I could lend you," I added, ever the schoolteacher. "Interested?"

"Yeah," he said—an unexpected response in this flashy man who must be hiding something nefarious.

Summer tourists in shorts paraded by outside, licking cones and studying the shop windows. Prescott's frontier hotels, their ghosts and the Western saloons lured the visitors here as they'd lured me a year ago. But I was not the same woman as I was in my first days here. Spirit Woman now laughed more, had fewer self-conscious worries, and felt at home with the changes in the high country outside her windows as clouds migrated and the land became white with snow.

Grant and I talked of his problems doing business in small-town Prescott and of his past career as a Hollywood minister. He set down a crate of glasses, and I smiled into his tanned face.

"Thanks for the 7Up," I said. "I have to get going. I'll stop by and see Rosemary soon." When I visited Grant's wife, I thought, I'd learn more about what really brought them here from Hollywood.

As soon as I got home I picked out *Incarnation*, a book of essays about Jesus by admirable writers: Annie Dillard, John Updike, and Mary Gordon, among others. Dillard expressed a sentiment I liked: "I had a head for religious ideas…They made other ideas seem mean." I put the book aside for Grant, trying not to judge his "get along" brand of religion. After all, I'd come here to learn where God, church, and I met. Grant could be on a similar journey. We were a funny pair. Could people like us lead a church where Joan of Arc and Martin Luther King, Jr. had gone before—not to mention Jesus? It wasn't up to me to decide who was worthy, but it would have helped to have a word from God: "Yep. You're the people I need."

On a street carving through a forest landscape, roofs of large houses emerged through the trees. Those were the residences of the Prescott wealthy, the patrons of the arts, the doctors, and judges. Birds fluttered courteously and the squirrels behaved themselves, unlike the snorting javelinas—wild peccaries—that plowed through our yard in Dewey. I drove slowly toward a mammoth pine tree presiding over grounds in front of Grant and Rosemary's home.

The quiet shaded avenue brought feelings of isolation. I'd followed my heart to Arizona, but I didn't anticipate that ministry in a new land would feel like exile. My friends back in San Diego seemed so remote. I missed familiar beaches, balmy air, good theater, and the energy in California. The lonely feeling may have come from the silence of the district I entered that afternoon. I saw no one.

Three years ago in San Diego I'd not imagined I'd feel alienation in Arizona. Back then I plotted and planned as if the idea of leaving was as exciting as a trip to Zanzibar. One critical day I invited Sally—secretary and jewelry adviser—to my office at the San Diego church, a space lit by a floor lamp to make it cozy, hoping she'd listen to my thoughts on leaving San Diego for parts unknown.

After she greeted several women leaving the Quilter's room down the hall from my office, Sally came in with two mugs of coffee.

"What took you so long?" I asked. "And close that door."

"Can't you manage five seconds without me?"

"Stick around for a minute." I pointed to a chair, "and listen to my rantings. I don't care if you've a thousand things to do. I need you here."

"Yes, my leader." She set a mug on the desk.

"Don't tell anyone but I haven't much to do today except think about my future—"

"Is that it? Can I go?"

"You know it isn't! I want you to hear this." I tried the coffee, sweetened to perfection. "I'm tired of managing kids' programs, of organizing and planning and then stepping aside for the boss to get the credit. Responsibility without the glory, I call it."

"Can I turn off the computer?" She started to get up, moving in her halting way. "This is going to take a while."

I put my chin on my palm and waited, studying the office with its two cartons of holiday costumes and children's drawings on the bulletin board. It looks like Kindergarten in here, I thought, and this thin carpet is symbolic of the value folks place on my ministry. I'm fifty-four years old! Time to move.

Sally returned and shut the door behind her. "Are you sure it isn't the carpeting?" she asked, reading my mind. "Those jerks carpeted the senior minister's office, my office, and the conference room and left yours with this old stuff. Bet you're secretly pissed."

"It isn't just the carpet. I want more to do. I want to make real decisions. I want to preach every Sunday. Are you getting the picture?"

She picked up her mug. "You like power."

"It's not power!" I protested. "Well, it's more like respect."

"Okay. I get it: time for you to go. You'll miss this place and its lovely new carpet, of course. Can a woman really get a job as a senior minister? I never met one." This was 1988. Women in the pulpit were rare.

"An astute question." I sighed and turned to the window and the view of the San Diego sidewalk, so urban and familiar. "I'll cast a wide net—all over the West—and see if some poor church that can't find a decent man would settle for a woman. It could happen." I clasped my hands, a gesture that always gave me comfort, excited by the decision and grateful to Sally for paying attention. "Thanks for listening. It's helped. Don't know how I'm going to tell John."

"You can throw him out!" Sally said on her way back to her desk.

Smiling, I reached for the phone to call the Congregational Church office that prepared information about churches looking for ministers.

In a few weeks I got responses from two churches, one in Oregon and one in Arizona—the only churches in the Western states willing to consider a woman minister— and read the information they provided, complete with photographs and words of praise for their churches and locations.

Taking the church materials home with me, I decided to see what John thought about moving away from San Diego so I could be a minister on my own. If it meant the breakup of our marriage, that no longer felt like catastrophe.

"Let's go out somewhere nice. I need cheering up," I said as soon as John came inside after he arrived home from work. I needed to confess that I was bored with my job as an assistant minister and wanted to move away from San Diego. He'd balk. This would not be a temporary time away to study; this would be a permanent change. I chose a romantic setting for disclosing my plans.

The sun disappeared behind the sturdy tower of the church across the street as we walked to his tan Toyota, parked in front of the house. John's tall frame was getting heavier, but he carried himself with the poise of a former runner.

"Why do you need cheering up?"

"Wait till we get there." I took his arm. "It's so lovely to just go out to dinner and not have to wonder whether Margaret's coming home." My daughter had moved away in a hasty marriage by then, and she was often in my thoughts. Her leaving felt like failure. Maybe I'd fail a church too, but I wanted to leave San Diego for a more challenging ministry.

A psychologist like Rosemary would know about unconscious motives, but mine were left unexplored until I sat down to write this memoir. All I knew was I was willing to change my life, to leave everything I loved about my home and city to find what I needed personally and professionally.

My venture into Arizona would be an odyssey of sorts, a wandering that I hoped would not only be enriching, but also lead me into wisdom. Ministry would change me, make me worthy. Worthiness, I learned, doesn't come from a role in a noble profession. It may come from stumbling over the rocks and falling into potholes on the journey. The best place for such an odyssey is the Arizona desert where I was watched by airborne creatures and scuttling ones, where I was overseen by Christians in a little church.

John and I drove down the hill into Old Town, a jumble of Mexican shops and restaurants. "I think Marg will be okay," John said, his deep voice a pleasing rumble. "She'll call one of these days."

After we were seated in an old adobe home converted to a restaurant and candle shop, John looked at me as if expecting the worst—that I'd changed my mind and wanted him to leave because of his love affair.

"Don't look so worried," I said. "I'm wondering about my ministry. What I want to do next." I realized with those words that the news would hit John hard.

"Are you kidding?" He lowered his voice and glanced around as if there were listeners in the room. The Spanish colonial atmosphere, with its low-beamed ceiling and smell of candles, reminded me of the Mission Archangel. "You've got things pretty good at the San

Diego church. The people love you." He leaned toward me. "What are you thinking?"

This was not Sally I was dealing with. I needed to take care with my words. As the red wine was poured—a fitting color for this Spanish setting—I said, "Truth is, I want to find a church where I can be the only minister." I fingered the stem of my wine glass. "The assistant work is okay. But it's not enough. It's too easy. I'm getting bored with it." John coughed and started to say something, but I interrupted. "I need to preach more and try the whole scope of ministry. I'll have to leave San Diego." If anyone could understand discontent, it would be my husband.

"You're thinking of changing jobs? Christ, I can not believe it." He coughed again, harder.

Before he could say more, I added, "I know you've never been thrilled with my being a minister. Mother sure can't figure it out. But I want to do real ministry on my own—that's the short version."

John picked up a piece of bread and set it aside. "I don't know what to say. I've been in so much pain with the knee. I can't seem to get any better." It was a whine, and I'd heard it before. How much more of this complaining did I want to endure? "My depression isn't helped much by the medication. If you would just—"

"Don't you think leaving here might help, might be exciting?" I was grinding my teeth by then. I'd get a migraine if I didn't get a grip, as Sally would say. "You could retire. Leaving your job might be a real boost." Did I really want him with me?

"Nothing—seems—to help," John said. "You do not have any idea what it is to be depressed. Nobody does. Moving will not help." He lowered his eyes and picked up his water glass, looking like our spaniel in her most disappointed mood.

Did screwing your secretary help? I thought, unable to speak such words out loud. I took a swallow of wine. "I'll visit a church in Oregon, but I'm most interested in a church in the northern part of Arizona, a small church with a commitment to grow, and they've invited me to speak the first Sunday in January."

"I do not believe this."

The waitress approached with our dinners. As soon as she left,

John leaned to one side, looking off, and added, "You mean you'd just go, even if I said no?"

I didn't answer. Candlelight flickered in wall niches and on tables. I drank some more wine, the rich color reminding me of sacramental blood.

"This is about Lois, isn't it, Elaine? I can hear your anger."

"I don't know." I was clear about wanting a new job, but not about whether I wanted to stay married. Why couldn't my life be a TV movie, with everything settled in ninety minutes?

"Would you rather go alone?" he asked.

"I'd like you to go with me to Dewey in January to see everything and meet the people. You could retire and join me if you chose to. It would be your decision. We'd take it from there." Surprised at what I'd put before us, I folded my napkin into a neat square, pleased I'd staked my claim.

We ate by candlelight, swallowing what seemed like sacramental bread in the Mission Archangel where mysteries fascinate and frighten us at the same time.

When I decided I wanted a ministry away from playing a secondary role to male senior ministers, I didn't think about being lonely. I didn't realize that a minister in a church has no real friends in the congregation. My seminary education had failed me in that regard. I know, though, that I would have gone into the desert anyway. I needed to stake a claim in an unknown mine that could be hiding rich rewards.

Rosemary Barringer was an unusual figure in Arizona, like an orchid flourishing among native brush. When she opened the door of their home, I heard soft music. About to enter a movie scene, I stepped inside, leaving behind the summer heat, and took it all in—a sunny room with baby grand piano, a plate of chocolates set out on a fragile side table, the aroma of Rosemary's perfume. Through a plate-glass window, granite boulders shaded a flagstone patio where round and pointed shadows met in cubist patterns.

"Would you like a tour?"

"Oh yes!" I handed her the Jesus book for Grant. "This is lovely!"

Rosemary wore a gauzy lavender leisure outfit, her blond hair combed into a French roll. Her clear skin had the pallor of a woman in a classic painting. She preceded me down the hall past a bathroom with a sunken tub encircled by candles. The sound of her feathery dainty mules—slippers I'd never seen on a human before—clicked on the parquet floor. I felt like a leather-shod ranch woman.

No photographs of family, central to the homes of other church members, lined the hallway, only art works that would take hours to study. Clunky earrings and golf togs were from another planet. How had these two exotic performers made their way into my church life? They certainly didn't seem sent by God. They were so out of place that I wondered again if they'd come here to avoid some scandal.

The canopied bed looked made for passion with a cascade of pillows in pinks and magenta. I pictured myself lying there, piles of books around me, a servant in the wings. I'd drift away from everything tedious into a charmed place like the secret garden of my favorite children's novel.

"I've just heard from Jack Paar," Rosemary said. "He's such a dear, keeps up with us wherever we are."

Background music wafted over the rooms making everything otherworldly. I felt transported to Neverland and was pleased to be there.

In the kitchen, outfitted with hanging copper pots, delicate porcelain dishes had been placed artistically on open shelves. The counters were inlayed with imported tiles. The tarantula exploring my bathroom counter yesterday wouldn't dare put his hairy foot on the hand-painted squares.

I noticed a series of framed certificates above the sink. "These plaques are awards for gourmet cooking! You've competed as a cook?"

"Yes I have. It's a hobby of mine. Grant appreciates it."

The telephone rang, and while I admired the dining table in front of the patio window—already arranged for the evening meal with green candles and wine glasses—Rosemary spoke endearments to Grant in a baby talk I'd heard used only with kittens. Was this pretty woman, who talked like a toddler, losing it?

"Sorry," she said, putting down the receiver, "we talk every afternoon. I'd be bereft without those calls. Grant says to tell you thanks for the book. Could you take tea, Reverend?"

"Thanks, yes. I'd love to hear about your career. I've read a lot of psychology—"

"You've no idea. My counseling work has been so rewarding." She began tea preparations. "I've a question for you, Elaine. I notice no gay people in the congregation—none out of the closet, that is."

The sounds of the background music seemed to mute.

I could hear perfectly but didn't know how to respond. The exclusion of gays from Christian congregations was not discussed in church conversations. Finally I managed, "You've come to the land of conventional thinking. All diversity of that kind is hidden." I studied my nails. "It bothers me, but people don't want differences displayed and they let me know it." I hated confessing to cowardice.

"Makes for a duller world," Rosemary said. "Grant and I miss the variety of our California life."

"So do I." I thought of my ex-husband, Carl, the secrets he kept and the self-loathing he felt. Complacent Arizona could use a dose of diversity, I thought, but reaching out to gays would cause an uproar in our church, and I didn't want to adjudicate conflict. Just as I avoided full disclosure at Easter about Jesus, I kept my opinions about including gays hidden from the congregation. I can look back now and claim that because I was a woman in a man's profession, I had to mind my manners, press for change cautiously or I'd lose credibility. That excuse doesn't work, of course.

"Is it a battle you'd take on?" the lavender lady asked, pouring the boiling water from her kettle into a flowered teapot. When I didn't say anything, she added, "To persuade people to accept gays?"

Who was this woman? My conscience? "Maybe you could counsel me on strategies," I said at last. With her bewitching figure and these surroundings, Rosemary could be a priestess in a temple, a prophet like Tiresias, speaking to a leader afraid to hear—*a model for the spiritual life*, I'd preached.

"I'll give it some thought," she said, her smooth hands arranging a silver tray with cups and spoons. "The stifling atmosphere of secrets is unhealthy."

I needed to change the subject. "Where did you find your clients? Were they movie people?"

"Oh yes, but I find clients everywhere. I'm fascinated by the human condition *in toto*."

"You did talk therapy? Freudian analysis?" I followed my hostess into the living room with its view of the huge pine outdoors.

"Whatever worked. My passion is dream interpretation, ancient mythology, that sort of thing."

"You mean Jungian thought?"

"I loved Jung." She poured the tea and offered me milk and sugar. "Met him in fact."

"You met Carl Jung?"

"It's a good story," she said. "Years ago, my father and I were in Madrid on a visit with the king of Spain, and I told him of my interest in Jung. The king up and sent me to Switzerland with an introduction!" She patted her hair and smiled. "I think Jung liked blonds." Whether this story was true or not didn't enter my mind. I accepted every word.

The king of Spain. The words brought back memories of the San Gabriel Mission and a Spanish king who gave a baptismal font to the mission church. I sipped the hot tea, feeling a cozy intimacy with this charming woman who couldn't possibly have anything sinister in her past.

The telephone rang again. Rosemary put her hand over the mouthpiece and asked if I'd take the call. It was Sarah at the church office. I shook my head. My hostess told Sarah I'd left, and we returned to the offerings on the silver tray. I felt refreshed, as if I'd found something I'd lost.

When I got to the church full of food and images of the king of Spain, Carl Jung, and a patio of shadows, Sarah met me at the door to announce that Bernice was trying to reach me. She'd called from the Northern Arizona Medical Center for Veterans.

I called Bernice immediately at the hospital number. "Fred's had a heart attack," she said, her voice rough. "I can't believe it. They brought him here in an ambulance."

"Oh my goodness. How's he doing?" While I'd been playing tea party, Bernice needed me. I sat, dizzy with guilt.

"He's stabilized, they say."

"Do you have anyone with you?" I asked, wishing I were stabilized too.

"Ah, no. We're at the Veteran's. I'm okay."

"I'll be right over. He's a strong man, Bernice, and a healthy one too. I'm sure he'll be fine." A trip to the veteran's hospital, with its ugly corridors and smells of sterilization, would be the right punishment for me after playing in Rosemary's garden of delights. *Shallow, empty, and easily led,* words from a sermon of mine, about covered it.

"I'm worried about Sunday's flowers, Pastor," Bernice said. "I'm not sure I can do it."

"Sarah's here. She can find flowers, I'm sure. She's been bragging about her roses." Sarah nodded.

I picked up my purse and a book of prayers, checked myself in the office mirror feeling embarrassed and unworthy to "untie the sandals" of the people around me—an image from the scripture for next Sunday. Spirit Woman indeed. Hungry Woman was more like it.

"You look rather shaken, Elaine," Sarah said. "Fred'll be okay."

"I hope so. If you'll mind the store here, I'll be back in about an hour." I thought of my installation ceremony when, to the angelic sounds of Mrs. Ogg's harp, I'd pledged to regard "all people with equal love and concern, exercise pastoral care, and undertake to minister to the needs of all." Was that possible for a skeptic from California in golden earrings partial to visions of kings and sweets on a silver tray? Equal love and concern? Is that possible for any human being?

I never took the necessary steps toward inclusion of people of all sexual orientations that Rosemary encouraged. I feared fiery debates, anger and gossip in the community, especially when we planned an addition to the church building. So I held back from changing the church into a center of welcoming. Rosemary never spoke of it again, and I was left with a guilt that haunts me still.

In summer we held our church service an hour earlier in the foolish belief that Arizona was cooler at the 9:00 hour. While fans whirred above our heads, people waved their service programs in front of their faces. The whole church fluttered. Some day, air-conditioning.

I told the congregation Fred Miller was cheerful and recovering at home. He'd greeted me with smiles when I'd seen him in the hospital, and I needed that blessing. Then I reminded everyone that our fundraising auction for Habitat for Humanity was next Saturday and thanked Mrs. Johnie Fain for providing ice cream at the recent potluck. She nodded her white head and smiled.

A woman I'll call Diane Merchant stepped to the lectern and spoke about plans for remodeling the church building to accommodate our growing membership. We wanted to enlarge the sanctuary and build a real kitchen and minister's office. An assertive woman, Diane took leadership of the building committee over the protests of men who'd grumbled about a woman in charge. They were unwilling to take responsibilities themselves but still felt entitled to complain.

While Diane outlined her plans, I sat facing the congregation hoping the spirit of goodwill would keep tempers in check as remodeling plans went forward. Noticing John sitting in the back, I realized how we'd changed since that evening in the candlelit restaurant in San Diego. I was glad he'd come with me to Arizona. His funny take on church life pulled me out of self-absorption often. We were managing together, and I laughed with him more. The healing I felt had something to do with the amazing seasons, the landscape, and a little church in remote Arizona where even mysterious beautiful people like the Barringers were welcome—though gays were not.

Diane stepped away from the lectern, and we sang "Morning Has Broken," a hymn about the natural beauty of creation. Mrs. Ogg's playing set a new tone in the sanctuary, as if a benign spirit had entered. The green banner on the side wall advised "Dwell in Peace," a message people needed to hear in a church where a strong woman had taken charge of the building committee.

I read from the Book of Luke and then began the sermon, "The Wisdom of the Chief":

Each of us is on a journey toward goodness, hoping to move from where we are to where we ought to be. The trip is not easy. We're in a way like the young Indian brave who went to the tribal chief and said, "In your great wisdom, Grandfather, can you tell me the most important steps one must take in order to become a chief?"

"Well," the old chief replies, "first, he must pluck the fur from the tail of the bobcat. Then he must bring down the great white buffalo with his bare hands. Finally, he must wrestle the brown bear two falls out of three."

The young brave thinks for a moment and then responds, "Whatever happened to wholesome good looks and a nice personality?"

The congregation laughed, and I noticed with pleasure that I'd brought smiles to the Godfreys' sober faces. I cleared my throat and John cleared his too, a friendly echo.

Not only are a nice personality and good looks not enough, but the wisdom of the sages in sacred writings reminds us that in order to become a chief—to become worthy—we require humility born of self-understanding...

John the Baptist was a humble man: "I am not worthy to untie the thongs of his sandals," he said after meeting Jesus. *I am not worthy.* Sometimes we ministers forget to be humble like that...

Near the two youngsters down in front, Rosemary and Grant looked delighted to be with us. Cal Appleton, complete with oxygen tank, grinned up at me in adoration. I knew them all, every person in this little church. Knowing them was part of my commitment. Most fun, though, was preaching for them.

I like to believe other's favorable evaluations of me. You see, I make a good impression because of my height. I am seen as wise and strong, and I happily accept that evaluation even if it isn't accurate...

> Self-knowledge is hard when people revere
> you for superficial reasons. All of us need to know
> ourselves honestly. That's about as hard as bringing
> down the white buffalo with bare hands...

After the sermon, Mrs. Ogg played the meditative hymn "Spirit of God, Descend Upon My Heart," setting a mood for prayer. I sat quietly and forced a smile, thinking of Virginia Regan's criticism before the service. She often treated me like a daughter she must supervise and today she stopped by my office to tell me she was disturbed by my sober frown when I faced the congregation on Sunday mornings. "Don't look so gloomy, Reverend. It's unnerving to us, the choir especially." I must unconsciously have shown worry on my face—about John's health or about my daughter whom I'd not seen since we left San Diego—and not realized it. The encounter with Fred's heart attack and my dallying in Rosemary's parlor made me frown too. Why wasn't everybody frowning? "My frown, dear Virginia," I silently told her, "is the mirror of a worried heart, and I'll continue to frown at the whole wide world if I choose."

Lighten up, Sally said to me numerous times. Now the same message came from Virginia. I refused to believe she'd been sent by the Holy Spirit to teach me to smile. Her critique hurt. As I viewed it, people like Virginia criticized their woman ministers to keep us framed as a perfect religious icon. I'd like to know if male ministers were criticized that way. Probably not.

We stood to sing a final hymn, and as I faced the congregation in their blue chairs, I silently prayed that everyone whose face I saw that morning might be blessed with mercy and love. I'd been reading of a holy monk who prayed for everyone he knew every day.

John chose to miss the fund-raising auction and instead planned a trip to explore old Route 66 with his friend, a church member also named John. They'd stop at diners and way stations that had survived the building of superhighways. When I left him to go to the church auction, he was making notes at the dining table surrounded by maps and an article from *Arizona Highways*.

The door of our church stood wide open that afternoon.

Trappings of worship had been removed, and around the edges of the sanctuary, tables sagged with articles for sale. Desserts were set out in the kitchen to sweeten impulses to spend, and the scent of chocolate chip cookies permeated everything. I wandered from table to table viewing the riches—a doggy pooper-scooper, an unopened set of playing cards, a landscape painting—and touched an imitation fur coat hanging on a rack. The used dishes could be cast-offs from a small kitchen with dim lighting and too many children. Folks around me chatted and appraised the fragments of their pasts.

I spotted the woman I'd prayed about on a recent walk, the one who so annoyed me that I had to ask God to change my feelings. I disliked her smile, her fake charms, and mannerisms I can't remember now. She smiled over a table of lamps and I realized my dislike had gone. I returned her smile, amazed that I'd ever judged or disliked her. The change in me felt miraculous, and I knew I'd never forget the prayers or the answer.

Grant Barringer, our auctioneer, called us to order. "I'm sure you know why we're here, my friends. The money we raise this afternoon is for Habitat for Humanity. Those homes cannot be built without sweat equity and these funds! Spend freely!" Dressed in black suspenders and a straw hat, Grant was a frontier snake-oil salesman. He picked up a small table lamp. Sold! He pointed to a stack of paperback books. Sold! He marched over to a scratched golf bag. Sold! A magician making objects disappear before your eyes.

Never mind my assumptions about Barringers' past, and questions never answered, the Barringers made magic happen that summer. They came like missionaries from the urban world, charming us with goodwill, urging me to bring gays into the church, and bringing snake-oil fun. That was all I needed to know.

At the craft table, Grant grabbed a hand-thrown pot with an ocean-blue glaze, a piece as big as his head. I decided to bid on it. Created by a widow in the church, it was a gleaming bubble in Grant's hands and would be perfect for dried plant stalks.

"Ten dollars," I said, raising my hand.

"Fifteen!" a voice called from the behind me.

I turned around. Rosemary Barringer was outbidding me.

"Twenty," I shouted.

"Twenty-five," she said and people applauded.

"Thirty!" I yelled. The applause rose.

"Thirty-five," she said, and Grant struck his gavel on the pulpit with a convincing bang. People cheered.

"You got it," I conceded, glancing at Rosemary. "God will punish you." That got a good laugh.

The next morning the luminous globe appeared on our doorstep. Startled by the gift, I picked it up, caressed the polished surface and carried the beautiful piece into the house. I handed it to John. "From the Barringers. She outbid me."

"Amazing." He spread his hands over the bubble, turning it to catch the light.

I placed the treasure on top of a bookcase. The piece reflected my troubled face—so annoying to Virginia—that I couldn't hide from the congregation. "Messages from people like Virginia are important," said some pompous voice in my head. "This is how you learn."

I didn't want to learn. I preferred to eat scones from silver trays.

"Our grandmothers give us connections to the past," I said in a prepared talk for the ladies of our Women's Fellowship. They sat at tea listening to me expound on the glories of family and the joys of parenting. "They lend us their energy, their faith."

The women smiled as always, pleased to be sitting in our breezy sanctuary at tea tables on a late summer afternoon. Bouquets of roses adorned each table. "My grandmother played the piano," I went on, "and inspired my risking my life to go to seminary." I told the story of the time she'd appeared to me after her death with a beckoning gesture as if to send me into a new life. "We are touched profoundly by a grandmother's love, by their caring and their attention." I smiled, satisfied with my winning words.

Then a woman I'll call Helen spoke up loud enough for all to hear, "*My* grandmother was a pain in the ass." Her words astonished me. The statement was aimed at our teacups—rather than my head, thank goodness—words never heard in church, certainly not over tea in polite company.

I looked into Helen's smiling face. She was pleased with herself. She'd been annoyed by my sanitized raptures about motherhood and angelic grandmothers, and I felt embarrassed that my talk avoided a more complicated truth that included many a pain in the ass. My platitudes helped me hold on to the fiction that grandmothers and mothers were angelic beings even though my parenting of my daughter, Margaret, had been a wild ride, leaving me with piles of guilt for my failures. I didn't take my audience seriously enough to tell them the truth, and Helen let me know it.

Helen sat with the rest, sipping and chatting amid pretty bouquets. The ladies looked alike—white cheerful faces, conventional clothes, tidy hair and an air of busyness. You'd think they were all related. They seemed interchangeable, and I characterized them as ceramic figurines, decorative white collectibles you keep on a shelf. People make jokes about women like that, "church ladies" worthy of imitation and parody with their casseroles and sweet voices. I'd accepted the stereotype and rarely saw the women of the church as individuals, including Helen. It was easier to lead when I made generalizations and was not burdened with the complexity of subtle differences.

At first I thought these matching housewives in aprons— whom I considered not very interesting—seemed a lot like my mother. Maybe that's why I assumed I knew who they were. They had Mother's gray hair, her modest way of dress, and they deferred to their husbands like my mother did, though most did not have Mother's caustic tongue.

I never really looked into the eyes of the ceramic church women, or listened to them fully. I was more interested in exploiting their abilities. Helen and her friend, whom I'll call Annette, did the work in the kitchen at potlucks, rummage sales, or church fundraisers. They took care of Sunday morning communion requirements and stayed after to wash the trays and cups. Who wouldn't lean on their skills and efficiencies? They tatted the handmade snowflakes for the sanctuary Christmas tree and stitched a lively banner that turned a plain church wall into a declaration of "Holy Holy Holy" on a field of green. They were keen on saving money too—like my mother.

All I knew of Helen and Annette was their duplicate lives. They came from Chicago where they'd worked at the telephone company before retiring to small-town Arizona, a rural setting so different from Chicago. They adjusted well to our pleasant golf colony with a little Protestant church where there were other women of retirement age, although Annette and Helen didn't play golf or wear golfers' attire. They were not as casual as that—more Midwestern proper.

Our gatherings were where Helen and Annette could breathe freely away from their overpowering husbands. A number of church women left their men behind when they attended church. A Christian sanctuary was more acceptable than a spa weekend.

Just as I avoided really seeing them, Helen and Annette avoided me too, or kept me at a distance, wearing smiles and talking with other women while they prepared decaf or set out the hot dishes. It was not their habit to speak of personal struggles, and I worried they concealed sorrows they should reveal to me. After all, I was their religious leader, a trained model of compassion.

Some ministers have a look of wisdom and caring that invites people to pour out their troubles and pain. These sympathetic pastors listen in the quiet of their book-lined offices, vulnerability and compassion expressed in their eyes. They seem to be born to ministry. I am not such a person. People looked at my tall take-charge persona and shaped up or found a sweeter soul to unburden to. I wanted to be the one in whom the world's sorrowing could confide. Never happened. I have the look of your high school English teacher.

These similar church women were not alike, of course. It took the twirling of the planet over some time for me to realize that church women like Annette and Helen were not a crop of stereotypes, nor were they sent by God to reassure me that I was a meaningful presence in their lives.

Annette wasn't anything like Helen. Annette was an artist with a studio in her home. She created silver jewelry using desert stones she and her husband collected. Many of us wore her pieces. How do you call a person *ceramic* who breaks open rocks to reveal gems?

I eventually saw Annette as a real person when she sang a solo for us during Holy Week, the liturgical season leading to the crucifixion. At an evening candlelight celebration of the Last Supper, she sang in her fine contralto voice "Were You There?" an expression of wonderment and pain that could not have come from a fragile figurine.

My assumptions about Annette and Helen make me wonder whether I ever knew my mother, a woman now dead. Mother didn't really look like Annette and Helen. Mother had an austere presence. She didn't tend the domestic fires at church as they did. She thought church was boring and attended hers only to be neighborly. I remember her wearing the uniform of a scout leader but never with apron attached. Mother must have been a good deal more than those descriptions, but my knowledge of her is as limited as my knowledge was of Helen and Annette.

I don't know whether we're able to know our parents fully, but I do know I had an obligation to regard the people in our church as individuals instead of figurines. Given my stereotyping and assumptions about them, I marvel that the church women accepted my presence in their homes and in the pulpit. When I wrote about models for the spiritual life, I should have considered them.

*For those of us like King Saul—or Erma Bombeck—who feel stressed, it's time to hear the song, to rest, and listen to the music. The singer will refresh us, reassure us, and speak to our souls. We have only to listen.*

## Harps and Harmony

## SIX

It was *time to hear the song* and find new choir leadership. Our heroic volunteer director Virginia Regan agreed to meet at my office to discuss how to campaign for a professional musician.

Our meeting began promptly. Virginia was reliable. Like me, she'd been a schoolteacher. Wearing a pale green golf shirt and matching skirt she made herself, she settled her short, tan figure into a chair opposite me. Her gray hair, cut short in a perky attractive style, topped a green-eyed intelligent face. The consummate golfing woman, her name was often listed in *The Daily Courier* as a winner of tournaments. With her champion confidence—like the blonde I'd envied in high school—she was a contrast to me, her taller, younger, insecure, bespectacled minister who was not a hearty golfer.

A powerful faction in the church, the choir demanded constant attention. Keeping them well fed was one of my duties, and I had a hidden agenda that afternoon: improving the quality of the music, but I didn't mention that to Virginia. She and I met to strategize ways to find a professional musician who'd work for little pay.

We decided to place free "Coffeegram" notices—printed on placemats at the Blue Hills Café—asking for anyone interested in a part-time choir director's job. We'd then advertise in *The Daily Courier* for a week and contact other churches to see if they knew of any loose musicians. We didn't expect to find a competent applicant, but we reminded each other that faith can move mountains.

In two weeks we unearthed one candidate, a man I'll call Timothy Haasen. When the young man walked into the office for his interview with me, I was surprised by his appearance. He defied all things Western, or Arizona, or even outdoors. This spectral man, with unblemished white skin, thin body, and long narrow fingers, had a weak handshake that would have annoyed my father.

After he seated himself, I asked about his experience in church music, thinking he could have come from behind the pillar of some cathedral.

"I have a doctorate in organ from USC," he said. "Do you know that university?" He moved his briefcase from lap to floor.

A doctorate? Here in Dewey? I could hardly believe my good luck. "Sure. I'm from Southern California. SC's an excellent university." Saying California to this man, I felt a familiar pang of nostalgia for the coastal views of San Diego. "I'm wondering what's brought you here to Arizona." Land of cacti and centipedes.

"We came here because it's cheap. My buddy and I live in Cordes. He does odd jobs all over the county." Cordes Junction, down the road from Dewey, was the site of Arcosanti, a commune of artists who'd come to the territory with the Italian architect Paolo Soleri. Haasen seemed too sober to be part of that carefree clan. "We like to travel," he added, "to explore holy sites actually. I'm a spiritual person. We both are."

"I see." A spiritual man. That sounded better yet. I glanced out at the clouds— gathering as if for a pillow conference—still wistful for California. "So, you've had experience with church music?"

"I've directed choirs and played organ all over the West."

Halleluiah. We'd been visited by the music angels, winged and playing zithers! Haasen handed me a folder, and while I scanned the impressive papers, we talked about his work history.

"Could I play for you?" he asked.

"I'd love it!" With his education and spiritual interests, this musician might be a real colleague. I needed a confidant. If I made friends within the congregation, it caused hurt feelings, and I spent only minimal time with other clergy in the area because of too many demands on their time and energy. I imagined lively conversations with this Californian and his PhD.

The altar and pulpit waited silent in the dim sanctuary. Eighty blue chairs vibrated as always with absent voices. Haasen made his way into the organ alcove, seated himself on the bench and removed his shoes. He had a movie-star Jesus face—a blond, handsome face that might be a sign that he really was a spiritual person. Or not. The real Jesus, an itinerant Jew, had to be a dark and passionate teacher, not a pale organist.

Improvising a meditative piece, the music man showed off his deft touch at the organ. Then he segued into the hymn "O God, Our Help in Ages Past," sounding the conventional notes with ease. "Our hope for years to come…" That was my kind of hymn, calling on God for "shelter from the stormy blast." We'd found a real musician, our hope for years to come. Hats off to Virginia Regan!

I leaned on the railing in front of the choir seats and spoke of what we expected from a music director. Mrs. Ogg played the organ and harp, I told Haasen, and he'd be free to concentrate on directing the choir. "The choir doesn't meet during the week," I added. "They rehearse a half-hour before the service, so—"

Turning to me in a swivel on the bench, he said, "That's not enough rehearsal."

"Up to you," I said, secretly pleased. A doctorate. A spiritual person. Choir practice!

Haasen stretched his fingers in a professional way, shut down the organ and left the enclosure carrying his polished loafers. "I'd like to have a look at your music files."

"Timothy," I said, leading him to a newly expanded meeting room adjacent to the office, "how've you gotten along with church folks in the past? Any problems?"

"I would like to be addressed as *Doctor* around here, if you don't mind. I think it gives me the authority I need."

"Oh yes, sorry. Doctor Haasen. About former problems?"

"Wouldn't call them problems, but I have to tell you I am sometimes impatient with the conservatism I find in local churches. I have a PhD and I can read. That can be a barrier."

"How do you mean?" I asked, playing dumb.

"Oh, you know. No one will accept modern music or even good music sometimes. Drives me nuts. And their politics can be Stone Age."

I opened a file drawer, delighted with Haasen's answers. I'd been frustrated by rural—even redneck—thinking in Arizona and was unhappy with dated church music. Placing a messy folder in front of him on the table, I knew I found someone who shared my attitudes.

As I bring back the memory of that first day with Haasen, I picture a sand-colored scorpion rushing out of the pile of music scores he's reading. I brush it to the floor and kill it. It suits my imagined recollection of that afternoon.

"Hope I don't offend," the doctor said with no hint of humor.

I smiled at his sober face. "We ministers have our difficulties with traditional thinking in churches too."

"I assumed a church that would hire a woman would be open-minded." Haasen frowned at the sheets of music as if they were too awful to touch.

"Um, depends." I joined him and folded my hands. "They're a complicated bunch, though they look like eggs in a carton." Pleased with my metaphor, I added, "They accept my gender but pay no attention to my critique of the Moral Majority and its threat to religion. I doubt if anyone around here voted for Geraldine Ferraro for vice president."

No comment from the gentleman at the table.

The choir accepted Timothy Haasen as its director, thanks to Virginia Regan, and with the addition of more singers and instrumentalists, the church music moved away from sexist, militarist hymnody. Choir members didn't object unless they were required to sing a difficult, unfamiliar hymn. Then they got mutinous.

It didn't take the wisdom of a Spirit Woman, however, to know that our problems with church music hadn't been solved. Warnings popped up immediately.

One spring Sunday morning, as the choir practiced their anthem for the service, I assembled papers on the pulpit and checked to make sure the appropriate place was marked in the Bible for the morning reading. Colored light fell on the carpet and chairs in capricious flashes, a sight that would move us toward contemplation of the source of all light.

To my right, Timothy waved his arms trying to extract music from his little choir. The singers were arranged in a bank of chairs, fenced off by the low railing Lew had built to give the space a finished look. Mrs. Ogg was at the organ. She'd not said a word of complaint about Doctor Timothy though it must have been hard to work with him.

I felt a jingle of guilt as I watched Mrs. Ogg because she dropped out of my consciousness as soon as she left the church grounds. She moved in an aura of music, an unreal figure. I thought of her as our Good Witch of the North, inspiring us toward Oz, a place we hoped was pure and beautiful. If she was the Good Witch, I was Dorothy trying to make sense of the adventure, God was the wizard behind the curtain, and my pet Toto was Jesus, of course. Timothy Haasen didn't fit into my scenario.

"I've asked you to listen to this!" Haasen said, glancing down at the music on the spindly stand. He spoke in his most commanding voice but couldn't command the people ranked in front of him—five sopranos in the front, six altos in the middle, basses and tenors in the back. The men bent over their music, their bald spots forming a row of shiny circles. The altos and sopranos talked over their director's voice. Some tittered.

"You must listen!" Haasen shouted in frustration. "I can only create the proper effect with your undivided attention!" No one cared. Timothy reminded me of a frazzled substitute teacher whose words are ignored by students who treat him as if he's an interfering bore. Poor Timothy. *The singer will speak to our souls.* Not this man.

Prospects for good music that morning were discouraging until I noticed Lew standing in the back of the empty church eyeing the rows of chairs making sure they were lined up. In his usual plaid flannel shirt, as reliable as the postman he once was, he gave me a reassuring smile, a gift of hope.

"This alto part is hard," someone said. "Could we sing it by ourselves?" I tensed.

"Yes, of course," Timothy said. Mrs. Ogg played the part for the altos. They studied their music and sang tentatively. They'd have to face the churchgoers in half an hour. Virginia, in the front row, frowned at Haasen as if their musical missteps were his fault. She and I had consulted about hiring him, of course, but she wasn't pleased.

I checked pulpit papers again—announcements, prayers, sermon last—and prayed for the faltering altos.

"My music's missing page three," Stan Mattson called out when the altos finished. Stan had a masterful bass voice despite his hearing aid. Right now he sounded like a nine-year-old.

"Will someone find page three on the music rack?" Timothy asked. You could hear his exasperation.

"I can do it," Stan said and leapt out of his seat as if released from homeroom.

Afraid to watch any longer, I finished preparations and hurried off to robe for the service while the choir tried one more time.

At first, my conversations with Timothy went well as we discussed innovations in the music for Sunday mornings. Then our discussions took a turn. His talk revealed belief in past lives and channeling the dead who, he claimed, gave him special insights about the future. I sometimes felt like laughing when listening to him but had to admit that the ideas I preached were no more reasonable than his. I was leading a congregation to follow the teachings of Jesus, a man who never wrote a word and is barely mentioned in early history. I represented belief in life after death, resurrection of a dead man, forgiveness of sin through repentance, and a host of ideas that do not bear the scrutiny of logic.

"God will complete the circle," Haasen announced as he stood angelic in his gold robe after the service one May Sunday. Everyone had left the grounds and we remained in the church building. The wind outside made restless rattling music that whispered "Listen! It's the southwestern wind that matters, moving the earth and raising the hawks. Listen!" Spring winds brought in an altered atmosphere, an upheaval of everything, as if we needed a stirring of conscience.

Timothy began to lecture, pacing, an odd figure who looked otherworldly as he moved about the empty church in his fluttering robe.

I knew he was confiding in me, trusting me to understand and support him, so I paid attention. Circles? Haasen's face betrayed nothing. I often categorized people, but Timothy didn't fit any category—too insubstantial to be grouped with the real-life church members. How about spiritual prophet? Not hardly. I wasn't in a charitable mood.

"I receive messages from my sources within the circle. The dead communicate with us, you know. If you're aware…" I said nothing as he talked about his messages from beyond. "My informants come to me from realms beyond the stars."

"Your sources. I see."

I tried to stay with the story and sat in a blue chair while he talked. Haasen's words made no sense to me, and I didn't take time to study his metaphysical language. It was hard enough to get a grip on the baffling world around me.

"I don't talk about it to everyone, certainly not anyone in the choir. They've no understanding of etheric planes where souls wait to be born."

Etheric? Would Grant Barringer, New Age minister, get this? I couldn't picture him chatting with Timothy.

"Etheric? I'm not sure. A spiritual plane?" I asked, grinning. "There's a mystery for you." Haasen didn't return my smile as he approached the cross in his dance.

Then the flapping fellow preached at me about problems with the choir, the arguing and complaining. He took no responsibility for the trouble he had managing the singers. He claimed their resistance was caused by something supernatural, something in their lack of spiritual knowledge. He didn't need agreement from me, fortunately, just nods.

I wanted, instead, to talk about the religious fundamentalism abroad in the country. There didn't seem to be time to talk with my clerical friends from churches in the area. Our monthly breakfasts were too brief. All of them had vast obligations, and Father Bill considered himself married to his parishioners—at their disposal day and night. I invited these men to our home for a lunch once, but even then they broke away after an hour, hurrying to save the people they served. God forbid they should help with dirty dishes.

Haasen sighed, his signature gesture.

"Let me know if you want me to say something to the choir, Doctor Haasen, but it's probably best if you tell them your concerns directly." Was this person really close to spiritual truth? I could be missing something. The windows rattled, and I pressed my agenda. "What with the increasing influence of the Moral Majority, it seems God's been pushed back into politics. I think—"

"Haven't got time, Elaine." He walked to the choir room door—or through it—and disappeared in a flourish of silken distress.

*The singer will refresh us?* Not today. I sighed, mimicking Timothy, and noted that he'd called me by my first name while not allowing me the same privilege.

The following Sunday, the music drama intensified. "Reverend Greensmith." Virginia stood in the office doorway, her short figure confident as usual. She had no compunctions about approaching my office to straighten out anything she thought needed adjusting, like my disturbing frowns. I touched the front of my dress, expecting to feel a wet dribble.

"I have to talk to you." She came in and closed the door. "About choir. We think the music's too draggy, and we're tired of being yelled at. Timothy—*Doctor* Haasen—won't listen to us." She folded her arms, showing the authority designated her from her constituents. "We'd like to get rid of him, frankly."

Already? I shuffled papers making my own gesture of competence. "I'm sorry to hear that," I began. "I'm partial to the slower music of Lent—sets a contemplative mood, don't you think?" High-spirited chattering from the choir in the outer room rose in contradiction.

Virginia's eyes narrowed. "Lent's been over for weeks! He continues to choose gloomy music we can't sing!" She stepped closer, a proud woman who never experienced low self-esteem. "I'd like to take this matter to the council." Her tan face was near enough for me to observe a delicate web of wrinkles like a spider's handiwork.

Opening the closet door to buy time, I shuffled the robes and colorful stoles hanging there, trying to think of a way to convince Virginia to accept a variety of choices in church music. Timothy and I had agreed it was important to sing mournful anthems to which our faith offers a response. Music like Mozart's "Ave Verum" stirs the heart at unconscious levels, brings us near to transcendent beauty, I believed. Some would say such music is a way to know God.

"Well, there are times when our music should reflect heartache," I said, shutting the closet door, "the suffering of the planet, the wars." I turned and faced a woman as determined as a drill sergeant.

Virginia paid no attention at my attempt to be philosophical and returned to her complaints about Dr. Haasen. I didn't want to encourage constant cheerful music that kept us smiling into our decaf. I hoped to introduce an awareness of the suffering around us. Emptiness and fear—evoked by sounds of sorrow—must be faced before reconciliation can happen, and the world needed reconciliation. I couldn't get this idea across to Virginia because at that time I didn't understand people's compelling need for reassurance from their church music. I carried a flag without a following.

"We've decided that he—*Doctor Haasen*—isn't working out as we'd hoped."

"Okay. Let me handle this, Virginia. I'll see if I can get Timothy to respond to your concerns." She and her troops might snatch Haasen away like the roadrunner plucks a snake from its den, and I didn't want to give him up. We might make changes, I thought, but we wouldn't give in to too much Lawrence Welk influence. I picked up my glasses, hoping the conversation was over. "Getting a new person is really hard out here. I'm sure you don't want to take over as choir director again."

"I'll let them know, but they're running—out—of—patience!" Virginia left the office with conviction, determined to follow through with her commission. The door snapped shut in agreement.

Seated in the armchair across from my desk, Haasen seethed with anger. "I've never known such ignorance and disrespect! All I hear is 'this music's too hard!'"

I explained that we'd need to make concessions to the taste of the congregation. The choir wanted no slow or sad music. I was hungry and my eyes hurt. The spring breezes scattered a yellow haze of pollen over everything. Even my car, parked outside under the office window, looked diseased, and I had a constant itchy nose.

Wearing a tan short-sleeved shirt and yellow tie, Timothy could be Uriah Heep in modern dress. "If it doesn't have *Jesus Saves* in it, they never heard of it! I couldn't sleep last night. These people are making me ill," he said, emphasizing *these people*. Then he said something like, "They don't understand how God needs us to complete the circle."

He was more upset than a spiritual person ought to be, I thought while I waited for clarification and blew my nose, aware that Haasen's "these people" remark offended me. Virginia might have been a critic, but she was my personal critic. He was attacking my family. I tried to frame a light remark but had no energy for humor nor was I happy about giving in to Virginia's demands. A white Kleenex box imprinted with the little violets was the focus of my interest.

"I've been told that necessary cruelties create a final gorge I must go through," Haasen said, and I tried to imagine the circles and gorges in some coherent way. "I'm being watched," he went on. "I'm not supposed to stay here very long."

Not stay where? At the church? In this reality? Enjoying my nasty thoughts, I blew my nose. "I sympathize with your situation, Doctor Haasen. We have the same musical tastes, as you know." I lowered my voice. "But we have to realize that many here can't understand your special insights, and they want to sing familiar and—I'm sorry to say—easier music. That's a lot to contend with, but—"

"I've been told by my spiritual sources that I'm here on a mission." His face looked pained. "I know there's a reason I must endure this. We who've been chosen…"

Chosen? This irritable fellow felt himself chosen of God? I took a breath to take in what I'd heard. "I'm so sorry this has come up. I like your choice of music; I hope you know that…Council will be voting on whether to approve your contract. In order to get their votes, you'll have to select music they're comfortable with, what they think of as upbeat." I smiled charitably, wishing he were more like me, more normal. "I've always liked 'Joyful, Joyful,'" I added, remembering that hymn from when I was a teen singing in church choirs.

"This choir rebellion is part of the time of darkness," Haasen said. He looked directly at me. "I've been called to speak messages from beyond, as you know."

Dear God, what did he mean? "No. I wouldn't call it a rebellion." I raised my voice, determined to make a point he'd hear. "They show up faithfully, and that's really kind of a miracle, don't you think?" If only he'd leave so I could research some topic for a sermon, anything far from this metaphysical business.

My clergy friends liked to say that difficult people in their congregations were sent by God to teach them something, and I had to admit that Timothy's righteous attitude mirrored my own righteous judgments about conservative Arizona. Not a happy thought. I wanted to be left alone with Kleenex, friend of my nose.

"I can't compromise my principles, but I'll see what I can find," he said looking down. "I know you understand."

No. I didn't understand, though I appreciated his affirmation. I couldn't fathom what made up Haasen's inner life, but when I saw him with his briefcase, I not only saw smugness, I saw California universities and exciting music performed in concert halls. I wanted to keep him at the church to march with me toward beautiful sacred anthems. *The singer will speak to our souls,* I thought, quoting myself. A bit overstated.

Later that spring, I noticed Timothy waiting at the Prescott Post Office counter. He'd made some changes in the choir repertoire, enough to avert a rebellion, so I'd been pretending all was well.

"Let's have coffee," I suggested, hoping to entice him into a discussion of *E.T.,* a new movie with spiritual overtones. Haasen talked often about planets and stars and might have an interesting take on this little movie. I found sermon material in the movie's story of a boy who makes friends with an extraterrestrial cut off from his home planet. If I preached compassion for E.T., the choir might see Timothy Haasen, our E.T., as deserving of sympathy. Or not. Peace in the choir would probably take something more on the order of a visit from Jesus, Moses, and Abraham.

We sat at a table in the Barringers' cafe next to the front window. On the side wall, Grant had placed a row of photos of nineteenth century Prescott, reminders of the town before the fire of 1900. Bow-legged, mustachioed men posed on Whiskey Row when the street was a jumble of wooden saloons. Outside we could see the same buildings now in red brick. This historic town should expand my soul, I thought, teach me to fly wide and free, but I knew I was more the cautious rabbit seeking safety behind a boulder.

"Have you seen *E.T.*, Timothy? I thought the movie hinted at other realities from which we Earthlings might learn." I tried on Haasen's way of speaking, thinking he'd hear me better, and I was encouraged by the tough guys in the wall photos to use his first name. He didn't notice.

Timothy stared out at the county courthouse across the street, a massive building with Greek columns. Clipped lawns surrounded the structure, and old elm trees provided perch to the hardy blue-black ravens that presided over the park with enough authority to bully small children.

"Can hardly wait for my vacation," he said. "Got tickets for India. You would not believe how easy it is to get a time-share if you go to a marketing lunch and listen to their pitch."

The skies darkened and thunderheads made ominous shadows on the streets.

"Oh. Yes. Your vacation. You mean you have free accommodations?"

Haasen turned from the window and focused above my head. "We do," he said. A young waitress brought my white mug of coffee and the teapot required for Timothy. "If you act like you're interested, they're all over you."

I stirred in cream and extra sugar. "Who'd imagine you'd find a time-share in India! It'll be quite the adventure. Won't there be other expenses?"

"Not for us." He waved his teabag back and forth in his cup. "I have my uncle's frequent-flyer miles, and we get rebates on meals and things—just by complaining about the food." He smiled.

"I see." Annoyed and uncomfortable about Timothy's travel schemes, I drank the coffee and gazed outside where a boy lay sleeping on the grass in front of the courthouse. A woman in a floppy hat walked by with a peace sign. She looked so alone. Clouds passed overhead and I saw myself reflected in the glass, dark eyes, thick brown hair with touches of gray, eyeglasses on my nose. I'd have preferred a blonde with a pink ribbon.

Thunder shook our building, and with a flash of lightning, the overhead lights fluttered and went out. Timothy and I were cast in twilight, waiting for the next bolt. We glanced briefly at each other, two Californians sharing a crisis in black and white. The world traveler drank his tea with a smile that comes of spiritual certainties.

I said, "Glad we're inside. What a surprise! Maybe this means rain." I took a sip of sweet coffee. "The *E.T.* movie I mentioned is about an extraterrestrial who comes to earth. The question of how we treat outsiders is one I'd like to explore with the congregation. What do you think?"

"Last year, in Italy," Haasen said, holding his cup in front of his mouth, "we went with a group to cultural sites, and we got a real deal." His face shone. "Heard great concerts too, got in with passes from church people there." He drank his tea calmly amid cracks of thunder. Still no rain.

I placed my mug on the table with special care. "Wasn't that a religious pilgrimage of some sort?"

His face sobered. "Right. We met with this hermit who's an incarnation of a Hindu teacher. Got a lot out of it."

Hindus in Italy? The lightning stopped, leaving an eerie stillness. Outside, the woman with the sign had gone. The ravens laughed, the lights came on, and we left the restaurant.

I drove the dozen miles back from Prescott to the church thinking of the varieties of religious folk I'd met in the area. I just left a man whose spiritual guidance came from channeling the dead. The Godfreys lived with an Amish-like religious austerity. Andy Follette followed his Jesus, helping and rescuing in every way he knew how. Conservatives were pestering our local school board for their version of strict Christian values to be taught in the schools. The Mormons placed family life at the center of their religious faith and gained followers all over the area. Members of a Unitarian congregation argued in letters to *The Daily Courier* against a nativity scene on the courthouse lawn, pressing their liberal agenda. This mass of differences was worthy of a sermon, a sermon that would need to touch on the turmoil caused by religious differences.

Back at the church a clerical woman nodded off at her desk. A flock of shouting ravens descended on the parking lot surrounding the building as if to keep it safe. They could be the ones she saw outside the restaurant when Timothy Haasen sat with her and sipped his tea. The gleaming black birds argued and chatted, no doubt about religious differences in the high desert.

I awakened with enough energy to start a sermon on religious diversity. When I'd made enough notes, I set aside my pen, turned to my new word processor, and began a sermon:

> I think we need healing, spiritual healing, because of our lack of acceptance of other people's religious opinions and beliefs.
>
> St. Paul prayed for discernment to see the goodness in all variations of spiritual gifts. He argued for acceptance of non-Jews in a time when tribal loyalties were strong. He'd have been a valuable asset at the recent debates when the Presbyterians asked for an end to bias against unmarried or same-sex couples. They succeeded only in heightening a hot-button conflict.
>
> We need more chaplains like the one who came across a dying soldier and asked him, "May I pray for you?" The soldier, seeing the chaplain's crucifix, said, "But Father, I do not belong to your church." The chaplain replied,

"You do belong to my God." The same God,
wrote Paul, loves everyone.

June pollen seeped into my office like a perturbed apparition. I
blew my nose and took an allergy pill, grateful for the cool water
in the mug on my desk.

> Religious conflict erupts even among those who
> claim the most indifference. I'm thinking of
> the overwhelming interest in Derek Humphry's
> suicide book, *Final Exit*, and in Dr. Kervorkian,
> who recently aided two women to end their
> lives. The act of suicide has caused yet another
> religious argument. Some say it's a sin against
> God, who must determine when we die. Others
> say we have God's approval when we choose to
> end our own suffering…

> In all aspects of life we need to connect in
> love with one another and learn to live with our
> differences. We might start with an awareness
> that we do *not* live in a secular world. We live in
> a world motivated by people's hearts, and their
> hearts are with their God.

More and more uneasy with Timothy Haasen over the next weeks,
I admitted he didn't belong at our church working with "these
people" whom he didn't respect. Then the day came when he
appeared with complaints about the Godfreys. They'd objected
when Haasen moved the lectern and pulpit chair for extra audio
speakers.

"That narrow-minded Janet Godfrey and her husband, Jim,
claim the speakers are now too close to the front," he said. "They
won't allow change even if the acoustics are terrible!" He sank
into the chair opposite my desk and put his head in his hand. "I
need a space in front for the cantata! They don't get it. They just
don't get it."

I felt like Timothy's grandma, pacifying the sensitive youngster.
"Well, Janet and Jim are very particular about maintaining order."

Scooting my chair back I folded my hands on my stomach and peered through glasses on the end of my nose, "They're probably afraid you'll make upsetting changes." Maybe he'd quit over this.

"I try to be patient, but I have to move ahead with what I think is right." He sighed audibly. "God knows we must use every advantage given the *total absence* of vocal skills." His features seemed to slip from his face and I saw him as only a blur. "I find it *so* difficult to work in these conditions! How do you stand it?"

How did I stand it? I not only could stand it, I approved of "these conditions." The church brimmed with patience, commitment, and lots of humor. The murmuring and nonsense—even the arguments—of "these people" were more comprehensible than anything I'd heard from this man who spoke of circles and ethereal planes.

"I need to move the speakers at least two feet!"

"I see."

The push and pull of chairs and amplifiers—back and forth—seemed to match our struggle with Haasen, never forward. We may have raised the standards of music sung in the church but at high cost. I picked up a tube of hand cream, squeezed out a generous amount and rubbed my hands together, trying not to think of Pontius Pilate. I'd ask Haasen to resign. "This isn't working, is it?" I began, "And perhaps—"

"You could say that!" He looked directly at me. "I want those speakers to stay where I placed them. Mrs. Ogg just sat there today and didn't defend me."

When he mentioned Mrs. Ogg's name, I found new resolve. "I'd like you to put the speakers back, and we need to discuss—"

"Fine with me." He got up and hurried out.

"Sorry," I said to the closed door, pulling my chair to the desk and putting the hand cream in the drawer. If only I'd been brave enough to finish my sentences and ask Timothy to leave us. I never told the good doctor that his brand of spirituality made no sense to me. Neither did I challenge his criticism of the church members. Instead of asking for his resignation, I used placating ministerial tactics that make me ashamed.

I'd killed a centipede and a scorpion in my house, cornered a snake in the carport, but couldn't speak truth to an unhappy man. So Haasen stayed on, and we both knew that without my cover the choir might capture, pluck, and roast his bony carcass.

*Our scriptures never promise us a rose garden, do they? They don't paint the picture of love returned, of children comforting us in old age, of the faithfulness of our loved ones. No, these texts are sacred because they reveal what we encounter down through our days—the good and the painful, the struggles and the triumphs.*

## I Never Promised You a Rose Garden

## SEVEN

I drove from my house to the church admiring the spring gardens of the country club homes. Front yards were landscaped with pots of geraniums, beds of tulips, and speckles of wildflowers. Roses abounded, crawling on fences, lining pathways. Here at least was the promised rose garden for a while, until snow, until death.

Sarah met me at the church to set up for our Women's Fellowship meeting. We dashed from our cars as rain started to fall and I unlocked the heavy church door.

"So, are you liking the music better now that Timothy—bless his heart—is picking easier pieces?" I asked. We turned on lights and started the fans moving.

"Sure, but frankly he makes it a pain sometimes. I'm glad you listened to our complaints about him." I swallowed my guilt about not dealing more forcefully with Timothy while Sarah brought a stack of white cloths to the tables Lew had arranged for us.

"How's your work going?" I asked. Sarah made bowls and

platters from found wood in the area. We placed two of her cottonwood goblets—a light-golden color with streaks of gray—on the altar, and they stood in rough, pleasing contrast to the brass of the candlesticks.

"Fine. I learn as I go." Her gray eyes serious, she looked attractive in a turquoise-colored vest with wooden buttons. "Cut myself yesterday." She held up a bandaged finger.

I winced in sympathy. "Did you make your vest?"

"Yes. Some made red, white, and blue ones for the Fourth of July parade."

"We'll go to the parade too. It's John's thing. I'm not a parade person."

"Me either." We had a common bond.

Sarah and her husband came to Dewey from Saint Louis with Sarah's aging mother—whom we saw only at potlucks—a disagreeable woman with a shrill voice. I wondered if Sarah would appreciate a chance to talk, but so far, her church life substituted for psychological counsel or therapy.

We straightened the table covers and Sarah went to the kitchen for a tray of the white cups with gold trim used by the fellowship group. Other women arrived with cookies while the storm outside sounded relentless. Inside the church, the bustle from the kitchen reminded me of the ladies of the Quilters Club at the San Diego church, a scene familiar throughout ages of American religious life when church women gathered to quilt together and talk. I was here in ministry partly because I liked to be with kindly women who smiled, worked their crafts, observed customs, and fed one another. These domestic comforts, provided in a stormy world, gentled my spirits.

LaVerne, Lew McLachlan's wife, came in uncombed, her blouse crookedly buttoned. She grinned at me, elfin eyes almost vacant, and reached for a cookie before the women were seated at the tables. While she munched, letting the crumbs fall to the floor, red-headed Ardith, in her apron, fixed LaVerne's blouse, murmuring to her.

The group of forty women assembled around the tables and Ardith announced, "Better leave your windows rolled up next month, or I'll put zucchini on the seat." As the laughter faded, Rosemary

Barringer—star of television and friend to the famous—opened the door to a clap of thunder. We laughed again, except for LaVerne, who grabbed Ardith's sleeve. Rain had not fallen on Rosemary. She was dressed as if attending a gathering at the embassy, high heels and a summer suit with a pink ruffle showing at the neck. Not one other woman in the room wore dressy clothes; polished brass next to cottonwood goblets.

After introductory words, I began my planned talk: "I'm going to speak of *sisterhood,* about *solidarity* with all women." I knew those loaded words reminded the women of controversial feminist ideas that made them uncomfortable, made them think of arguments over salaries, mannish assertive women, sarcasm from husbands and fathers. They didn't want to hear anything feminist in 1993. Still, I'd been with them long enough to know they'd listen because they were reliably courteous, if not sympathetic.

A woman I'll call Tina Everett came in late wearing a plaid shirt and jeans. She dropped her furled umbrella by the door. Disabled from the complications of surgery, Tina moved awkwardly to a table. She blushed, staring at Rosemary who nodded. Desert Dweller greets Beverly Hills Beauty.

I resumed:

> One quarrel I have with life in our church is the sameness of faces. I wonder: Is the poor, struggling, single mom in our church? Would a lesbian woman be welcome here?
>
> We know of women too poor to get their children to doctors, women in gangs, women who live afraid of their lovers or husbands, some who have no dreams because they're overwhelmed with grinding work and child care.
>
> I know we look past or around women not like ourselves and stay protected from seeing their pain. If that's true, we must change. Keeping to ourselves limits our ability to offer comfort. We ignore what we cannot see...
>
> The Spirit of Love asks us to be with all people

who need us and to regard them as loveable and worthy. We are called to compassion for the world and its strangers because we are knit together in what Martin Luther King called a "network of mutuality."

"A diverse congregation offers expansion of the soul," I said in closing. Rosemary smiled and LaVerne wiped away tears.

Was I trying to start a discussion on welcoming gays and lesbians into the church? My unconscious may have been teased by Rosemary to start a process I was running from. The thought made me uncomfortable, as if God were tapping me on the shoulder.

Light through church windows left color drops on the tableware. We chatted over tea, and conversation tumbled out like a cascade of rainwater. The women shared truths about their lives, mostly about the trials of raising children. I like to think my sisterhood speech transformed the atmosphere and made us able to expose real feelings, but, more likely, the women were inspired by strong tea sipped in a pleasant space protected from a thundering monsoon.

My private truth included a story I couldn't reveal to the women of the church because I was too embarrassed. The women hadn't said a word about what it was like not to bear children. The subject of infertility carried painful memories of a bitter day—during my marriage to Carl—when I stormed out of a gynecologist's office.

That morning, Carl and I were in the kitchen—a flashy male with long sideburns smoking a cigarette and a prim female holding her favorite porcelain teacup, a wedding gift.

I gazed outside at the backyard, the view as suburban as my pretty kitchen: green lawn with tree. Our black cat Bardahl, named after motor oil, tiptoed through the dewy grass shaking the droplets off her feet before each step.

"Connie's bought a cow," I said, referring to my sister who lived on a Michigan farm.

"Oh." Carl took a drag on his cigarette. Dressed in tight, bell-bottom trousers and silky shirt, Carl looked at ease, but I couldn't talk with him about my fear of a medical procedure that afternoon. We didn't share private thoughts. I took a sip of tea from the pretty cup.

Connie not only had a cow, she had four children. The fact was absurd. She was two years younger and had given birth four times while I taught at the high school. Four babies! She raised her brood on a farm. With her husband and family, she'd gone back to the earth like so many others during the sixties. Absurd or not, I wanted my sister's life—mother to adorable children.

When we were youngsters, my sister wore toy guns in holsters and pretended to be a cowboy. She liked to climb on to the roof of our house while Mother shouted for her to get down. Connie would wave to us from up there, a sprite framed in blue sky. I played with dolls and should have been the one with babies, I thought. I could do a better job. We wouldn't live on a farm. We'd live near a library, and I'd read to my children every evening.

Carl and I had been married ten years and our sex life had become a task as we tried to create a child. Each effort was mechanical, desperate, prompted by a doctor's program for successful intercourse, whatever that was, and I worried that I wasn't a good lover, whatever *that* was.

I'd been having fertility treatments for months. A gynecologist I'll call Dr. Brighton had tried painful procedures—that he'd never explained—like injecting me with a long needle and cauterizing the cervix, a horrible process with smells of burning flesh. Nothing worked to help me get pregnant. I needed to confront him with questions this afternoon after school.

I buttered two pieces of toast and thought of Connie's cow, barns, livestock, the smell of soil. "Want one?" I asked. Carl shook his head. I turned away to face the window again. The cat had disappeared, and the kitchen felt deserted. When I returned to our vacant house in the late afternoons, I suffered with headaches. A friend told me the pain might have something to do with my marriage. I preferred to think my miseries were brought on by infertility, a condition easier to understand.

Carl lit another cigarette and snapped the lid of his Zippo lighter. The sound had the crack of the last word, a steely pop. Case closed. Then the screen door slammed as he left with his coffee mug, headed for work. "Take it easy." Maybe he'd be home for dinner or maybe not. I didn't know where he spent time.

I wouldn't leave Carl over his lack of interest in me. In my universe, women didn't divorce unless they'd been attacked or found their husbands locked in the arms of a floozy. My options did include a cozier solution: a baby would bring warmth and love into our marriage. I can blame such innocence on the times, on a culture that assumed women were fulfilled only by motherhood.

Gazing out at the empty green lawn, I sighed a dramatic sigh and took a last sip of tea from the wedding cup. Then I made my way along the path through the grass to the carport. No black cat. No glance from her yellow eyes. When I opened the door of the car and raised my foot to get in, I was startled to see my white terry slippers instead of the high heels I wore in those days. Slippers kept me in a soft retreat from fertility doctors but would not do for the classroom, so I retraced my steps to the house, regretting having to return to a hollow place.

Driving to the fertility doctor's that afternoon, I wept at the sight of my dreary face in the rear-view mirror. While my sister nursed a baby—or milked a cow, for God's sake—tears flowed and my nose ran. This young teacher wept in every setting: our empty house, in bed, fixing meals, the privacy of a car.

The brick medical offices were set back on grounds landscaped with red and pink camellia bushes. Only trained gardeners can grow camellias, Mother liked to say, so I chose to believe that the doctors in this blooming complex were trustworthy, though I wasn't comfortable with Dr. Brighton. He seemed to look through me, as if he'd heard my story many times and it bored him.

At the doctor's office, a row of silent women sat focused on their magazines in the hushed, windowless waiting room. Only the whisper of turning pages broke the quiet. Sporadic giggles from behind the office wall. We were being laughed at. Though I wasn't heavy with child, I nursed an oversized paranoia. I wish I'd spoken to the other women and said some silly thing.

When I was ushered in to the inner office, the doctor was sitting at his desk in front of a plate-glass window. An afternoon glare behind his head put his face in shadow. It didn't occur to me that I was an inferior being in that office arrangement, but I did know I was uncomfortable facing the powerful man with the big window. He didn't get up or welcome me but tilted back in his chair, nearly touching the glass, his arms behind his head. I sensed an annoying cheeriness in him.

"How's it going?" he asked.

"I…I've been crying a lot. I'm not pregnant." I had difficulty breathing. "What's this medication? Why does it make me so tired?" The tears came. "Some odd hair is growing on my—"

A screech of chair and the doctor's face appeared out of the darkness, grinning. "Your clitoris should have enlarged. Wasn't that a bonus?"

I sat up straight and stopped crying. Shadow Man became a leering Jack Nicholson and innocent teacher changed from Cringing Child to Wolf Woman. She'd use her fangs and attack Dr. Brighton's throat. He'd fall back through the window leaving a severed corpse for his giggly secretary to find in the morning.

But mayhem didn't suit. Lady school teachers didn't murder people.

Saying nothing, I left the doctor's office, slipped past the secretary's office and rushed to my car. I'd never submit again to that arrogant bastard. I'd never bear a child. Case closed.

In those years every doctor we women saw was a man who treated us as if infertility was a sickness. That doctors would prescribe my sex life appalls me now, even though they did it in good faith, most of them. Would a woman doctor have seen it differently? I wish I'd had the courage back then to fight for myself and my wounded spirit hurt by insult.

At the tea table in Arizona no one gave any sign of anguish from infertility, though several of the church women didn't have children. Sarah's thoughts were probably in a forest where she'd find a burl to transform in her woodshop. Rosemary, childless too, looked as if the conversation at the table was all that mattered at the moment. A woman I'll call Mary Wilkens, a childless shy woman who never missed a meeting, seemed content with talk of child rearing. I wish now that I'd shared my infertility experience, giving permission for more disclosure by the church women on a rainy afternoon.

As I drove up our driveway after the meeting, rainwater surged in the culvert beneath my car with echoes of unspoken secrets. I stopped to pick up *The Daily Courier* and realized that soon I'd be watching a Fourth of July parade—zany enough to distract from memories of doctors and infertility.

On the Fourth, John and I ignored the threat of monsoons and turned out for the Territorial Days parade in downtown Prescott—John in a patriotic hat. We stationed ourselves facing the parade route under an elm on the grassy courthouse square where the ravens squawked near the trash bins like barkers, calling us to step up and toss treats.

Across the way I spotted Ardith—who'd traded her apron for an American-flag vest—sitting on a lawn chair beside the Mattsons. Above their heads, red awnings shaded the windows of the St. Michael Hotel, a landmark from the last century. Next to the hotel stood a brick building with a wooden sign, Prescott Museum and Gift Shop, 1903.

We waved, and I fretted that our friendly greeting would bring Sandra across the street to dominate the afternoon with talk. Before she could make a move, though, the parade advanced down Montezuma Street led by a Boy Scout color guard.

Festooned cars of dignitaries moved past. A high school band played Sousa music. Remarkable horses in flashy trappings, ridden by aging ranchers and their wives, followed a whooping group of women—in slinky dresses and feathers—representing Prescott's high-flying saloon days.

Then I stared in shock as a truck approached with a huge wooden crucifix on the flatbed. Jesus hung strapped to the crossbeams, blood streaking down his body. "The Potter's House" sign flapped on the side of the float, and men walk alongside singing hymns and smiling at the crowd. What had this to do with the Fourth of July? Why were people cheering? I could include this bizarre Arizona custom in the sermon on religious diversity—or not. First I'd have to understand it.

When the Shriners came toward us—middle-aged male show-offs wearing fezzes and seated in miniature cars—they zigzagged to either side of the street. They'd never pass us. Sighing a martyr's sigh, I decided to leave the noisy crowds, careening Shriners, and the suffering Jesus. John waved good-bye without looking away from the parade, and I headed for the best women's shop downtown, Solt's Clothing Store. I'd buy a heavy bathrobe to protect me on snowy mornings. Something new to wear would reward me for staying—with John, with the church, with Arizona. If I couldn't have a reassuring pat from God—"Good job!"—I'd settle for a bathrobe.

As I meandered through the racks in a store empty of other customers, I could hear the parade and thought of Hank Wilkins, a Shriner member of the church who wouldn't be riding in the parade in a toy car because he'd suffered a leg amputation due to a circulatory disease.

When I visited Hank and his wife, Mary, at home, he greeted me—leaning on his crutch at the door—with a jolly insult, his usual practice: "Here comes the pastor. Hide your wallet."

We settled in the family room where Hank rested on the couch with his partial leg propped on an ottoman. Dumpling, a standard poodle, folded herself into a black heap on the floor beside him. Mary joined us with cross-stitch handwork in her lap. A quiet couple who treasured a collection of Kachina dolls and portraits of Indians, they had no family except the church—and the Shriners, of course

"You pay a lot for those shoes, Reverend?" Hank asked. He had a way of starting a conversation meant to disarm me. He sounded like John.

"Ah, well. You see. They came from the preacher's barrel," I said. "We live by pitiful handouts, you know."

"Not likely. I seen your good-lookin' Chrysler out there."

"A gift from an admirer. We live on crackers and milk."

He shook his head and pushed his glasses higher on his nose. "So you don't need money? Ministers are dumber than I thought."

Mary kept at her cross-stitch and observed, a tiny smile on her face.

Many in the congregation like Hank were bitter about the financial machinations of greedy ministers. The church members told stories of trusting clergy with their money only to have it melt away along with the minister. In my biased opinion, ministry was a male-dominated profession that needed the purifying influence of more women. I kept this idea from Hank, though I wish now I'd offered it and heard his response.

As I drove away from the Wilkins' home, Hank waved to me from his large vegetable garden, a one-legged man guarded by a black poodle—an unforgettable image.

I tried on some bathrobes at Solt's store while the faintly audible parade continued on its way past the patriotic crowds. Having decided on a bulky blue terry-cloth wraparound, I hauled it to our car and deposited it, like stolen goods, in the trunk. The purchase brought Mother's accusing voice: "In the old country we didn't have bathrobes." Mother had lived in poverty in Alabama after the family emigrated from Europe, and she'd not been able to go to school after the eighth grade. I have a photograph of her standing in an Alabama dirt yard, feeding chickens. Deprivations left her irritable about what she viewed as the easy life my sister and I enjoyed. "You kids better appreciate how lucky you are, getting to go to school in new clothes."

As a child I felt guilty about my easy life—but still wished for fine things, like party shoes and bracelets. I especially loved my purple lunchbox the year I turned ten. I loved the feel of the metal handle and the promise of food that feeling held. "No one had lunchboxes in the old country," Mother admonished, "only a piece of bread wrapped in a cloth." I was glad I lived in America where a person could carry a real lunchbox. Mother provided enough guilt coins to make me feel I needed to make amends with a commendable life. I'd been trying ever since.

Back at the parade route, John leaned against a tree waiting for me. Around him the lawns of the courthouse square bustled with red, white, and blue families moving to cars or restaurants. A storm hovered in the lowering gray clouds.

"I'm still reeling from the Jesus float," I said. "Do you know anything about a Potter's House?"

"I think it's a church near the high school." We made our way to the car.

"Boy, have I been sheltered." Here was a stream of religious life in our area I'd never noticed. I learned that the Potter's House Church started in Dallas and was growing into a huge operation with churches all over the nation. Enthusiastic, emotional, and evangelical, their services were televised widely. I've no idea why the local group entered a float in the Fourth of July parade in Prescott, Arizona.

"Let's go home," I said. "I need to walk off my guilt for leaving you alone."

On the drive back to Dewey, I asked, "Did I miss anything after Jesus and the Shriners?"

"Not unless you like mountain men in spurs. I will say their women on horses were fun to watch—lots of bouncing boobs."

"You can put that patriotic hat away till the next Fourth." I lugged the bathrobe up the stairs to our front door.

Out of breath after the climb, John said, "Just hope I'll be around next year." He switched on CNN, muting the sound. "You know why I wear the hat, don't you?"

"Yes. World War II, the Navy."

I concentrated on John's face as if to memorize it. He was pale, his blue eyes sad. This man was dying! In a matter of months, he'd disappear from this room, this land, this planet. A fresh sadness rose up, more penetrating than guilt over the purchase of a bathrobe.

We managed John's illness in the only way we knew. We went to the doctor weekly, followed the protocols and advanced toward the inevitable with routine and some humor. Like my former headaches, memories of his unfaithfulness seldom erupted to the surface, no more than the occasional exposed root in the asphalt in front of me. God's grace, some would say.

"I miss WW II," he said.

"I know."

"Seemed like a simpler time—bad guys, a heroic general for president. I wear my hat to remember." He went to the television and retreated.

Wishing I had ready words of support, I chose to take a walk and get in touch with the spirit of the desert. "Be back in a minute." I put on a straw hat and sunglasses, kissed John's smooth cheek, and hurried down the stairs. Even Jesus retreated to the desert to clear his head.

Thunderheads gathered, and I worried I'd be struck by lightning—for lots of reasons—and walked with my head down.

At the end of summer, a call came from a Phoenix hospital. "I know he'd like to see you," Mary Wilkens said. Hank's kidneys had failed and he was in intensive care.

"I'll be there this afternoon."

When I arrived at the Good Samaritan Hospital in the center of Phoenix, a dirty haze filtered the sunlight but didn't mitigate the 110-degree heat. The walk from the parking lot was long and uncomfortable, but I stopped to glance up at the side of the building with its mural of Jesus standing beside a lamb in a desert landscape. The painting reminded me of Hank in his garden with Dumpling beside him.

I made my way to the intensive care unit, pushed through the double doors and spoke to the nurses behind a high counter. Because I wore a clerical collar, the staff didn't question my presence. They pointed to one of the curtains that divided the patient beds and I stepped into the cubicle. Mary, a little woman, seemed childlike in this institutional setting as she came forward, her hands outstretched.

We turned to Hank's bed, a high platform attached to banks of monitors, all bright lights and whirring sounds. Covered by a white sheet, he might have been sleeping, but I could detect awareness in him, as if he watched us through his eyelids. Dumpling should have been with us. Hank should end his life with his friend nearby.

"Hank, it's Reverend Elaine. I'm here with Mary." He turned toward me, his face pale, his lips dry.

I leaned down and caught a whisper: "Hide your wallet." So much like John.

"Did you hear that?" I said to Mary.

"Oh yes." She appeared composed, a look in her eyes as if she remembered something pleasant. A nurse came in to check dials, hoses, and linens.

In a few minutes, Hank was gone.

"Would you like a prayer?" I asked. The space wasn't made for prayer but was adequate for blowing your nose, which I did, as softly as I could.

"No need," Mary said. "If you'd just wait with me until the nurse finishes here. I'll be calling the Shriners after a bit."

At Hanks' memorial service, I joined a large group of his lodge members and their friends at a Phoenix funeral home. Mary asked me to read scripture; the Shriners would do the rest.

Embarrassed for having judged the Shriners harshly, the woman minister sat in a clerical robe with the Shrine officials who wore badges in many colors. She looked like a black raven next to tropical songbirds and felt as small as the girl in a Brownie uniform who reached over the shop counter for Jesus and was refused.

A trio of Shriner women sang "Abide with Me," and the melancholy words, "Though the darkness hide thee, Lord with me abide," stirred a yearning for unity with God that the black robed minister shared with the mourners. Could she continue to stand for love and hope as a Christian minister when she made unfair judgments about Shriners?

After the service, I drove the same highway we'd traveled when we'd headed the first time into northern Arizona. This time I noticed the low buildings of a prison in the distance. My vision seemed to have improved from that January day four years ago.

As I ascended into high country, blue sky appeared through the haze of the valley as if the air has been wiped clean with a mop. Cooler temperatures too. I felt I moved away from hot urban stress toward the baptism of a purifying rainfall. Lord with me abide.

"I'm not used to summer rain." I said to John from my post at the living room window. "Puts me off balance." This was my fourth summer in Arizona, and it was monsoon season again. Menacing dark clouds exploded around us. Jagged wires of lightning flashed along the mountain-rimmed horizon, and the thunder sounded like the cannons of war. We were at the mercy of unseen forces.

John stepped outside onto the front deck to enjoy the storm, but I moved outside only for short glimpses before returning inside.

I had to take the noise and bursts of light in small doses. That's who I am, one who lets in the unexpected a little at a time.

"Worse than off balance," John said. "You get literary."

"I know. Surprise frightens me. I wax metaphoric to make sense of it."

"Metaphoric? Is that normal?" It was good to hear the familiar sarcasm in his voice, and it was good to hear the heavy banging of rain after a dry spring.

"I've no idea, but I know that surprise makes me want safety." Childhood fears of attack from bombs and submarines during World War II must have lingered in my consciousness.

Suddenly, flames flared up out of the ground on the hillside next to our house, igniting the wet ground. A blaze five feet high burned in the soggy soil despite the rain. John called the fire department, and they attempted to stifle the flames but finally decided to give up and monitor the blaze. Men in elaborate gear gathered around the fire, a circle of day glow Druids. The fire reminded me of the Moses story when God spoke from a flaming bush and told Moses he was standing on sacred ground—like the Arizona earth sacred to native peoples. It seemed as if their spirits lived in the land around us still, the flames rising from their hidden world.

After the firemen left and the rain stopped, we walked down the slope of the drive and over to the black circle of ashes. "This is really spooky, like a witches' coven has met here," I said, and John teased me about my tendencies to see omens in ordinary business.

"Does anything really keep us safe?" he asked.

"Are you kidding? I'm a minister. That's a complicated question." I took off my hat and wiped my forehead.

"Answer it," John said as we walked back to the house. "You're the only minister I've got. Can we trust anything to keep us safe?"

We started up the stairs to the deck of our Halloween house, John in front. I waved my hat to create a breeze in the heavy air, feeling I'd been walking for hours. "Well, safety is an illusion, of course, but we have to hope that something beyond understanding is holding things together. Keeps us from giving into fear, I think."

Why do bad things happen to good people? John was really

asking what he'd done to bring on his serious disease, Myelodysplastic Syndrome. The Mayo Clinic in Scottsdale verified the local doctor's opinion—that the syndrome would develop into leukemia and result in death. We'd no idea how much time that would take. John accepted the diagnosis calmly, but I couldn't believe the awful news. I had to accept the verdict in stages. *I never promised you a rose garden*—words from an old sermon I'd taken from a novel by Joanne Greenberg— was God's comment on our lives now.

"Okay. But what about the bad things that happen to good people? To quote the rabbi. How can you believe in 'something beyond understanding' in the face of that?" He went to the deck railing and gazed out at the wet land.

Trying not to hear the anxiety in my husband's voice, I said, "You're hitting them all this afternoon," and hugged him around the waist. "I'll get us some iced tea."

Flames of anger about John's unfaithfulness seldom erupted in me now. The hurt from his love affair was nearly gone. We'd just learned that he had a serious illness, and perhaps I felt it was time to let go of self-pity. There were other reasons too. He'd become lovable in Dewey, transformed, I chose to think, by Arizona. He liked the church people too, laughing with them and working alongside them to solve church problems.

Like the time we held a meeting to make final decisions about whether to go forward with additions to the church building. Tensions were rising over a fundraising campaign. I nervously watched the proceedings. Diane, the forceful chair of the Building Committee, presided over the discussion, tapping her pencil. The group debated underneath pathetic overhead fans in a hot, stuffy church. Questions were asked about how we'd raise funds in a congregation with many retirees on fixed incomes. The church treasurer quaked. Jeremiah Jim could have risen to shout and shake his fist but he merely whispered, "All we need is a storage shed."

Dr. Stan Mattson stood to speak. "We're overreaching! We'll incur tremendous debt!" Tap went Diane's pencil. "I won't stand for it! This is a foolish plan. The church is fine like it is." He sounded frantic, his booming voice extending to the golf course and over the earth to distant continents. He spoke as if he owned the church, as if he held special authority in the congregation.

I'd expected all the church members would be like the nice church folk in an imaginary quaint village, behaving with an orderly propriety. Movies of the fifties exerted too much influence on my views of church. Seminary certainly hadn't taught me much about the real people in churches either. We'd studied religious history and literature as if the psychological drama of a human communal enterprise like the church was not suitable for serious attention.

Tap Tap. I suppressed a desire to chew my nails. People stirred and muttered. No one had the courage to disagree with an angry Stan. Would fear govern the vote?

Then my husband confronted the red-faced Mattson. "Stan, you can't control us, even with shouting." John used his James Earl Jones voice. "You don't need to worry." He spoke slowly, pausing between sentences. "We're going to raise the money. There'll be no debt."

The doctor said nothing in response, his face relaxing. It seemed he needed John's reassurances like a child needing a parental pat. Diane took a vote and we committed to a building project with John in charge of raising the funds. I was surprised—at my husband, at the way Stan folded, at the miracle of a democratic process. In time, Stan apologized to John.

I thought of the surprises around me in church work: people's burning fears of change, smoldering conservative attitudes, and fiery anger from adults needing attention. A person in the robes of the church could bring hope and calm fears, a fire extinguisher in a robe—with help from John.

Our conversation on the deck over iced tea was not finished.

"Are you avoiding answering me? Must I phone a rabbi?" he called to me in the kitchen.

"Okay. Okay." I raised my voice. "The reason I'm trying to duck is that my answer won't satisfy you." I returned from the kitchen and handed him a tall glass. "I don't think God's in control of the laws of nature or the evil in people. God doesn't punish and reward, like Santa. The suffering of good people is an accident of fate, or nature."

"Are you saying, 'Shit Happens'?"

"I'm afraid I am, but I'm also saying I believe in a God who suffers with us and offers comfort no matter who we are, that prayer matters—somehow—because if we turn beyond ourselves to holiness we are responded to with love. Boy, that's all I can think of in this weather."

"How do you do that, believe what makes no real sense?"

"Don't know. I am continually helped by prayer, when I shut up and listen. Music sends me into belief too, I think. And then—something began in me when I was a kid in a beautiful old mission."

John didn't ask whether he could pray himself into wellness. He knew I didn't have an answer for that, and he went inside to the television while I stayed at the splintery table on the deck surrounded by the odor of soggy earth. I drank my diluted tea wondering how you explain God to anyone.

Back in San Diego I'd pictured God as a farmer. In those days it was part of my job as an assistant minister to lead Sunday morning children's chapel services to help the children feel comfortable with altar, candle, and hymns. At those simple chapel rituals, the children expected me to tell them who God was and where God lived. They filed into a dimly lit small sanctuary with an altar in front adorned with a single candlestick—the girls in their Sunday dresses and shiny shoes, the boys in washed jeans and pressed shirts—and their presence turned a sunless interior into a bouncing, attractive space.

After lighting the candle, I strolled up and down the center aisle greeting the crowd of about fifty youngsters. Sally had insisted I wear the gold earrings, saying that too much modesty was inhuman. Nancy Hernandez, a large cheerful girl, waved at me, grinning. Over my dress I wore a red stole with a design of fish and shells.

Pointing to one of the stained-glass windows in the side wall, I talked about the glass figure of a farmer in his fields, his sack of seed strapped to his side. "God's like that planter," I told the children, "giving out love from his sack to everyone who's scared or alone." Enjoying the pleasing smell of candle, we watched the planter in the glass until he seemed to move over the furrows.

After I added a few more words and settled a squabble over who'd pass the collection plate, Colin, father to one of the children, came forward with his guitar and we sang "We Shall Overcome," including the verse:

> We'll walk hand in hand
> We'll walk hand in hand
> We'll walk hand in hand some day
> Oh, deep in my heart,
> I do believe
> We shall overcome some day.

I blew out the altar candle and the children noisily adjourned to their classes, leaving me alone in the quiet wishing I might walk hand in hand with my daughter some day, a daughter like the adoring Nancy Hernandez, of course.

On a summer afternoon in Dewey, I swallowed the last of the tea and thought of the farmer in the chapel window. For now, I'd let that be my image of God—a planter who places seeds of love in human hearts.

Indoors again, I asked John, "Didn't that lightning fire scare you?"

"I'm not afraid of fire. I'm afraid of dying."

"So am I," I said and went to him.

*We need to be lifted into a child's reality so we can see differently, find some sparkle, some silliness, some childlike honesty in our lives. That's the lesson of THE CAT IN THE HAT. We can't listen to the practical goldfishes all the time…We must enter the Hundred Acre Wood with Winnie the Pooh, a world of creativity, imagination, and energy—to free the spirit, open us to new truth, and turn our faces to God.*

## Memories of Childhood

## EIGHT

Hank's death and John's diagnosis set a tone in my thoughts, and a heaviness of spirit stayed with me into the fall season. We had only to look out at leaves fluttering on the streets to be reminded of the end of things. By now, John needed to be monitored by doctors and had constant blood tests. At the same time, my first husband, Carl Ludlow, was hospitalized in San Diego with a serious infection. Doctors couldn't control some mysterious germ in that large, active man.

All I knew about Carl's illness was that he'd been stricken with a microbe that invaded a cut on his leg. He'd escaped AIDS but not some insidious new germ that didn't have a name. His collapse was unbelievable. Since our divorce he'd been living a flamboyant gay life in his La Jolla hotel overlooking the Pacific Ocean, where he entertained our children, collected beautiful art pieces, and made friends of the celebrities who lived in La Jolla.

A fan of easy money, Carl had managed to slide away from prosecution for being a bagman in a Ponzi scheme—a felonious money-making game one of his friends devised—but none of this mattered to Joey, who lived with his dad in those years. I've no idea how Joey managed to fit into Carl's La Jolla life. He would never speak of it when he returned to my home at sixteen. Now in his twenties, and called Joe, he made critical decisions for his father's hospital care and spent hours at his bedside.

I needed to call my son and check on how they both were doing, but I dreaded hearing his account of Carl's torments. I preferred memories of when the children were small, of Carl playing songs by the Carpenters or Pete Seeger on his stereo. Carl sang and danced— while smoking a cigar—with Margaret in his arms. Lord with me abide.

I made the call, and for some reason told the receptionist in Joe's office I was his mother. She laughed, and in a moment I heard Joe's exuberant "Mom!" His voice had enough energy for both of us. My heavy spirits began to lift.

"Remember me? I've been thinking about you and wondering about Carl. How are you doing?"

"Hanging in, Mom. Hanging in. He's worse every day." Joe sounded older, taken over by responsibility.

"Oh, Joe. It must be hard."

"I can handle it," he said. "Um…Dad's going to have to stay in the hospital, they say." He stopped, frightened by his words.

"My God. Sorry I don't call much. I've no excuses."

"It's okay. I don't call much either. How's John?"

"Pretty good. He has to get to the doctor's often, but he manages pretty well. You must be very worried about your dad."

"I have to stay over at the hospital a lot."

"Oh my. Are you having to manage his properties too?" I loved this boy so much and could see his worried face.

"Partly," he answered. "Two of Dad's friends are helping me and we've got a lawyer." He stopped. "I'm coming to Arizona over Thanksgiving if I can get away. I'm going to shoot quail. I'll borrow a rifle, and—"

"What! If you bring a gun around here—"

"Cool it, Mom. Just kidding."

"No sane person could hurt the quail. The tiny chicks follow behind their mothers like bumblebees." I stole that metaphor from Marjorie McLellan, my funny neighbor who loved birds.

"They still wake you up in the morning?"

"A small price to pay, kiddo." Carrying our new cordless receiver, I wandered over to the window to see if I could spot any Gambel's quail, their tassels bobbing as they scratched the earth beneath the pines. Just a lone rabbit munching beside a boulder.

After I said good-bye, I kept an eye on the rabbit, thinking of Carl's suffering. I noticed I was shivering. Supporting church members in crises couldn't compare to the challenge of this horror.

When I visited the hospital in San Diego in later weeks, I found Carl paralyzed. By my second visit, his legs had been amputated and he was heavily sedated. He begged me to come to him as soon as John died and care for him. I declined with as much grace as I could, feeling pity and grief. I had no obligation to Carl and was shocked that he asked me to give up my life in Arizona for him. Instead, I left him in the care of our young son whom I would later hold as he wept at his father's bedside.

I wanted a merciful death for Carl, but treatment choices were not up to me. Joe had full responsibility. Because Margaret was considered too irresponsible, she was left out of final decisions. I knew she had the insight and compassion to have been a strong support to her brother and father, but they couldn't appreciate her when this horrific event was unfolding.

Some time after my talk with Joe, I heard from my lost child.

"Hi Mom," Margaret said over the phone. A long time had passed since she'd left. I'd not heard Margaret's voice since she stopped by our house in San Diego accompanied by a scruffy man with dirty hands and a scratched leather jacket. She introduced the stranger as her husband, Brian, giving no details about a wedding. Brian said he wanted to live in Oregon to be close to a forest, so he took my daughter to the far north that night in an awkward, incomplete parting from me and John and San Diego.

Now she startled me with a friendly tone and surprising words:

"I'm going to have a baby. Next April. I want you to come."

I could hardly absorb the news. I'd carried an image of my daughter as a troubled teen shouting furious insults at me. This sudden message took a rearranging of the furniture of my heart.

"That's wonderful, Marg! A baby. I wouldn't stay away. I take it you're pleased. You sound good." A baby!

"Yeah, I'm good," she said in a quieter voice. "You gotta be here. I'm sorta scared."

"Of course I'll come. I'd love to see your place and all. How're you managing?" I thought of Brian's dirty hands and wondered what kind of father he'd be.

"This house is kinda broken down, and Brian works most of the time doing body work, but I've got friends here on my street," she said. "He collects Grand Ams, fixes them up, and sells them." I could hear her fears. The prospect of childbirth would have scared me too.

"I see. So you've a house and everything. Good for you."

"Yeah. I have a doctor, and I'm trying to cut back on smoking. How are you guys?"

"We're fine," I said, pleased to be asked. "John's been photographing Indian drawings. This is Indian country, you know." I waited, but Margaret said nothing about her heritage. She was of mixed background: Comanche and Fox on her Mother's side. "I'm busy being a lady preacher…You know about your father?"

"Yeah. Joe called." She started to cry. "He…he…shouldn't…"

"I know, honey. I know." We couldn't say more. I wanted to talk instead about her pregnancy and enjoy that good news. "We'd love to come up when the baby arrives. Send directions and have Brian call as soon as you go into labor." I felt a twinge of envy. My pregnant daughter was going to give birth; I never had the privilege of calling my mother with news like that.

"Okay. Send me one of John's photos of a horse or something. I need stuff for the walls. I'll keep you up on how it's going here."

*I want you to come.* Margaret's words brought a memory of a day in seminary when, at fourteen, she asked me to come to a performance of *The Rocky Horror Picture Show*. Her young image came back, an overpowering girl with dark hair and eyes, wide mouth, and mature body.

"We have to go on Friday," Margaret said. "You see, it's this great thing. We're going to dress up and everything."

I was at the typewriter in our Berkeley apartment trying to get inspiration for a paper on the Old Testament prophet Hosea by gazing out of the window at a gray cat walking along the top of a wall.

"What are you talking about? Costumes?" A breeze lifted the heavy fur of the cat.

"My friends and…We have this movie we go to." She stood behind my chair, aiming words at my ear, making sure I paid attention. "It's *The Rocky Horror Picture Show*! We go to the Berkeley Theater every weekend at midnight."

I turned and faced her. She looked like an Aztec princess with her tawny skin and wild hair. "You have to explain, Marg. I'm afraid I don't get it." I headed for the kitchen, a tiny place suited to one skinny person. She and Daisy trailed in behind me. "You want to go to a midnight movie wearing a Halloween costume?" My daughter often spent weekends with her pal Diana whose mother evidently was unable to prevent their escapes to midnight movies.

"No! We go at 10:30 to get ready. We wear the clothes they wear in the movie. We know all the parts."

"You know what?" I started preparations for our meal, macaroni and cheese out of a box, and waited for the water to boil. The cooking instructions were more clear than talk about late night costume parties.

"We know every word of the movie! We talk it with them." I could tell she was trying to contain her frustration, and I enjoyed drawing out the tension.

At the refrigerator I gave Daisy some limp French fries. She was delighted. "I see. Do you want dinner?"

"I want you to be there tonight."

I stopped fussing. "You must be kidding. Go with you?" We'd been in Berkeley for a year while I studied at Pacific School of Religion. Margaret attended school only when inspired, and she and

Diana had once been caught stealing. She bragged about panhandling in front of La Val's Pizza and would surface only long enough to tell me stories of her exploits, enjoying my shudder.

"Mom, it's fun. I want you to see it."

"I don't know. I've got this paper to do, and I can't possibly stay awake that long and wouldn't your friends think it funny to have your mother there?" I brought plates and forks to the table under the window, moving the typewriter to the side. Margaret arranged the plates and Daisy arranged herself on my bed in the corner, a Cinderella arrangement next to the fireplace.

"Mom, I want you to see me in my costume. You'd really like it. I can say all the words."

We ate our macaroni, Margaret watching me. The Bible—with its account of Hosea's trust in God despite everything—lay open on the table. "Alright, I'll go," I said finally. Outside, the gray cat on the wall must have continued pacing.

At the movie theater—it was midnight!—a group of five girls, fully costumed and joined by four boys, sat in the front rows. The attendance was sparse so I could see everything from the back. When the movie started, the kids stood and shouted lines with the actors. Margaret recited the words with everyone else, a Native American version of an outrageous housemaid, as I recall the scene. The kids sang along too, tunes like "Hot Patootie."

At home I tried to sleep, but a rerun of scenes from the movie and the frolicking kids in the front rows played out in my mind. Margaret was so different from me, a respectable seminary student in glasses. I sensed what it must be like for her as an adopted child. Every time she looked at me, a pale schoolteacher type, she knew we didn't match. She felt a kinship with the wanderers of city streets because she felt like a transient herself, a "wayfaring stranger," the song goes. Over time, we talked about finding the Native American birth mother she'd never met, and we started a search.

And now. A baby.

Musing through memories of my daughter now, I see our former life together similar to a "rocky horror" rather than a romanticized movie scenario with cookies and suburbs and hair ribbons, the motherhood I'd imagined as a young college graduate wearing corsages and white gloves. I never imagined a call would ever come from a runaway daughter far from home. I never imagined an ex-husband suffering in a hospital, or that I'd take leadership in a congregation living and dying around me.

After Berkeley, life with Margaret in San Diego kept me writing in a journal and talking to therapists to stay sane. She was as restive as the turbulent sea that rocked ships in our harbor. She hated school and by the time she was sixteen often ran away for days with young men, appearing back home to taunt me or beg for money. I was preoccupied with concerns about her welfare but couldn't think of a way to change or help her. I tried doctors and therapy for her, but the best advice came from a blonde church secretary, blue-eyed tough Sally, who pulled me out of guilt and worry with reassuring words as brilliant as her jewelry.

At the church where we both worked, I leaned on a kitchen counter watching Sally as she began her ritual of making strong coffee out of a supermarket blend. The steel surfaces of the wide oven doors reflected our movements

"Margaret's making me crazy," I admitted. "She's impossible to live with, and she runs away and stays away." I took two mugs from the high cupboard. "If I'd been a better mother…" A self-pitying sigh.

"I thought you'd been out of your mind lately. Must be hard." Sally's pointed, coral fingernails flashed as she arranged the filter. She made coffee with the same competence she used at the computer. "I like Marg," she said. "She's a funny, tough girl. She'll be okay."

"Hope so. She's a troubled kid. John likes her too." I fingered my gold earrings, still not used to such finery.

"When I think of what my mom went through."

"You miss her. I'm sorry you lost her so young. We all need a mother—except Margaret, I guess. No. She needs her missing birth mother. I wish we could make contact. Seems like we're all whirling around our mothers, trying to keep holding on or struggling to get free."

My mother's hold on my soul was strong. Besides the guilt coins she dropped into my pockets, she told me many times how much she'd suffered with my birth, sparing no details. I wondered if that shivering story of her painful labor left me resistant to pregnancy at some unconscious level, fearful I'd not survive.

"Margaret's into drugs. I know it," I said as we monitored the scratched Mr. Coffee.

"Well, Pastor Lady, I used plenty of drugs in my day," Sally said in her rough smoker's voice. "I got over it." She poured from the glass carafe and handed me a mug of coffee. "The earrings look good."

"Thanks." I took a sip of what felt like an elixir taken after confession. We carried our mugs into the deserted conference room where we staffers planned the church programs. I set the mug on the polished table and looked around wishing the room had a window. "I could have handled things better in Berkeley," I said, remembering the gray cat parading on the seminary wall while I pondered religious ideas. "Margaret got out of control and I kept my nose in books." My voice got weaker. I blew my nose.

"Is that why you're a minister, 'cause you feel guilty? You don't have to answer that. In fact I'd rather you didn't." She squinted as she sipped her coffee. "You've got to stop blaming yourself for the kid's troubles, Elaine. You give yourself too much credit for Margaret's stuff."

"What would I do without you?"

"You should come to Quilters. You'd learn something about real life. Those old gals have seen it all. With my various husbands and history of financial disasters, I fit right in with them." She twisted the five antique rings on her right hand.

"I know. It's just that, well, I can't help thinking I could've been better with discipline, kept better track of—"

"If you're going to minister to anybody, lady, you'd better realize everyone feels like that. Come on! Since when should a minister be better than everyone else? Is that what they teach you in those seminaries? If it is, they should get a grip."

I'd expected my role as minister would transform me into a saint, a good person without hatred or boredom or impatience with people I couldn't like, let alone love. It was a burden I had to drop, and Sally knew it.

I studied Sally's face—blue eyes lined in blue mascara, cheeks and nose dotted with freckles, streaked blonde hair cut in a stylish wedge. Goddess of Wisdom chats with Marian the Librarian. "I'm glad you're here, and deep down I'm glad I bought these earrings... How'd you get so wise and to be such a good coffee maker? You cut hair and use a computer. You ought to get more money."

"I know."

Sally laughed at my Snow White innocence, deflated my pontificating ego, and gave me perspective on my daughter and husband. She helped me get a grip if I took myself too seriously and was still with me in my head in Arizona. Like Mrs. Ogg, she was an angel sent from heaven, or so I thought before our friendship moved to a different place.

Soon after that conversation, Margaret was caught by police joyriding in my car without benefit of license or permission. Because I chose to press charges, on the advice of a detective, she was moved into jail and rehab. Somehow that institution and a phenomenal probation worker—and time to grow older—brought change. It took a year for her release, but after her strict program ended, she was able to control impulses and maintain a civil attitude.

Now, a baby. I had to tell John. He was trying to plant a honeysuckle vine in the hard clay by the downstairs doorway, hoping to make our wooden barn-looking house into a New England cottage. The day was white-hot, "Indian Summer" they called it. I shaded my eyes and watched him. The sight was pleasing, his body appealing. I couldn't imagine his absence and wondered who I'd be without the love and laughter, anger and annoyance John awakened in me.

"You'll never guess," I said. "We're going to have a baby! Marg just called. Can you imagine?"

He kept digging. "Grandparents. I'm not ready. I'm too young." He picked rocks out of the dirt, sweating over the job. "Pay no attention to this grunting."

"Your bald head is very sexy. Oh John, I'm floored. A baby. Next April. What's a Grand Am?"

"A sporty Pontiac. People collect them, I think. My back is killing me."

"See, you talk like a grandpa already. Marg's got a home and neighborhood friends. I can't believe it."

John picked up the potted vine, removed the plastic container and placed his plant in the hole next to a wall. "She'll be a good mother," he said to his scrawny plant and moved the tendrils of the vine so they'd climb gracefully on the wall. Then he stood holding his watering can and admired his work.

"I think so too. She has a big heart."

After my daughter's call, it seemed easier to return to the church and its demands. Her request that I go to Oregon to be with her healed my feelings of guilt about failing her and somehow lifted my confidence that I was where I should be, preaching and praying in Arizona. I felt a release in my neck and shoulders, as if someone lifted a hiker's pack from my back. *I want you to be there.*

I turned to thoughts of a sermon about humor, gaiety, and gladness. A good place to find humble cheer was the outdoor rummage sale in the church parking lot the following weekend. When I arrived, the church was surrounded by the detritus of modern life, from construction materials to doilies. Tables were heaped with the innards of homes and garages. Members brought linens, used tires, televisions, books, clothing, pots, pans, and plants. Church workers—in red neckerchiefs—stacked, arranged, and chased articles scattered by bursts of desert wind. Arched above them, a giant earth shovel waited ready to work on a construction project. The huge machine looked like a Charles Addams cartoon monster that might reach down and snatch one of us to dangle above the teeming swarm below.

Virginia, the cashier—positioned under a billowing awning attached to a fifth-wheel rig—handed me a red neckerchief and started counting the accumulated money piled in a cigar box. I tied the neckerchief over my hair and began tidying the piles of rummage. While keeping an eye out for baby clothes, I could monitor the children playing with items from a pile of used toys.

Young Becky waved at me as she and Dana crossed the street to shop at our sale. They picked up trinkets and set them down carefully as if handling precious artifacts. "We each got a dollar to get stuff," Becky said and reached for a filmy shirt on a rack. "Hey Dana, look at this!" The wind yanked the shirt out of her hand; it skipped away, trying for one last moment of freedom. She handed me a quarter for the shirt—that we retrieved—and headed for the heap of shoes. Her black baseball cap stayed planted on her head, untempted by wind gusts.

When I wandered over closer to the church building, I overheard the familiar voice of Jim Godfrey say, "I had this hot fudge sundae yesterday—first time in ten years." Pausing at a table of old radios and walkmans, I listened to our fire-breathing Jeremiah describe his sundae—the sweet chocolate, the whipped cream, the nuts. Jim never ate anything as unhealthful as a hot fudge sundae. He and Janet walked miles every morning and went to bed at eight. They didn't even have a television, our mainstay in this distant land. This was a miracle of conversion. It sounded like the war had ended, the hurricane passed, and the Red Sea had parted. Jim had lightened up and was given over at last to fun and sweets, fitting for the sermon on joy I planned.

At Virginia's cashier table, I said, "I want to buy a flashlight. You think there's one around here? We have blackouts during monsoons, and our flashlight supply is puny. I wonder if Jim—"

"Ask him. He's inside," she said and returned to her responsibilities.

I found him helping a crew sort through boxes and pile rummage into categories. Church women marked prices on everything before another crew carried the refilled boxes outside. Everyone looked ludicrous in neckerchiefs, like aging extras in a Roy Rogers movie.

"Got any flashlights in here?" I asked the man of the hot fudge. "We need a raft of them—no, a ton of them. That's wrong—a flash? Never mind."

Jim straightened his thin frame and squinted at me. "Can't imagine not having plenty of flashlights," he said, as if we neglected to install toilets in the house. I could read his outlook on life in that frown: God wants us to live according to strict Biblical teachings— tithing a tenth, judging everyone around us and surrendering joy for Jesus. A gloomy Eeyore in a red neckerchief.

Jim pointed to a box and went back to his appointed tasks. "Okay," I said, and wondered if I imagined the ice cream sundae.

Taking a mammoth red flashlight to the car, I spotted Dana and Becky heading down the street with a full plastic sack each. Lew hurried toward a truck with a stack of window frames. I picked up two infant sleepers on my way and paid Virginia fifty cents. A baby. Just think. A baby.

The next Tuesday I got a call at the church from Jim-of-the-hot-fudge. "Made fifteen hundred on the sale."

"That's amazing. I never thought—"

"We've got to improve the speaker system this month," he said. "Council's asked me to check it over."

"Come on by," I said, thinking I'd rather have air-conditioning. "I'll be here at the church until three. Lew's borrowed the extension ladder, so you ought to bring one if you think you'll need it. Fred and Stan are under the building checking out plumbing. We'll make it a party."

Jim was not amused and said a serious good-bye. In a few minutes he was standing in the sanctuary with a notepad and screwdriver.

"Glad you're taking a look at this. That pulpit mike has never worked right. It sounds to me like the organ's hooked up to all the speakers." Timothy Haasen, doctor of music, had probably messed with the system to enhance his part of the service, but I didn't mention that possibility to Jim.

"I know," he sighed. "Might be expensive to fix." He turned his plaid back to me and stepped up the ladder to reach a speaker.

"We'll find the money," I said to his lean form, a few feet above me.

"You always say that."

"And the money appears every time!" Laughter from the plumbers under the building offered a chorus of support.

"Been lucky so far, I guess," said the lone adult overseeing us toddlers.

"You could call it God's grace, Jim." He didn't answer so I added in a sing-song, "If God wants the people to hear the sermons, God will provide the money." I must have smirked.

Jim didn't turn around to see me leave the room.

I could hear Sally saying, "You need this guy. Keeps you funny."

At the church service that Sunday, John spoke to the congregation updating the congregation on the building fund project and the rummage sale. As liturgist, he led a call-and-response litany then announced, "Free cookies are available to any visitors willing to join the church next month!"

You have to love someone who can make you giggle in a church.

I still hoped Jeremiah Jim would lighten up when he heard the uplifting Bible stories in my sermon—the dancing David, the dove welcoming Noah, the return of a prodigal son—though I tried to stay aware that I should leave revisions of human beings up to God.

> If we read carefully, we discover in our Bible words
> like this: "the eyes of the blind shall be opened, /
> and the ears of the deaf unstopped; / then shall the
> lame man leap like a hart, / and the tongue of the
> dumb sing for joy/...They shall obtain gladness;
> and sorrow and sighing shall flee away..."

*Sorrow and sighing shall flee away.* I loved those words and felt better saying them, a Sunday sundae. I wished our music man, Timothy Haasen, could feel a gladness of heart. Healing laughter seemed out of his reach.

> We can come out from under the clouds newly
> born. It's a matter of becoming more fully alive,
> as I read the Bible and other religious literature.
> Joy is what God wants for us, I think. Those who
> refuse to lighten up are like Shakespeare's Malvolio,
> a judgmental cuss who found no joy in life. Listen
> to his name: Mal-vol-io. Dour people like him miss
> much and need a rebirth of humor. We in the
> church call this process "spiritual renewal."

Of course I was describing Jim Godfrey, hoping he didn't take my words personally, though I may have hurt him. As I revisit my days in the pulpit I see that I thought being a minister gave me the right to define and judge people. It isn't only doctors who have a god complex.

Proof I'd made no changes in anyone with my sermon on joy came when Jim's wife, Janet, materialized in my office doorway on Monday morning. Her sudden stern appearance—in gray polyester slacks and print shirt—stopped the movement of the stars in the heavens. Janet had a presence. I envied her slim figure and told her so, hoping it might lighten the moment. She thanked me and tried not to smile.

This prim lady came on a serious mission, probably to tell me how I failed to meet her religious standards. She disapproved of the fact that I'd been divorced. She said I didn't quote from the Bible when our church committees require guidance, and she objected to prayers for AIDS patients since she thought AIDS to be the curse of gay men. My yoga practice was suspicious too—the gyrations of a pagan?—and she said I avoided looking at people directly.

Janet was right on that one. I had trouble really seeing the faces of people if they were anxious or sad. Their eyes triggered fears in me, known and unknown. I was working on it.

Like Virginia, Janet felt comfortable criticizing me as if a woman minister needed to be coached. Our male counterparts inspired awe in the congregation, but we clerical women had to be reminded of our duties. The thought made me want to press a lever and send Janet down below into the basement, like you do in melodrama.

My stern visitor began with a stern lecture, saying that Lew McLachlan made changes to the audio speakers in the sanctuary without permission from the church council. Though her husband, Jim, had the authority to fix the speakers, and did an evaluation last week, Lew had gone ahead and made the necessary adjustments without consulting Jim or the council.

"We can't let this go by, Reverend," Janet said after explaining that Lew's hasty work insulted Jim's authority. She had a point: Lew should have called Jim first, but Janet wanted me to bring down justice upon Lew's head, my dear Lew who volunteered faithfully at the church and had a wife in the early stages of Alzheimer's disease. "I'm sure you can see we must take this matter to Council," she added. "People can *not* act without authorization." She put down her purse and regarded me sternly.

I glanced away. "I'm sorry this happened," I said, barely able to contain sarcasm. "I'm sure Lew didn't mean to cause problems. I don't feel comfortable criticizing Lew for—"

"Lew should have checked with Jim. If we let people go ahead on their own, things can get out of hand."

I protested and she interrupted me again. "Your avoidance of problems around here is a namby-pamby way to do God's work."

Namby-Pamby? Namby-Pamby? I felt a surge of anger and told the earnest messenger in one breath, "Lew's a trustee of building and grounds and they take care of repairs. Please remind Jim that they don't have to submit a request to the council every time they make alterations unless they cost over five hundred dollars." I met her dark eyes this time. Before she could speak, I added, "I knew Jim had started on the project, but when Lew decided to see what he could do, I encouraged him."

"You talked with Lew about the speakers?" she asked, sounding fed up with me and my yoga-practicing-AIDS-praying soul.

"Yes I did. I guess I failed to mention to him that Jim had already made some assessments. My mistake. I'm sorry."

"He knew."

"Janet, I'm grateful for Jim's attention to repairs, but I'm also thankful to Lew who's at my side every Sunday morning. I take responsibility for the mix-up. Please tell Jim I'm sorry. This is not a Council matter." I waited for a reaction. Janet left without comment.

As the tension of Janet's visit lifted, I hummed a lullaby to any listening angels in the office and started work on a sermon about the Holy Spirit. I was intrigued by popular spirituality movements—the efforts to find the divine in nature and in human hearts. I could weave in new feminist thinking, suggesting that God can be thought of as a Mother with attributes more maternal than judgmental. Still, Janet's visit reminded me that the traditional Christian woman is alive and well in the church. I must tread cautiously if I meant to shatter familiar images, an idea that appealed to me that morning.

Punishment for being namby-pamby came within the week.

"I removed the cartoons from the bulletin board in the entry," Janet said from my office doorway without a hello. Dressed for janitorial work this time, she carried a bucket of rags and brushes.

"The narthex looks better now without all those tattered scraps. They're really not appropriate for a church."

Did I hear her correctly? She'd taken down my religious cartoons in a cleaning fit? Janet was an artist. She did a nameplate for me in her excellent calligraphy. How could she not appreciate the drawings of cartoonists? "Oh? I've been collecting those religious cartoons for a long time," I said in a desperate effort to defend my turf.

She had me, and she knew it. The tattered collection from *The New Yorker* were hard to defend. Janet would never accept that they lightened the church atmosphere or were necessary to my sanity. I stared at her and her broom thinking how much I treasured those drawings—like the one of a hoary Moses leading the Hebrew people through the Red Sea after stopping to let a family of ducks pass through. Janet didn't approve of making fun of Moses. Janet didn't approve of fun period.

"I thought the cartoons livened up the atmosphere," I said, still trying. "That one about the chicken and the lemmings…" Knowing I'd get nowhere with feeble argument, I longed to be out of the building away from disagreements over cartoons. I once was obedient and well behaved, and now I felt like The Cat in the Hat who'd messed up the parlor for the fun of it while the practical goldfish warned of trouble.

Matters between me and the Godfreys had become strained a year before when I supported the membership's decision to build the addition to the church. The Godfreys sided with Stan Mattson and voted against the project, letting everyone know that the truly faithful Christian is a "frugal steward," as Jim put it. Plans went forward anyway and—to my surprise—the Godfreys accepted the vote. If they'd protested we might have had a division in the church.

Bucket, broom, and Janet disappeared into the new church kitchen, rejuvenated with new dishwasher, huge sinks, mammoth refrigerator, and a stove fit for a hotel. I heard her begin an earnest sweeping as she attacked the invisible dirt of a spotless kitchen. Give back kindness, I told myself as I took my mug and followed the earnest cleaner.

Afternoon light from the kitchen window shone on Janet's tight chest as she began her work. We'd never understand one another. I thought she lived in a puritanical muddle, taking the Bible to the point of absurd narrow-mindedness. She thought *I* bordered on New Age liberal frivolity.

"I hope you saved the cartoons for me." I reheated some decaf I found in a carafe on the counter.

"No. They're in the dumpster," she said, as I knew she would. It's satisfying when people act according to your script.

I smiled. "Isn't anyone coming to help you this morning? Mary was saying —"

"I don't need help," she muttered, her back to me.

The bag of Oreo cookies in the refrigerator looked like the perfect antidote to this conversation. "I appreciate your support of the new building project," I said, tearing the package. "This is a beautiful kitchen."

"Hope people keep their pledges," said Practical Goldfish.

"I do too," I said, musing that my black-and-white cookie was a perfect metaphor for Janet's thinking.

Mug in hand, I left the sweeping Janet and returned to the office where I rocked side to side in the desk chair. The Godfreys reminded me of the farm couple who stand glowering at us with their pitchforks in the Grant Wood painting *American Gothic.* I stood my ground stubbornly too, of course, holding—what? A fountain pen? A chicken cartoon?

I twirled in my chair, a fitting gesture for The Cat in the Hat soon to be a grandmother.

*We've scoured out so much of the visionary in ourselves in favor of our*
*rational sides. We forget that the world needs us to be visionary as well*
*as realistic. The church, in fact, ought to be a place that encourages us to*
*imagine and visualize. Let the schools mind the growth of our rational*
*brains; here we will enjoy and encourage visions.*

## Visions of Change

## NINE

"I've planned a spirituality retreat!" I exclaimed during a Sunday
service at the end of summer. "We'll stay at Friendly Pines, a camp
only a half hour from here. They'll provide all our meals. We'll have
a leisurely two days together sharing our thoughts and feelings." Mrs.
Ogg played an emphatic chord on the organ as if I'd announced the
Second Coming of Christ.

With the additions to the church building done, including a
larger office for me and a choir room with lots of cupboards, it was
the perfect time to put aside concerns about money and facilities and
launch a program to enhance our religious life. Inspired by popular
New Age talk about nurturing the inner spirit and a book about
spiritual gatherings, I decided we needed to develop our spirituality
in an all-church retreat. It was easy to find a camp in the nearby
foothills with comfortable cabins and good food.

I hoped to persuade Mary Wilkins, who'd lost Hank, to join
the retreat, and the Mattsons too—though Sandra's talking could

overwhelm the quieter folk. The Godfreys might learn to relax in a Hundred Acre Wood, and Fred and Bernice Miller seemed ideal people for a cozy escape where they could share a hidden pain that was a burden to Bernice.

After the service, Lew and LaVerne signed the clipboard in the entry, and theirs were the only names. No interest from the Mattsons or Mary. The Millers were probably too reticent to share personal stories. The Godfreys no doubt guessed my plot to conscript them and wisely avoided the opportunity.

The next Sunday I expanded my pitch. "Our spiritual retreat sign-ups have started! It's going to be a chance to get to know each other better. I'm planning quiet conversation, great snacks, easy walks."

That day we added Helen and Annette, best friends, and Millie and Curtis, a couple who told me they wanted to get to know more people. My husband chose to sign up, perhaps to talk about his illness. Our neighbor, Marjorie McLellan, added her name, saying she wanted healing for an incurable golf swing. Not the response I'd hoped for, but it was enough to pay the fee at the camp.

Later that month, nine of us in colorful sweatshirts—except for John in a beige windbreaker—headed into the forest above Prescott where Copper Basin Road winds into stands of pine and juniper trees, some stunted by drought. A pickup sped past with a shotgun visible in the rear window and a German shepherd pacing in the truck bed. "Made out your wills?" Marjorie said. Wearing baggy shorts and huge binoculars around her neck, she had the humor and energy of an adolescent.

Soon we assembled in our cabin—one of eight log structures in a forest clearing with a knotty pine main room, a woodstove, a variety of chairs, and an abused couch. I announced, "We need to bring our own touches into this place. I'd like you to explore the area for fifteen minutes and bring back small forest articles." The painted wood table cleared of coffee-making clutter would be our shrine for the symbols of the outdoors. "Make your explorations in silence to get the feel of the place."

I took the advice of Dolores R. Leckey's *The Ordinary Way*, a book about finding spirituality in group experience. The cabin was as ordinary as you could get. Leckey writes of the Rule of Saint Benedict: "The revelation of self is a revelation of God." That would be my direction, self-disclosure, finding the holy within our shared stories. I marked the passage that said, "Christian spirituality and community are intertwined."

The group returned bringing woodsy smells and cool fall air. They placed their forest articles on the table: an acorn, two enormous golden leaves, a yellow wildflower, part of a nest, a tiny stone. Hope came into the room, and beauty—of course, beauty. Now everything, including the torn curtain at the window, was perfect for spiritual explorations.

We pushed the assorted chairs into a circle. Lew and LaVerne chose the couch and John grabbed an upright kitchen chair. Mine was overstuffed; I tried not to see a metaphor in that. Helen and Annette took the recliners. Marjorie settled into a wicker armchair and put her bare legs on an oversized ottoman.

The room quieted and I was aware of the trust in the faces around me. LaVerne, whose memory loss had worsened, watched her husband, Lew, for clues on behavior. Millie and Curtis turned their faces to the window, as if longing to return to the outdoors. Marjorie refused to be subdued by the shyness in the others and jumped up to get the cookies she'd brought. The food eased our discomfort, and the group was ready to hear me out. What else could they do? I'd seized them and brought them to this hideout.

I gave everyone a small green spiral notebook and asked them to write about the question, what gives you courage? They bent over their laps and we continued in that way—writing, reading notes aloud, eating cookies. I raised more questions and we talked of neighborhoods we'd lived in, people we admired, our love for Arizona.

At one point I asked, "What kind of religious teaching did you have as a child?"

John told of his childhood as a minister's son, emphasizing how he'd disliked church and the righteousness so admired there. He talked with a sober energy that surprised me, but he didn't share anything about his illness.

Curtis said, "My parents pushed me to go to a church that forced us to memorize Bible verses and recite them in front of people." He took a breath. "I was so frightened I wet my pants and that ended my interest in church forever. I came to our church here because of Millie, and I'm glad I did. Get something out of it every time."

"Sounds tough," Marjorie said. "We kids had to read the Bible aloud at home every night, but I remember it as funny—especially when my younger sister said things like 'Jesus spit.' We thought that was hysterical." Marjorie always cheered me. One time I collapsed wearily into a chair in her living room and she offered me a martini—"Will you take it intravenously?"

After we tittered at Marjorie's story, she pointed outside. "Look at those balloons!" We followed her outdoors to get a better view of three hot-air balloons faraway over the tops of the pines. Launched from our valley, they looked as if the clouds had suddenly burst into colorful pieces. The distant striped drops seemed to be symbols of joy sent up by people celebrating, drinking martinis. The break was a relief, and I tried to believe we were making a joyful noise ourselves.

People told more stories about their lives. In keeping with their preference for privacy, no one exposed secret pain, and I wasn't sure we'd moved toward the deep sharing Leckey writes about. The most spiritual sound I heard was the haunting call of a quail.

"That's the daddy quail trying to attract strangers away from the nest," Marjorie said. "He's saying, 'Over here. Over here. No one is home. No one. No one.'" I remember her voice imitating quail as only a birdwatcher would do.

The next morning, after breakfast in the common house, we wandered back to the cabin. Marjorie had awakened us too early—by mistake, she said—and I wasn't cheered by the weak coffee or greasy food we'd just eaten. I kicked at the pinecones on the path feeling I'd done a namby-pamby job on what was supposed to be a spiritual experience.

Inside, the cabin looked dismal with morning haze before the dappled sunlight reached the windows. The place was strewn with green notebooks, two hats and empty snack containers. Except for the little acorn and stone, our forest mementoes had dried up. My plan was to take another three hours for writing and discussion, but I doubted if things would get more intimate.

Again in our respective chairs, everyone seemed cheerful, and we teased Marjorie for waking us so early. "We could take her," John said. "It's eight of us against a skinny blonde."

In a better mood now, I began, "If you could envision the perfect church, what would it look like? Put down ideas and I'll make a prayer for Sunday from your thoughts." Everyone except LaVerne started writing.

Curtis read his contribution. A businessman, he held his green notebook as if reading from a company document, back straight and throat cleared: "How about 'Give us a church that serves people outside our doors'?"

John added, "And a church that has music God would like." He was thinking of some dubious anthems from the choir. "Timothy and the Blue Notes," he sometimes called them.

Lew scratched his chin. "I want a church building people take care of, show respect for, like a shrine, sort of." LaVerne beamed. He was her Indiana Jones, revealing secrets from the Arc of the Covenant. I wondered what their home life must be like. Lew no doubt took care of everything while tiny LaVerne followed in his wake, sweetly confused and dependent.

I prompted the women to join in with suggestions about the ideal church, and Annette said, "I think church should not be terrifying to children." Helen agreed.

"You got that right," Marjorie said, "and I think a church is best when it tries new things." She got that right too. We needed new ideas and discussions of how to be a more inclusive church. Maybe she was conscious of our need to encourage open-minded acceptance of the gays and lesbians in the community. She didn't name it, but she expressed a willingness to break free from old church customs—like a youngster poking fun at our old-fashioned practices.

My retreat memory brings back the time I made an attempt to lead another group back in seminary. At a session of a counseling seminar at the Pacific School of Religion in Berkeley, my presentation had an impact I didn't anticipate, though the experience felt like failure. We were studying trauma.

Seven fellow students—some middle-aged, like me, some young, like my friend I'll call Georgia, some Asian, like Yoshi—came into the classroom wearing heavy backpacks, as if they'd been thrown out of their homes and made to carry all their belongings on their backs.

I handed around a summary of information about the effects of infertility on women—scanty in those days. I intended to center my presentation on my firsthand experience, taking my lead from another student who described her life married to a Vietnam war veteran broken by post-traumatic stress. We students of religion needed informed insights to understand the people we would serve, their suffering and struggles.

"It was my dream after college to have a baby," I began, "to become a mother." I started to sweat. My voice got weaker with each word. "After a year of trying, I realized I couldn't get pregnant. I didn't know what was wrong. I went to a doctor who tried painful and humiliating procedures, but they were unable to help me. I want to give you a picture of…of what it means not to be able to—"

Starting to cry, blowing my nose, I took a deep breath, but speech was impossible and the awful grief gained momentum. After several futile attempts, my efforts stopped. The professor made no comment. We closed our notebooks and left the room, dismissed by my weeping and sputtering.

Georgia and I emerged into fresh, cold air. "I'll have to apologize to the class. I'm afraid they didn't learn much about infertility."

"I'm not so sure. They probably learned as much as they need to know. I don't think I want any more details."

Infertility defined my psyche profoundly. While I may have turned to the church as a safe refuge and for approval, I also sought some way to fill the emptiness of my body with the sustenance offered in church. I think the sacrament of communion—sharing bread and wine—replenished me. "Do this in remembrance of me" we say as we swallow the elements of earth and fertility.

In the Arizona forest at our little retreat, John helped me load my duffle into the van. "I think a good time was had by all," he said, knowing how much it meant to me to have succeeded in a small way and enriched the lives of the small crew at the retreat.

On Sunday morning, the choir sang a cheerful anthem in four parts and the altos outdid themselves. The congregation spontaneously applauded. During quiet preparation for prayer, I thought of Sally back in San Diego; she was not doing well. She'd been forced to wear a contraption around her neck, called a *halo,* that fastened to her skull with bolts to keep her spine rigid. I included her in the prayer, along with the ideas of those at Friendly Pines on retreat.

Following a contemplative hymn, "Spirit of the Living God," I began the sermon, "The Golden Age Passport":

> It is not necessarily true that the older we get the more we grow in character. Gray hair and bad backs don't always make for gentleness. Sometimes they give us permission to be selfish, demanding, jealous, or self-righteous. We are unfinished people. I don't care how old we are, there's always work to be done. Thank God for our sense of humor…

Each person present that morning seemed vibrant, each tiny difference between them—hearing aids, clumpy shoes, a wristwatch—mattered. I wondered how ministers of gigantic mega-churches could serve congregations of large numbers. This complex, varied group in front of me was all I could handle.

> Our ultimate golden-age trip is to another realm, and we need to go prepared, I think, by carrying with us the passport of an active conscience and a willingness to learn. We can be *ready* to go—bags packed and everyone kissed—or we can stumble in the dark, never having thought about what it means to be alive or to see holiness…

Janet Godfrey, an excellent alto, sat in the choir looking like a model Christian. She was much like me, I realized. I saw in her my fear of exposure and identified with her efforts to be noticed by God. We were both trying to project a perfect image to a deity we hoped was paying attention.

Being mature also involves being what St. Paul calls *steadfast*—holding to faith and hope and joy, struggling with our doubts, renewing our spirits again and again. That renewal comes, for me, in a church service that reminds me that God is with us. Church offers us a bit of time to renew and rest in an atmosphere of holiness.

The church looked beautiful, now decorated with a green banner depicting a waterfall, symbol of outpouring love.

I would not have come to this church if I'd not been touched by the holiness I feel here. That's why we make an effort. We try to arrive tidied up, show better manners than at home. Little is required of us except to speak a little softer and let God be here in the quiet and the music. That is our way of showing respect, instead of removing our shoes and bowing, as you might see in a sanctuary of another religion.

We can return again and again here for refreshment and renewal at the fountain of peace where we are cooled and empowered for another week out there. There are reminders here, even though I am well aware that many of you also find God at home, or in nature as you walk and feel the wind.

The sermon ended with a summary of Benedictine teachings from Leckey's book about God in ordinary daily work: if we do any task with awareness of God and respect for the dignity of our task, God is with us. I liked that. By the end, worries over my imperfect efforts to lead people toward spirituality in a forest retreat were gone.

Then fall turned into a time of weeping. I sat in the church taking time to marshal the strength I needed before the congregation entered. It was late afternoon, and soft colored light from the glass windows didn't lighten the somber mood. The altar was decorated with fall leaves and a drawing of a quail next to Sarah's hand-turned goblets. Candles flickered. The evening voices of women preparing sweet food sounded a low hum of mourning.

Marjorie McLellan, our comic birdwatcher, was not among those women. She'd caught a chest cold while helping the school nurse process incoming junior high students the first week of school. Within days, our energetic funny Marjorie collapsed with pneumonia. She died a few weeks later.

I'd checked with Marjorie's husband, Orville, as her illness progressed, and he assured me she was getting better. Suddenly she wasn't. Suddenly she was hospitalized in Phoenix. Giving in to doubts about rural medicine, I suspected her local doctor had been negligent. I needed to blame someone.

We were at the church that afternoon to celebrate Marjorie's life. From now on—forever—the church would lack a spirited melody. The memorial service began with Mrs. Ogg's music, and we sat unbelieving as the hymns washed over us.

When she was stricken, Marjorie's adult daughters came from California and Oregon to be with her. I drove them to Phoenix to visit their mother at the Good Samaritan Hospital. We found her unconscious. I spoke to her still form about the balloons drifting over the pines and the birds she taught me to recognize. The hummingbirds are gone now, I thought, flying their way south. Finding a metaphor in that, of course, I touched Marjorie's pale face and said a prayer as her daughters, standing back from the bed, tried to face the reality of a mother near death: "The Lord bless you and keep you. The Lord make his face to shine upon you and give you peace."

I felt the loss of Marjorie every time I opened the drawer in my kitchen and saw the cake spatula she'd given me. Every bird in every tree reminded me of her. Every martini reminded me of her. She'd been such a treasure to have in the congregation, so light-hearted—a "moonbeam in our hands," the song goes. Making the effort to write words for the memorial service had been like working under water. I stared out at the mountains, seeing nothing and hoping to see her again in her shorts and binoculars.

A friend of Marjorie's read a passage from the book of John: "And when I go and prepare a place for you, I will come again and take you to myself, that where I am you may be also. I will not leave you desolate..."

The choir sang two of Marjorie's favorite hymns, and I told the story of her life, using information from her husband and daughters:

> I cannot explain the ways of God, the reasons why our neighbor, mother, wife, and friend has left us too soon. We've lost a bird-lover too, a fine musician, and a funny lady. Learning to accept loss is the hardest of lessons. Those words from the Book of John assure the Christian—and Marjorie was a Christian—that life does not end at death, that we will not be abandoned by God.

> Marjorie came from a family of California pioneers—literally, the covered-wagon pioneers. Her great grandfather was the first doctor in San Bernardino County, a huge area of California. Her life there was just what you might think—sun and oranges and smudge pots and school and bare feet and as much fun as nine children could have living away from town.

> Marjorie's father was a citrus grower, working a dairy as a sideline. He believed that church was an important family focus, and there was Bible study every day. Even the little ones had to read aloud. "Jesus spit," one of them mistakenly read.

> The family's Scottish heritage came out in their frugal way of life, and Marjorie was a frugal person herself. I'm sure you knew that she stalked the golf links in the evenings to find lost golf balls.

> She will be missed everywhere. A charming spirit is now missing from this church, our neighborhood, and the planet.

Church members recounted their memories, and after the service we gathered at the McLellan home where Orville sat in a recliner chair staring out at the pecking quail. "No one is home. No one."

After the guests left, Kathleen, the McClellan's older daughter, went to a side table and picked up Marjorie's green notebook. "You should read this," she said.

On the first page, in Marjorie's handwriting: "What gives you courage?"

Her answer: "My minister's sermons."

Overcome with gratitude for this affirmation, the fretful minister held the notebook to her chest, and—embarrassed to face Kathleen—moved to the window. In the silence of that quiet room, worry lifted from her heart and floated off like a hot-air balloon drifting in the September sky. Suddenly she could believe that a gracious God did brood over the world. As vulnerable as the quail Marjorie loved, she'd been given a moment of faith by a kind remark.

It used to be that a minister was given a plucked chicken in payment for officiating at a funeral or wedding. I'd rather have a few words in the handwriting of a neighbor. Marjorie's gift soothed a doubting, self-conscious, weak reed, and her compliment gave me energy to better appreciate life in Arizona, its stones and nests and multi-colored leaves—and to keep trying to live my vocation.

In the next days it was difficult to concentrate on duties. The mail stacked on the corner of the desk needed attention, so one morning I reluctantly picked up papers from the denomination's office in Phoenix, a flyer encouraging participation in a downtown protest against military incursions into the Middle East. I'd have to skip that one. It would offend John and take an entire day. Another page reported a meeting to be held at our national headquarters in New York about re-envisioning our image of God to include feminine qualities, not just father and judge but also mother, nurturer, and comforter. I made notes and planned to discuss the idea with our Bible study class.

A separate page of the mailing called all churches to begin a process called "Open and Affirming" in which congregations discuss ways to accept gays as members in local churches. The suggestion was that each church launch a year-long study followed by a vote of the congregation to decide whether to be open and affirming to gays. If the decision is to be open, the church then advertises to the community that they welcome people of all sexual orientations.

It's easy to be full of progressive ideas when you're not in the trenches, I thought, annoyed by the resistance in the church members—and by my fears of confronting them. We weren't being asked to sleep with gay people; we were being challenged to expand our church. Excluding anyone violated the teachings of Jesus. Hermits can live peacefully in their caves, I thought, but it's not easy to live in a community.

I phoned John and told him about the "Open and Affirming" mailing. "Can't face it. I feel like such a wimp, as Margaret liked to call me." When John said nothing, I added, "It would cause a fight at the church, I know it. Last month—I think I told you—the Arnolds left the church when they learned our denomination ordains gays. What do you think?"

"That's easy. You do what you can, what you've the strength to do."

"I'd like to see Marjorie again."

"I know. Me too," John said and hesitated. "Feeling weaker these days."

"I'm so sorry. I'll speak to God about it."

"The birds cheer me up, the muttering quail and these finches." John still sounded basso, a vigorous voice with a sexy edge. "They get all fluffy in the cold."

"Fall is so beautiful. And you sound strong this morning."

"Wish we had a dog. I'd like a greyhound, a retired racer."

"I know. Might be the very thing. We'll talk about it later." John loved the sleek greyhounds and followed some of their careers. In a way, the tall slender dogs with gentle manners resembled him. On a vacation once we visited a ranch in Iowa where greyhounds were trained, and I watched John—starting to show his frailty—crouch down to speak with one of the dogs.

John and greyhound

"I'm so damn tired," he said. "Dr. Caccavale thinks I need to go to the blood specialist at the Mayo Clinic in Scottsdale. It'll mean a drive down into that wretched hot valley."

"We can do that. We'll buy fresh grapefruit." I felt helpless over what was happening to John, the inevitability I couldn't change or fix. As mother and teacher I thought of myself as a fixer of troubles, but death obliterates all sense of control, at least it did for me. "I'm sure Mayo can help you. Caccavale's a smart guy...I have to get to my sermon—been thinking about miracles."

"Don't forget the Gipper," he said, identifying himself with the dying sports hero of a Ronald Reagan movie.

The stretch of desert outside my office window, the wide silence, looked otherworldly. I scanned the area for Marjorie's quail, always cheerful, always busy. Instead, I saw a land resting and quiet, waiting. John and I were in that mode now, a waiting time.

"I need to see you, Reverend Elaine. Something's happened. I've had…can't say right now." Tina spoke softly. A single mother who looked like a woman of the open range, her tentative words were out of character. "Can I see you tomorrow?" she asked.

"Of course. This sounds important." Tina and I made plans to have breakfast together. She'd pick me up the next day at the church and we'd go to Steve and Cathy's Blue Hills Diner. My thoughts were at last distracted from the shock of Marjorie's death, and I was soon to learn about a matter I'd not confronted before.

"We're quite a pair," I said the next morning. She wore boots, jeans, and a tight-fitting snap-front plaid shirt. A lighted cigarette dangled from her hand. I looked more suited to parlors in a purple and rose jacket, glasses, and modest skirt. Pampered Parson greets Wrangler Woman. I touched her arm. "Have you had bad news from the doctor?"

"No, no. That's not what's bothering me," she said, and we got into her Jeep. "I called because I've got to tell you about what I saw. Couldn't think of anyone else." She took a drag on her cigarette. "I hoped there'd be cloud cover, but the sky was *clear* that morning." She told me of a visual experience she'd had. "It was early—about five—and I couldn't see any hazes or mist. I was sitting on the front deck and there it was, right in my yard! I thought the thing might be coming from my mind." She exhaled smoke as if it had been held for days. "All I know is I saw one tree all lighted up, glowing. It frightened the hell out of me. Excuse the language."

When she finished, I realized I'd been holding my breath. Tina lit another cigarette, her hand shaking, and started her four-wheel drive. After a moment she explained that the explosive sight in her yard couldn't have been real. Her story reminded me of the time I saw my dead grandmother in my backyard. Something bright had broken through to both of us.

"Are you still frightened?" I asked, watching her startling bright eyes still imprinted with a magical vision.

"I think I am." She regarded the morning. "That's why I'm here. It was so strange. In all my days of sitting on my deck, I never saw anything like a...a heavenly tree." She paused and gazed outside. "Gives me shivers. I couldn't look any more and went indoors and paced the floor, telling myself it was my imagination."

"Tree of Heaven. Wow." She turned the jeep onto the highway, and I grabbed the dashboard to steady myself. "I saw something like that once," I said, "and it can get to you. Tell me more."

"I was afraid, but I went back out and my yard looked normal. You've seen stuff like that? Tell me what it means, Pastor." Her voice had an unfamiliar pleading, and the word *Pastor* felt like it came from her need for a shepherd. I was learning that competent adults under stress could be reassured by a person representing the cross, a place of suffering and redemption where no evil could invade.

"The fact that you were scared," I said, "only means it was beyond...I mean, out of the ordinary—not something bad."

The October slant of the sun on the elms cast long shadows as we bounced along in Tina's dirty SUV on the potholed back road to the diner. The autumn air was wonderfully cool and the leaves golden, a fine setting for a mystical experience.

Inside the cafe, I looked around, wondering if the hefty gun-toting man I saw on the first day we drove into Dewey was there. Would he be eating breakfast with us? No sign of danger. Cathy—owner/waitress/cook—moved around the café carrying dishes and joking with patrons.

We ordered major breakfasts, Tina's with biscuits and gravy and mine with lots of bacon. The atmosphere was smoky, since in Arizona there were no separate non-smoking sections.

"What was the best part about what you saw?" I asked. *We will enjoy and encourage visions.*

"Nothing," she said. "It scared me too much. I've seen sunlight on trees a thousand times, but this was something different."

The cooking odors from pork and pancakes clouded the unventilated space, and my brain felt hazy too, but I reached for coffee and focused on this woman who'd requested pastoral care in the Blue

Hills Café. Tina's tough appearance made her helplessness more touching. I wanted to put her at ease, to offer her an explanation she could believe. "We often think of such visions as inspiring feelings of warmth and love. None of that?"

"Nope." She shook her head and glanced at the nearby table of men smoking and talking. "I'll tell you what gets me. It's all this bad luck. My husband leaves me, and then the surgery was so messed up. Now this. It makes me feel like I keep causing trouble that gets me punished." Her eyes filled, and she leaned over her plate. "Maybe God's after me and the tree is like a warning."

"Oh, Tina. That's not it. Bad luck like yours *isn't* a punishment." I silently asked God to help me explain this vision. Then, over what was left of my rye toast and sour coffee, I found my way. "I know this is just the opposite of a warning. The tree was gorgeous in that heavenly light, wasn't it?" She nodded. "This is reassurance! This is God's way of saying, 'Tina, I care for you, and I think you're managing very well—with all you've endured.'"

I meant every word. *The world needs us to be visionary.*

"It didn't feel that way. It felt threatening, except, maybe, not hurtful I guess."

"Remember Moses," I said. "He was terrified when he saw a mysterious burning bush, but he was chosen by God." I swallowed a bite of my breakfast. "You've been given this vision for your special gifts too. Nothing to worry about. All that's asked of you is to continue to be who you are."

"It's nice to hear you don't think I'm crazy." She attended to her disappearing biscuits. "Are there books where I can learn more about these things?"

"Not that I can stand. There are books about miracles that'll tell you if you expect a miracle you'll get one, putting you on alert to keep the right attitude. That kind of message irritates me—blames us when things don't work out."

Tina lit a cigarette and stared into my face. My cynicism startled us both.

After breakfast I let myself into the church to begin my day, feeling that despite a few setbacks—like unwanted criticism—I enjoyed my ministry. "Church can get so boring," Mother liked to say. I disagreed. Complicated, funny, sad, infuriating, yes. Never boring. I hung up my purple jacket. No, Mom, this is never boring.

I surprised myself that morning, coming up with a ready biblical reference about Moses that helped explain a troubling event. I realized I had a hallowed biblical resource to share, stories for healing and comfort. I liked that view of ministry—sacred storytelling.

The meeting with Tina increased my sense of belonging at the church. I'd been of use to her. She showed faith in me and the church. My doubts about theology didn't matter that morning.

I picked up the phone to talk with John. "You doing all right? Did you manage breakfast without me?"

"How was tippling with Tina?" He cleared his throat, sounding sleepy.

"Quite interesting. I'll tell you about it later. The coffee's ready to go; just flip the switch."

"I know. I'm watching the birds right now. They like my peanut butter on the pine-cone arrangement."

"Of course. I'm about to tackle the miracle sermon, and I've decided that miracles happen in Dewey."

"I could use one of those miracles. Feeling weaker these days."

"So sorry...God loves you."

"Sometimes you sound like a believer."

"Sometimes I am."

During a church service that fall, Diane Merchant asked me to pray for victory for the Bradshaw Mountain High School football team. I was startled by the request.

"We'll pray for the success of both teams—that no one gets hurt," I answered with a smile.

Diane, a stubborn woman, was not done with me. She took my answer as a namby-pamby response. Before long, she and her husband invited John and me to a high school football game to show off the Bradshaw Mountain Bears and teach me what it meant for your team to be blessed by Jesus.

The fall afternoon was perfect, chilly, and sunny. Simple wooden bleachers surrounded the unlighted field, and the fans were the usual crazed teens and parents waving pennants.

"You'll appreciate this," Diane said as the team ran out onto the turf, formed a huddle and prayed to Jesus for victory, their voices amplified for the respectful crowd. How could the school district ignore the laws against prayer at public school events? Easily, it seemed. No one here gave a fig. Diane and Phil beamed with pride—and a note of triumph.

Here was my chance to stand up for minority rights and neutral school grounds, but I said nothing. The issue felt too academic, and I didn't want to upset the Merchants with pompous proclamations. I felt as out of place as E.T.

A few days into the month I got an invitation from the Prescott Valley Town Council, a growing community near Dewey, to give the invocation at their next meeting. Each month a different Christian minister offered an opening prayer. (Only Christians were invited.) I was surprised they'd thought of me since I was the wrong gender, but I was flattered by the request and couldn't resist accepting. Ever the actress ready to charm an audience, I hoped my appearance would cause a stir. How could they bring religion into a civic meeting? As easily as praying at a football game.

John and I went to the town council meeting on a Friday evening. I'd make my public debut in a humble place, a cement-block building in a small park. At the doorway we passed a couple having a last-minute cigarette, and we entered a hall lit with florescent lights, much like public school classrooms. The officers of the town sat behind a table on a dais, microphones in front of them, important papers at each place. The mayor, a dapper fellow with handlebar moustache, smiled and came down to shake my hand. We'd have the prayer after the salute to the flag, he said.

I nodded to the one female council person, a church member, and John and I took our seats to observe from the audience, a crowd of about forty people who'd come to observe and comment upon matters that affected their town. They looked tired from their workday but eager to have their say.

The pink agenda sheets on our chair seats reminded me of the song sheets at my church youth group meetings led by Carl Ludlow. I'd married my true love in a flutter of adolescent romance, and he now lay paralyzed in a hospital, barely alive. Lord, with me abide.

Reading the agenda, I learned that there was much to discuss: sewers, the hiring of an attorney, paving the shorter streets. After the opening ritual I stepped to the podium:

> Be present with us this evening, O God.
>
> Lend wisdom and compassion to the work done here. Help these leaders—whose responsibilities affect the children, the poor, and our seniors—to be mindful of the needs of those who do not speak for themselves.
>
> Inspired by the sight of peaceful antelope which roam our lands, may our work include protection of our valley and its beauty. Amen

No one rose to object to a woman minister praying at the meeting. No one cared. My hope was that Marjorie knew I'd prayed for our town. A pioneer birdwatcher with a booster spirit, Marjorie had lived in this little valley for years. She would be proud of me.

Driving the unlighted rural road toward home, I realized I could find my way around in this territory as I never could in sprawling San Diego. In the years I'd been in Dewey, the names of landmarks—the Mayer smokestack, the Ironite Mine, Fain Ranch, the Blue Hills—had entered my vocabulary, and the bursts of cloud punctuated my sky. This was now my world, a place of vacant spaces presided over by hawks and mayors with moustaches.

"Dark as the inside of a cow," John said.

*Jesus taught that in order to be fully righteous we must not just be lawful, we must also be compassionate. We must stop judging everyone who we feel is in error, and remove the log from our own eyes. We must forgive, he taught. The protesters are models of true righteousness for me—the Beyond War people, the non-violent followers of King, the disarmament groups. They are confronting systems that delay the reign of peace, the message of Jesus Christ.*

Letters from God

## TEN

The drive from the country club neighborhood to the Fain Ranch took me along a dirt road through open land, a short trip to meet two women who'd lived in Dewey all their lives. Johnie Fain used her respected position as *grande dame* of our church to influence decisions, so when she called and invited me to visit her and her daughter at the ranch, I didn't hesitate.

Johnie was a cherished favorite in the congregation, our oldest member and deeply loved. She was a member of the ranch family who'd given land for the church, and she was beautiful and generous and a woman of confident religious faith. Our respect for her was automatic, a part of who we were.

On either side of the road, fields of dry grass stretched to the horizon. I searched the area for a glimpse of antelope. Instead, a hoard of grasshopper-like bugs streamed across the road, millions and millions of them, moving swiftly in tiny ranks from my left and into the field on the right. I stopped the car, thinking how biblical it looked, like the locusts that swarmed on the crops of the Egyptians. I felt privileged to be in a wilderness of sorts—far from the pavements of California—where primal urges moved hordes of creatures according to the slant of light. Thank God for the birds who'd take care of this lot, I thought. Finally I did the civilized thing and drove my ordinary car over the extraordinary plague. Behind me the insects kept marching on, creeping over the bodies of their kin. There's a metaphor in that, I thought, and made a note.

The Fain Ranch could have been a Western movie setting. Two chestnut horses grazed in the nearby enclosure, a colt posed next to a mare. Cool breezes caught their manes, and I sensed the coming of winter. Standing next to my car, I was Maureen O'Hara, the red-headed actress of Western sagas, a more romantic figure than a clerical woman in sensible shoes.

The ranch house had a long front porch and low roof held up by hand-hewn posts. My father would have loved the place. He designed our suburban California home where I'd grown up, an imitation ranch house with the same long porch as the Fain's—but no paddock or cattle noises, only a wagon-wheel resting against an orange tree.

Johnie's daughter, Sue, smiling as always, invited me into an understated living room with an imposing fireplace. A woman in her fifties, Sue wore slacks and a white blouse, her graying hair in a messy permanent. She'd returned home after a failed marriage, and she and Johnie made a life together. Sue drove the Mercedes, did the cooking, and managed everything, including their two large dogs. When she opened the door, soft hymns sounded from a distant place as if I'd entered a monastery.

Ushered into Johnie's peach-colored bedroom, I found her in an upholstered chair waiting for me. Johnie, now in her eighties, had been a hands-on rancher and raised three children—though she had the bearing of a white-haired British royal. Wearing a lush rosy robe, she said, "I'm having a lazy day. Sue, can you bring tea? Then come join us."

I sat next to her side table stacked with books. She may have called to talk about a book, or she wanted to promote the chapel she planned to build using stained glass religious windows from the old Mercy Hospital in Prescott. I wondered what chore she had for me.

"Have you read this?" Johnie asked, patting the Christian novel on her lap, a popular book called *Joshua*.

"No, I haven't. I've heard of it though—about a young man much like Jesus?"

"Yes. Like our Lord. Oh there's so much here, so much. I'll loan it to you when I've finished." Johnie read Christian books and gave them away to anyone, including young Dana and Becky, our acolytes in sneakers. Fortunately she never quizzed me to see if I'd read her selections.

When she didn't explain why she'd called me, I said, "I've been listening to the audio tapes of your ranching days. They're fascinating. Helped me get a feel for this area before it was developed." Johnie smiled and tilted her head, her light eyes serene behind her glasses. No comment. "'Jackass Flats' you said this area was called. And 'Lonesome Valley' is the perfect name for our valley. I wish we still had those colorful names. Dewey is dull."

"What about Humboldt? Now there's a silly name." Johnie referred to a nearby town with crumbling buildings and a thriving ice cream parlor. "Glad you liked the tapes, dear," she added. "It was a fine opportunity to talk about those days with the museum people. They brought out memories I'd almost forgotten." Still no request.

The audio tapes filled me in on Johnie's life. Proficient in Spanish, she'd been about to accept a job offer with an oil company in Mexico when her high school sweetheart, Norman, arrived home from Stanford and she married him. He then went on to become a leader in ranching interests and Arizona politics, and Johnie spent the following thirty years at his side, raising their children, riding the range on horseback here in Lonesome Valley. The couple then divorced, an ending out of keeping in this American ranch setting where marriages should be happy ever after.

I'd been thinking about marriage and weddings as a topic for a sermon. Divorce had to be part of the picture. Collapsed expectations, like squashed grasshoppers. My divorce wasn't sad; it gave me new freedom, and I was able to leave behind suburban dreams that never worked for me. I felt released. From a lonely home. From desertion.

After divorce from Carl Ludlow, I went back to work in the San Diego schools and Carl slipped into a new life as a gay man. I took the children to a small house on Jackdaw Street where Margaret, Joey, and I fit perfectly. The day we moved in everything looked splendid—a big kitchen, dirty shag carpets, a noisy staircase. My furniture belonged too, including my upright piano.

My friends rallied to help with the heavy lifting.

"A rite of passage," Faithful Ingrid said as she lugged a heavy load of clothing up the stairs.

"The end of an era," Rugged William added, carrying the coffee table into the living room.

Joey, in his leather vest, watched the bustling activity, hoping for a role in the moving project. "Hey kid!" I called. "Could you find the step stool and hang the birdfeeder outside the kitchen window?" He took the bottle and tray, pleased to be asked to do a real job.

"You're looking good, Elaine," Incredible Iris called from the laundry room. "What's that old joke about losing two hundred pounds with a divorce? You look less preoccupied, less unraveled."

"I feel quite raveled, in fact. Never felt better." Carl and I had been married twenty-one years and he'd not been affectionate for a long time. He was playful, cheerful, full of ideas for excursions, but we lived together as distant friends. His absences at night felt like abandonment, and I was pleased never to have to feel it again.

After an hour of arranging and unpacking, I stopped and watched Iris polish my coffee table. Her hair tied back with a kerchief, she revived my table, making all things new.

"Watching you work on that table will be my most treasured memory of this day," I announced. Pat went to the piano and played the "Hokey Pokey," a theme song for a left-handed divorcee:

I put my left hand in; I put my left hand out

I put my left hand in and turn myself about.

The tune ended, we ate a picnic supper, and the work party ended. While Joey and Margaret entertained themselves out in the front of the house scribbling on the sidewalk with colored chalks, I slipped out the back door to take a walk around the block. Daisy joined me unleashed that evening. The quiet of Jackdaw Street didn't require leashes.

We turned the corner on our return, and my new home came into view. "Daisy, we've done a good thing here. We've come to Jackdaw Street, named after a bird." I blew my nose. "There's plenty of symbolism in that name—freedom, flight, nesting." We walked on and I lectured my dog about the joys of a new life.

Back on the Fain ranch, I didn't tell Johnie Fain about my happy divorce, but she observed me as if she knew everything about me.

Still waiting for Johnie's request, I said, "I like the story of the time you taught the cowboys how to coax a calf that wouldn't move."

"Stuck out my thumb, the little guy started to suck, and we were on our way." She grasped *Joshua* and her eyes twinkled like granny in a children's story.

An open Bible rested on the side table. "Did you want to talk about a scripture passage?" I asked.

"No, dear. It's about family, I'm afraid."

Sue came in with a tea tray and gave her mother an encouraging glance. They had something on their minds, but Sue didn't introduce the subject. Johnie placed the *Joshua* novel next to the Bible and reached over to touch my hand. "I've asked you here because Norman's Vivian is very sick. I want you to visit her."

"Oh?" I turned to Sue, hoping for an explanation of why Johnie would want comfort for Norman's young wife.

Sue gave no hints and poured the tea into pale celadon cups, saying, "You know we played bridge every Wednesday night with Vivian and Norman—until she got so sick."

Who could imagine it? Johnie, Sue, Norman, and Vivian played bridge together? "I didn't know. It's a surprise." Now this request for me to visit Vivian. "I'm not sure what you have in mind," I said. "Vivian's not a member of our church."

"I know, Pastor, but you see Vivian's a Christian Scientist and she's very sick. I can't visit, for lots of reasons, and I don't even know if she'd welcome you, but I like her, and she's a fine bridge player." She chuckled.

Amazed at the easy way Johnie accepted and forgave her husband—or so it appeared—I admired her crinkled face and wished I had her kindly spirit. *We must forgive, he taught.*

Sue handed us our cups on delicate saucers, smiling as always. For Sue, her mother's request was common Christian goodwill. "Vivian's very sick, and we feel so bad," she said with no change of expression. "She's in a lot of pain. It's her lungs. I imagine her Scientist beliefs have added to her difficulties, Pastor."

"Hard for us to say. Christian Science has ways of dealing with suffering through prayer." I caught myself lecturing. "Doesn't she have support from her own congregation? Someone who visits regularly?" Johnie and Sue stared at me in silence until I got the message. "I'll call Vivian and see if she'd like me to visit." A friendly telephone call wouldn't hurt. That Johnie Fain would trust me with a mission to speak with Vivian touched me and I felt valued. Out of respect for Johnie's selfless request and her faith, I'd make the effort.

That afternoon, back at the church, I said a silent prayer for guidance before telephoning Vivian. Lord with me abide. When she answered I imagined her speaking to me from the living room of Norman's spacious home with its high ceilings and mammoth furniture. She'd be seated propped by pillows wearing a heavy black sweater, dark hair pulled back, a blanket covering her legs.

"I saw Johnie today," I began. "She wanted me to stop by."

Vivian breathed with effort. "Norman warned me—that Johnie would be after me to have a minister in—but I'm sure you know—I can't do that."

"Of course. Do you have a practitioner?" I asked, referring to the Christian Science people trained to pray for the sick.

"Yes. She comes—almost every day. I always feel better when she's been here." She coughed.

"Well, Johnie's concerned about you, and—"

"I know. Don't worry. We Scientists are full of hope." Her voice was faint. "Johnie, Sue and I—get along just fine. Kinda funny, isn't it?"

"It did surprise me."

"Me too," she whispered.

Vivian wouldn't complain about her condition. She'd chosen

to limit her medical options and had no need to explain herself. "I should let you go," I said. "I want you to know I'm here, and we'll be praying for you at the church. Johnie will see to that."

"Thank you." She coughed again.

The familiar feeling that I'd not done enough came over me as I said good-bye.

When Vivian died, I worried with Johnie and Sue that the consolations of her religious beliefs may not have protected her from suffering, though we couldn't know the relief that came from Vivian's spiritual counselor who supported her belief in God's power to restore all wounded people into what her church taught was the perfection of creation.

At the time of Johnie's death, I imagined she must have gone to a reward that was complete with angels, harps, and golden streets. Before she left us, when she was confined to her bed at home, members of our church choir joined me one afternoon at her bedside in the peach room. She loved old hymns, so we stood around her bed and sang them while she smiled up at us, her face a shining witness to the power of her Christian faith, rising as it did from belief I'd never known.

A wedding sermon.

The chilly weather did not inspire sermons about weddings. The cold fall air felt more suited to divorce. After fortifying myself with a cup of real coffee, I opened the New Testament wedding passage in the Bible. The account in the book of John—just twelve verses— tells of the day Jesus turned water into wine at a wedding in Cana. Jesus not only performed the miracle but on that festive occasion he said to his mother, "Oh woman, what have you to do with me?" A bitter question. Made Jesus sound real. I liked that. Jesus not only turned water into wine in a generous gesture, he rebuffed his mother with a rude remark that exposed his self-absorption.

A wedding sermon.

I'd try for something whimsical. Whimsy described some ceremonies I'd been a part of—like the time guests gathered in a small Prescott backyard, listened to a solo of "Bridge Over Troubled

Waters," and out of the kitchen door came two figures from *Gone with the Wind*: Rhett Butler in black tuxedo with Scarlett at his side, her bouffant skirt blooming over a hoop. The best man stood next to me chewing gum. I've taken leave of my senses, I thought, quoting Scarlett herself, as the couple approached over the rocky desert yard through a bower of paper roses.

A wedding sermon.

"Oh woman, what have you to do with me?" I said aloud. If Jesus were addressing that question to me, I'd brag how a woman serves a church in his name, a church that raises money for Habitat for Humanity, gives provisions to the food bank every week, cleans trash from the roadway, helps the school nurses and provides comfort for each other in times of crisis. Triumphant as I felt, I knew that the teachings of Jesus asked us to do far more, like protesting war, welcoming persons of all sexual orientations, and providing refuge for the lost, homeless, and despairing. We'd not met those obligations. The Catholics did better.

Johnie Fain would answer Jesus differently. If he asked *her* what she had to do with him, she'd say, "Lord, you have died for me, and I live in faith that I've been saved," relying on her conviction that Jesus cherished her soul and would do so after her death. I didn't see Jesus in that way, but our religious disagreements didn't matter. We desert Christians kept our versions of theology to ourselves.

A wedding sermon.

I remembered the time two young people from the flight school in Prescott held their ceremony on a field where a hot-air balloon waited. Protected from the sun's glare in dark glasses and wearing a white robe, I faced a handsome couple in flight gear and goggles. After the kiss, they climbed into the balloon-basket and were launched upward into the hot wind and blue sky.

My stories weren't going anywhere.

Footsteps outside crunched the church parking lot. It had to be a stranger. No church member would come around and disturb my work on a Monday, the quietest day for writing. No one needed to fix the heater or sand down a peeling front door. Most of the remodeling was done. I had no secretary. Timothy Haasen wouldn't appear on

Mondays to interrupt my work with his complaints. Volunteers came around occasionally, but I was usually the only Monday staff at Faith United Church.

I heard a knock and got up to answer. Our church had to be locked if I was working alone because of the stream of callers who came asking for help. When you try to do as Jesus would have done you want to open doors and welcome whoever's there, but this minister needed to use caution because people sometimes got threatening in their desperation. She looked through the peephole. I think we women in ministry do that more than men—take a look before swinging wide a church door.

A small whiskered man in grimy clothes waited in the parking lot a few feet from the doorway. "Where's the preacher? Gotta see the preacher." He could be Gabby Hayes, the time-worn sidekick of the clean-shaven hero in Western movies. He wanted to speak to the lovely lady at the church (me). I smiled. Here was a chance to meet a real mountain man.

Before I could identify myself, the grizzled fellow spoke again, "I got these troubles, need money." He looked down, embarrassed.

"I'm the minister here," I said, pleased to help out a man of the Wild West. "I can give you some—"

"You ain't no minister!" His eyes widened in panic as if confronted by a sorceress. "I wanna see the real minister!"

"I assure you—"

"You're a woman, for Christ's sake!" He scanned the area frantically.

Ever the actress, I put on a clerical face, reassuring and saintly. "Well, yes, but I'm the minister of this church, and—"

"I know why this church is going to hell, lady. It's because of people like you!" Backing away to protect himself from the evil eye, he added, "I can't talk to you. You ain't even got a Bible!"

So much for my kindly pose. Johnie Fain would give this guy the perfect response. I wished I had her cowpunching spirit but had no comment for this Western man who believed our church was going to hell. The lady minister stood speechless. Over his retreating figure, the Arizona skies looked a colorless white. A lone hawk swayed above hills scattered with bits of snow. Nearby, normal folk played golf.

My visitor had defined me as a trespasser on this sacred site. If he was right, I didn't belong among true believers. I'd had this criticism before. The Baptists declared in a public notice that I was an inappropriate choice to represent clergy at the Good Friday community service. One time I was asked by a groom if a wedding performed by a woman would be valid. Before an ecumenical service featuring ministers from several denominations, the Anglican priest looked at me through squinting eyes and announced to the four clergymen waiting, "I've never approved of women clergy." His words sent me right back to self-conscious days in elementary school.

"I'm the best priest you'll ever meet," I said aloud to the empty parking lot, wishing my poor visitor had accepted help instead of leaving me in a doorway feeling awful. "Ask Nancy Hernandez!" Nancy, my Sunday school supporter, was probably in high school by now. She'd spun out into the future and left me here to confront nasty reality.

You're a woman, for Christ's sake. Some day I'd think that was funny.

Why was a woman minister more frightening than a woman doctor or pilot? Some people thought the Devil lived in me. The matter was worth exploring. I set aside my wedding sermon to write about this visitor and proclaim the injustice of his indictment.

A place to talk about my experience was already arranged. An organization of women professionals in Prescott asked me to speak about coping in an occupation dominated by men. The women knew that all the congregations in the county—a territory composed of hundreds of churches—were led by male clergy, except ours and the Science of Mind church, so they expected some good stories. I could take the subject in any direction and I'd get a free lunch at the Prescott Mining Company, an attractive restaurant.

Within a few weeks, preoccupied by thoughts of revenge— Where's the real minister? Right here, buddy. Right here—I drove the familiar road into town to speak to the Prescott professional women. I passed hills covered with healthy, rain-watered brush.

Rows of cottonwoods, now with yellow leaves, lined the creek beds. In contrast to that natural scene, a pock-marked paneled van was parked next to the road with a crude sign on its side that read "Swords, Blowguns, Silver Jewelry. Gifts that say I Love You." We'd been invaded by knights. Funny knights.

Those empty stretches of land would one day be covered with homes, and blowguns would no longer be available. We Californians know what invasion means.

Near Prescott was the entrance to Fort Whipple, a former Civil War fort. Johnie Fain told me she saw a hanging there when she was a child. John loved the American citadel, now the veterans' hospital set among old shade trees. The compound stirred his imagination as much as the San Gabriel Mission did for me in my childhood. Built to hold the territory for soldiers and settlers against Indian raiders, the hospital's older buildings were preserved with Civil War authenticity.

Above the hospital, a mammoth heap of black and white stone loomed like a pile stacked by giants, Granite Mountain. The small town of Prescott huddled below it, a cluster of buildings that barely made a statement in the expanse of high country. It pleased me to be near the Civil War, as if I lived in early America before urban settlements, dirty air, and fast cars.

In a glass-enclosed atrium at the restaurant, well-dressed women sat at an array of tables next to a desert garden of evergreens and bursts of pampas grass. Noon light came to us a pale green through the glass walls. The scene looked like Rosemary Barringer's patio. I was pleased to see a good crowd of women attending this luncheon. Sandra Mattson sat at one of the tables—the only church member present.

After our meal and an introduction, I thanked the group for inviting me and confessed that the opportunity to speak answered my need to be heard by women who might have had similar experiences. Then I told the story of the man at the church door and his fear of a woman minister, saying that I'd shattered his sense that in God's house there'd be sublime order no matter what fell apart around him. I must have represented the end of his hopes.

"Does that make sense?" I asked the women at the pretty tables.

"Can you think of another reason I'd frightened this stranger? I'd like to hear what you think when I've finished."

Not long ago, when Bertha Knox died, Knox Farm was bequeathed to the local Methodist Church. You see, the Presbyterians had hired a *woman* minister, so Mrs. Knox left her estate to the Methodists—when her lawyer told her she couldn't leave it to her dog.

It's still a man's world in my profession. Let me assure you, I believe Anita Hill and I believe Senator Packwood's accusers—because I've seen what goes on behind closed doors to women in my profession. Some are being sexually harassed by male senior pastors. Many are not getting promoted above assistant. The truth is, women are not taken seriously as ministers. We are called by our first names, told we cannot be heard in the pulpit, ignored when part of a clergy group, and perpetually asked to take the notes and make the coffee...

The listeners didn't look offended. Sandra smiled at me as she always did. One woman put her hand to her mouth and coughed.

But here I am today. I got hired! I've done a difficult thing, partly because I thought prejudice against women didn't apply to me. After all, I'm tall, over forty, and look assertive. But I was wrong. I learned after I was hired that the congregation was desperate to get a full-time minister without paying a complete salary package...

Women belong in the home, the Bible teaches, and I submit to you that those biblical rules were written to curtail the rise of female influence in the early church. They are not the rules of a compassionate God...

At the end of my talk we discussed why women frighten men if they take on a responsible job. Some felt that if women could work any job, men would think they weren't superior. One woman said it frightened her to think all women might not want to raise children; such deviant behavior could bring down American society. I hoped that when they heard themselves they'd take a new look at the dominance of men in their lives.

In front of me on the drive home through Prescott, a landmark mountain—called "Thumb Butte" for its characteristic shape— loomed in the distance. All roads in Prescott lead to that gigantic crag with its gesture of support, "Thumbs-Up!" Today it was all mine. I'd told the story of my visitor who said "You're a woman, for Christ's sake" and the audience had laughed.

Prescott was named for William H. Prescott, who'd never visited Prescott but was considered an American patriot to those who made the decisions in 1864. The town became the capital of Arizona territory, complete with Fort Whipple, a school, the governor's mansion, and some impressive homes. Some of Prescott's streets have Spanish names—Cortez, Montezuma, Alarcon—taken from W.H. Prescott's book.

I turned onto Mount Vernon Avenue, a picturesque street with classic Victorian homes and charming gardens. Driving slowly along the avenue, I enjoyed the fluttering leaves from pampered birch and aspen as they cast trembling shadows on the pavement. A storybook street where you could pretend. Never mind a mountain man who came to our church door with his fears.

Back at the church office I worked the wedding sermon to include some feminist thinking. With clever maneuvers I could use the story of Jesus changing water into wine and say that what was inadequate and watery without women is made rich and tasty when the feminine is included in church leadership. Yes. The sermon took off like a hot-air balloon into a western sky.

Fall proceeded in triumph. Never had I experienced such a beautiful season. My walks were full of surprises, my window-musings more prolonged. The colors and new light inspired courage to see into faces—though the season brought some concerns; one was Sally's health.

I scribbled a note to her. She'd recently undergone spinal surgery and I needed to know how she was doing.

Sally, you better get well. I need
you, and so do the Quilters! I'm
okay, but I'm not always courageous.
Surprise. Surprise. I don't know how
long I can do this. Part of me craves
to be away from John and church
people to a remote place of my own. A
dirty little man came to the church
door and cursed at me last week. I
know I'm supposed to love him. Who
can do that? Courage and super-human
compassion are needed in this job.
            Let me know how you are.
                    Love, the rev

As I wrote the note, I'd no idea that Sally would not recover from
her surgery and the pain would continue as she lost strength. She so
often was beside me in spirit with her sarcasm, advice, and friendship.
I wasn't wise enough to imagine she'd never return to her computer
or my life, that she would die in a nursing home.

Sally was addicted to prescription drugs, a truth I didn't accept
until after her visit to us in Arizona the fall before the surgery. She
could hardly walk by then so her teen-aged daughter assisted her on
the trip. When they arrived, Sally looked as pretty as ever. Tinted eye
shadow intensified her blue eyes, and her blonde hair was still stylish.
She wore her mother's jewelry, of course. I was delighted to see her.

My friend had little time to listen to my stories or give me advice.
She needed more pain killers and was frantic. I had to help: I was
a minister, for God's sake. I offered my migraine meds, but they
didn't work. I called a church member who was chronically ill and
borrowed some drugs from her. She could spare only a few of the
controlled substance, but they were enough to bring Sally some
peace. I felt proud I'd provided relief, never imagining Sally was
severely in trouble. We took a drive to Flagstaff the next day and
admired the quaking aspens in their autumn glory, as gilded as the
jewelry Sally loved. She and her daughter walked a short way with
me through the quiet forest, crunching psychedelic leaves underfoot.

I couldn't see Sally, or my first husband, Carl Ludlow, as they really were until they were nearly gone. The truth, with its unhappiness and miseries, was too dark. How a real minister could serve people with that much avoidance appalls me.

On a Sunday that fall, as I started to preach the wedding sermon, I was glad to see Johnie Fain sitting in her usual place on the aisle, her smile reassuring. I had a genuine supporter in this courageous forgiving woman who saw me as a *real* minister.

Another of my champions, Cal Appleton, usually sat next to the aisle too, his oxygen tank on the floor next to him, but he was not with us that Sunday. He'd left for parts unknown. Cal adored me, his lady minister, and he was a married man. Before Sunday services, he'd catch me in the church entry to hold my hand and give me a hug. He managed his oxygen with tube attached to his nose, but he was not slow in trailing after me. I'd skitter away, a black clerical mouse, as my geriatric admirer searched the building.

Cal tested my pastoral patience. During church services he'd speak up in moments set aside for prayer requests and thank God for another birthday or his new car. You weren't supposed to thank God for a new car; you were supposed to thank God for blessings, like a birth or recovery. Cal didn't attend to unspoken rules. Sometimes he got up in the middle of the service and trudged to the men's room trailing his oxygen tube and tank. We'd hear the flush of the toilet and anticipate his disruptive return no matter what was happening in the church service.

He knocked at my door early one cold winter morning.

"Morning, Pastor," he said, shaking dirt from his well-worn boots. He noticed my bathrobe and added, "Hope I'm not too early." Retirees like Cal held to imprinted farm schedules. They rose at dawn.

He looked like a bundled-up prospector—wrinkled face, stooped body, clutter hanging from his belt. He fit the rustic scene better than I did in my blue robe and slippers.

"Cal! Not at all. Just having my coffee."

"The church's shut up tighter'n a drum," he said. He'd arrived with no oxygen tank that day and his breathing took effort. He stomped his feet and made wheezy foggy puffs with each word. "Got a little—electric organ to drop off."

Cal haunted the rummage sources of the area searching for castoffs from garage sales and swap meets. He tinkered with his treasures until they were ready for resale, and if he thought his riches had any religious meaning, he gave them to the church. The level of his gifts rose like Noah's flood, and I struggled to control it, giving away much of Cal's bounty as fast as the items came in—the video tapes on sign language, the gigantic Bible made for gigantic people, the *Guidepost* magazines from the 1960s.

"Okay. You can leave it in the trunk of my car." Our feet crunched the gravel of the drive, and I opened the screeching door so Cal could haul the organ into the trunk. We had no room for such a gift at the church, of course, but this was a ritual I chose to continue.

"Can I make a phone call, Pastor?" he asked wiping his gloved hands on his pants. For a second I worried that he wanted more than that. "I wanna call Dick—see if he's going to the Donut Hole." Cal and his friend enjoyed the donut shop, their hangout, every morning. He trudged behind me up the stairs and into the house. "My sister's got a thing about you, Pastor," he said. "Heard from her again yesterday. She don't believe in—wheeze—such a thing as a female pastor." He laughed. "Said I shouldn't go to your church. I told her to mind her own business." He winked.

That news was no surprise after I'd been accused of not being a real minister, a fake who didn't even carry a Bible. Women like Cal's sister were going to thwart feminine efforts to serve in the priesthood and ministry for a long time. If it hadn't been for the acceptance of my congregation, I'd have felt hurt by Cal's report from his sister. As it was, the wink was all I needed.

After making the call to his friend, Cal left, speeding down our driveway faster than seemed safe. I turned to see John standing in the bedroom doorway. "Just Cal," I said. "Had to drop off an organ."

"You're kidding."

"It's one of those electric things."

"I see."

Within a week, the telephone in my office rang and I picked up to hear a choking noise. "Pastor, I'm dropping out of church." I knew by the end of the sentence it was Cal. "Take me off the rolls. I ain't comin' back."

"What's the matter?"

"I'm quittin' the church," he said. "Take me off the rolls."

"Has something gone wrong? Are you okay?" I imagined his sister told him he was destined for hell if he stayed at a church with a lady preacher, especially since he made his affection for me so obvious.

But it wasn't about me.

He blew his nose. "Today at the donut shop…can't talk about it."

"You mean something happened over coffee this morning, something to make you want to drop church?" I asked, wishing I had a maple sugar donut.

"Yeah." He blew his nose again. "Dick told everyone about my going to the toilet during church, made a joke of it. The guys laughed, said I was avoiding the collection."

"So, you don't want to come to church anymore. I'm sorry," I said with genuine regret.

"Can't do it."

Hesitating a moment I asked God's help for Cal and me and got an impulse to stay passive, let Cal pour out his pain. He told me he'd never had such a terrible morning, never been mocked that way before. He cried.

"Cal, do you want me to speak to Dick, tell him how you feel?"

"Course not!" he said. "Dick's okay. Most of the time he don't hurt me." He blew his nose hard.

"I'd miss you if you never came to church again."

"We'll see about that."

Cal was in church on Sunday, all smiles, and asked me to visit his home and meet his wife. The request surprised me because his wife was never seen around the country club. I wasn't even sure she existed.

In the next week I drove the winding street toward the section of the country club reserved for mobile homes. At the Appleton's there'd be collections of junk. There'd be a garage for a treasured vehicle. There'd be Cal and his oxygen tank and a mystery wife I'll call Betty—an alcoholic, I'd been told.

The day didn't have the sunny brilliance that we often enjoyed year round. Cloud cover made everything gray. The occasional pine tree stood black in the filtered light. Most homes looked well kept with combed yards and landscaping, but some seemed as if they've been part of the desert a long time, sorry looking units in need of paint.

Cal's corner lot had no plants or graded rock. He'd placed remnants from an abandoned mine—rusty tools and an iron wheelbarrow—out front, making the house a mountain man's quarters. Would Betty be Calamity Jane, wielding a rifle?

As I got out of the car, I could see Cal standing behind a screen door wearing a cowboy hat, his oxygen, and a wide grin. "You got here okay," he said in amazement, as if I'd driven from Colorado.

"Yes. I recognized your yard and all your collections." He seemed pleased and escorted me inside. The darkened room smelled of tobacco and dust, suitable to the old-timer who lived there.

Off in a side room, Betty sat at a table next to a window holding an empty jelly glass and a cigarette. She turned to me and grimaced, exposing large teeth in a tanned face. She could have been a thirsty gray-haired Native American woman, a striking contrast to Johnie Fain in her rosy robe.

I joined Betty at the table, and Cal stood in the doorway, nodded to me and disappeared. Betty was unlike any other women I'd met in our complacent community near the golf course. She wore no apron. She offered no food. She didn't chatter about bridge games, golf, or gardening. She seemed to be saying, I'm managing. I'm not dead yet.

I didn't know what Betty needed from me except that it wasn't religious counseling. We posed in the window for Cal. My presence may have made her uncomfortable, but I didn't think so. I was the uneasy one, stranded and awkward. I felt I'd been dropped off the boat at the wrong port. Was there anger in her face? Was she jealous of me? She didn't look bothered. Both of us glanced from time to time into the gray skies, searching for the sun.

The universe of this couple felt as unfamiliar as the amazing snowfall that transformed the desert in winter. Betty and Cal didn't appear connected in ways I was used to. All I could guess was that they lived separately and Cal sold his junk to buy her liquor—a scenario I couldn't accept.

Betty eventually disappeared. Her existence was not mentioned by anyone, before or after she evaporated. She was one of a number of people in Arizona I never understood because of my limited background. They came to me from a long way off, another country. No amount of training told me what I needed to know about their lives or their suffering. I'm amazed by their patience with an inexperienced minister whom they'd allowed into their lives.

I'd chosen ministry to learn where people find faith and courage, how they love. Choosing the church to learn of the human condition seems an odd decision, but I thought it was where people took their troubles, their secrets. Not so in Protestant churches, I discovered, where we honored privacy, pretending, and hiding. I had to do some guessing and learn the hard way—by standing still and letting the spaces between us tell me what I should know.

Cal drove sporty late-model cars, acquiring them like his other collections. He must have longed to drive home to Illinois because one day he did just that, leaving Dewey in a red sports car. Before he roared off he parked his gleaming toy on our driveway, knocked on the door, and asked for a hug. He regretted his decision to leave Arizona and wrote me a despairing letter about his mistake. Maybe his sister had not been welcoming. Maybe there was no donut shop in Indiana, let alone a woman minister to whom he could give his gifts.

Cal had an admirable way of making his way in our rocky landscape. I remember him with fondness, even gratitude, for his adoration. I wish he'd stayed at the church in Dewey. His departure left more emptiness in the Sunday morning service.

It occurs to me now that I tried to serve a God who was a lot like my adoring prospector. Both of them gave me unwanted gifts, tested my patience, loved me more than I deserved, and left me on my own to confront a lonely table and an empty glass.

That year my sermons explored the person of Jesus, the

heart of the Christian Bible, the main man who stood with me in homes, hospitals, and pulpit. I liked making him come alive for the congregation. To imagine Jesus in Arizona was easy. We wandered the same burning earth, endured the same storms and wind. I felt I was an interpreter for him, a translator like those in the Middle East who trail after the military trying to turn Arabic or Persian into words Americans can understand. I liked the challenge, and the church members may have valued my interpretations—but they also needed a believer who came to them confident that Jesus sacrificed himself to redeem every believing soul. To pretend I was that person became more of a struggle as the Sundays went by. The role required too much theatrical pretense, and I sensed I was cheating the congregation.

I knew how it felt to be deceived.

*I'm going to tell you a story…Then Barrington Bunny shared the gift of his warmth with a tiny freezing mouse, and he saved its life. After Barrington died, no one in the forest noticed the great Silver Wolf who came to stand beside that brown, lop-eared carcass. But the wolf did come.*

## Seeing with My Heart

## ELEVEN

"Can you come over, Reverend? The place is overrun with cops!" Millie Thornton's voice sounded worried. "You won't believe what's going on here."

"Of course I can be there. What's happened?" Millie would need handholding if cops were swarming. I felt parental toward her ever since the council meeting when she was so distressed by Jim Godfrey's clipboard complaints about children with clumpy shoes.

"You'll never believe this. Ah…hard to talk about over the phone. You see…" I heard muffled words, "Should I tell her what we know?"

"Yeah," Curtis answered. "It's okay. It'll be in the *Courier* tomorrow."

In a lowered voice, Millie said, "Um, you see, the man next door has had this freezer in his truck and they've found a girl's dead body in it." She stopped, shocked by her words.

"Millie! I can't imagine."

"You see, um, he must of murdered her and put the body there. He's had the freezer plugged into his house by an extension cord. We noticed the cord but never thought—"

"Sounds unbelievable."

"The police are using our garage as some sort of investigation center, and we don't mind, but it's hard to get used to."

"I should say. I'll be right over." I cancelled an appointment and put on my heavy red jacket, anticipating winter cold and shudders from the sight of violent death.

On Saddleback Road I parked as close to Millie and Curtis's home as I could and walked past the police cars, thinking of the man with the gun I'd seen my first day in Arizona. He belonged in the cold where dead bodies are found. He'd become my symbol of fearsome unknowns as he stood leaning and guarded, waiting.

Neighbors milled across the street from the Thornton's home, chatting and staring at the garage where police talked on walkie-talkies or conferred in clusters of khaki, moving in and out of the dim interior to speak with onlookers. My interest spiked: a drama of violent death! A heroic team working to apprehend a killer! I wanted to walk into that garage and listen to every grisly detail.

On the Thornton's flagstone patio, bordered by potted succulents dusted with snow, a gleam of sunlight highlighted the spiny paddles of one dominant prickly pear, a fierce beauty in a cold desert.

Before I could ring the bell, the front door opened and Millie and Curtis stood in the entry, eyes fixed on me, two round cherubs in winter wear. "You can see what we mean," Curtis said. "It's a mess. Can't believe it. At least they've taken away the freezer."

We settled in the living room and Millie went to the kitchen. She returned with a mug and silver spoon, her flowery scent mingling with the smell of good coffee. "A little cream and sugar, as I recall."

The room was overheated and full of furniture. Striped upholstery and a silk bouquet on a side table provided a dressy contrast to the cacti of the entry patio. A glass-fronted case displayed Millie's angel collection.

"Thanks for coming over," she said fingering her necklace of turquoise beads worn over her satiny white blouse. "It helps."

"Not much you can do, I suppose. It must feel strange—to be spectators at your neighbor's arrest. My goodness!"

Millie patted her silky, black chignon. "It's unreal, Pastor. But I was out there a minute ago and the police were so nice." She smiled at Curtis. "They make you feel like they're going to take care of everything."

I stirred my coffee. "That's good to hear. We think we've left murder behind in the big city, and we're hit with this. A wake-up call, they say these days."

"Yeah," Curtis said. "A wake-up call, alright." He put his thumbs in his belt, securing his bulging stomach. His brown hairpiece made him look a bit comic. "Murder at the Country Club."

The nervous couple told the murder details over and over, a story as unbelievable as Rosemary's romance with Carl Jung. Sipping coffee until we felt more comfortable, we eventually accepted the truth of this murder—even in a room with angels on the shelf—and turned our conversation to memories of the forest spirituality retreat and a funny Halloween now marred by murder.

By the time I left, the police had gone except for one patrol car. Neighbors had retreated too, and the empty street looked more frightening than when it was full of the curious and efficient. I sensed an eeriness in the vacant murder house where the windows were blocked from the inside by stacks of cardboard or crates. A killer had lived in that darkness.

Eventually we learned more details: John Famalaro, age thirty-nine, kidnapped and bludgeoned Denise Huber, a twenty-three-year-old woman whom he accosted when her car's tire blew out on a California freeway. He packed her body into a freezer, stole a truck to transport it, drove to his home in the Prescott Country Club in Dewey and attached the freezer to his house with a long electric cord. The body was not discovered until now, three years later. (Convicted of murder, Famalaro resides on death row in California.) He was never part of the society of retired golfers and gardeners, bridge players and choir singers, of course, but his violent act invaded their lives, leaving a haunted house on Saddleback Drive. A wake-up call indeed. We residents would never again feel distant from malevolence.

Then the season became Thanksgiving. Early on that snowy weekend morning I called Lew to take me to church on his way in his pickup. If I drove myself, I could be stranded in a snowdrift! He chuckled. "Be right there."

I'd never get used to deep snow. The white mounds covered everything familiar. I feared losing my way and felt relieved when the snow disappeared and reality returned. Thank God for Lew.

Bernice had decorated the altar at the church Sunday morning with a cornucopia spilling with colorful gourds and fruits. We sang "Come Ye Thankful People Come, Raise the Song of Harvest Home" and admired the arrangement of autumn leaves around the candles. Never mind the snow outdoors. The church felt warm and looked filled with abundance, lifting our thoughts from cold, darkness, and murder.

The number of attendees in the congregation was larger than usual, always a pleasing sight. After we introduced family and visitors, I led the congregation in a Thanksgiving prayer of gratitude. Aware of Millie and Curtis Thornton sitting near the door, I added a word about the murder whose aftermath continued as authorities sorted out the facts:

> Gracious God, be with us as the strong white of
> winter advances. Come to everyone burdened by
> grief and fear because of the murder of a young
> woman. Be with those who knew her and her family
> and with the one who struck her. Bring comfort
> where there must be despair.
> In thankfulness for courage, for family, and for
> each other, we begin our service this morning…

The prayer came easily. I could now sense the worries of the congregation, breathe with them, and pray for them.

I had no idea, as I prayed that cold morning, that in a few days I'd be leaving a Thanksgiving snowfall for a trip to California.

Within days, my father's heart failed. His death was impossible to accept. The last time I'd seen him, at my seminary graduation ceremony when I was awarded a Master of Divinity, my father had the bearing of a fit, tanned leading man. I had to go to California and be with family, especially Mother who'd planned a memorial service. My father understood my wanting to study religion and claimed my fascination with religion came from his German father, Gottlieb, whose name he translated as "godlove." My religious heritage on Mother's side was more entertaining: we were told that my great-grandmother was the illegitimate daughter of the village priest.

Preparing to leave for California, I was preoccupied with memories of my father and my California childhood. His competent strength during wartime kept us safe. Losing him ended so much of the past—scents of citrus blossoms, warm evenings of neighborhood street games, funny aunties in pretty dresses. A certain security was gone, as if I now lived unprotected on Saddleback Drive next door to catastrophe.

Many Christians feel that after death they'll live eternally in a heavenly place, and as their minister I affirmed their belief, preaching the certainty of God's love after death and the promises of Jesus from the Bible, but I didn't believe in the Christian promise of an afterlife. All I could truly accept was that my father's life mattered—to us and to God.

On the plane I breathed a full yoga breath, trying not to give into sadness that would spill into fear and worry. How would John feel about a trip to a memorial service? His shins were covered with the red petechial dots that we learned were indications of internal hemorrhage. The back of his neck had a deep crevice between the muscles, a sign of very old age, though he was only sixty-eight. Still, he seemed at ease, and he'd brought his camera to record our visit.

I checked my appointment book to see if I'd thought of everything so that programs at the church would continue smoothly in my absence. Grant Barringer, café entrepreneur and church auctioneer, would preach for me. He'd charm the congregation. Lew would see to the comforts of the building. The Reverend Strickland would answer any emergency requests.

If only ministry were that simple—preaching a message, answering calls, maintaining a building. I'd been challenged in my ministry by moral crises more difficult than those chores, like the day I walked away from a dying woman in a hospital.

I rushed into the three-storied brick hospital wearing my heavy red jacket and boots. Invigorated by the bite of cold, I hurried upstairs to the room of a woman I'll call Jeanine. She was not a church member, but I'd been sent by her friend who knew Jeanine was alone. At her bedside I was startled by a repulsive odor, tempered by a sweet powder the nurses used.

"Oh…Elaine…help me!" I'd not expected this.

Jeanine's body lay naked except for her belly, hidden beneath a white flannel cloth. A nurse hovered and told me, "It's the cancer. We can't cover her." She adjusted the cloth, revealing open sores—probably for me to see so I could understand—and left. Jeanine looked like she'd been blasted by a bomb. If she'd been on a battlefield, medics would be shouting for help, but no surgeons from a MASH unit came running to this hospital room. Hospice had not been called as far as I could tell. All Jeanine had was me.

I put my coat on a chair, the crimson heap too bright for the misery in the white room. Leaning over the tortured form, barely able to breathe, I said the words of the Twenty-Third Psalm, "The Lord is my shepherd…Ye, though I walk through the valley of the shadow of death, I will fear no evil…Thy rod and thy staff they comfort me." The swollen patient couldn't hear poetry. Her consciousness was given over to suffering.

"Help me. Help me," she moaned again, her eyes opening and closing.

Jeanine was a vibrant person who'd loved her husband, now gone, with a convincing passion, but no family or friends were with us. How could that be? "Jeanine, I'm so sorry," I whispered.

At the nurses' station I waited at the high counter decorated with paper turkeys and a bowl of candy corn. When a young nurse looked up, I asked if she could give Jeanine a shot to relieve her pain.

"Nothing more to do," she said, looking down at an open ledger.

"But she's suffering so!" I said loudly, hoping to be heard by anyone who might help. The girl stood silent and turned a page. I noticed her bitten fingernails.

"Yes she is," agreed an older nurse standing in the back, "but

Dr. Helms is the only one who can change orders, and he's opposed to giving her more morphine." We stared at each other for a second. The gray-haired woman looked away first.

So that was the issue here, giving a stronger dose of morphine to end Jeanine's pain and probably her life. If I'd been the patient, I'd want to go peacefully, aided by a drug, rather than lie in that agonized state. I assumed Jeanine longed for that peace too. I'd alert this gentleman I've called Dr. Helms.

Before I could ask to use the telephone, the young doctor came down the corridor. He was my personal physician. He'd listen to me, an older person of the cloth with a loud voice. I fell into step with him and asked if Jeanine could be given enough morphine to alleviate pain.

"That much would not be possible, Pastor. She wouldn't survive." Helms moved ahead of me to the nurse's station and leaned over the counter, turning his back so I'd take the hint and go away.

"Does it really matter?" I asked of the doctor's back.

Helms turned, his face close to mine. "You know I can't do that. I'm a Christian."

How could this man's biblical religion—based on forgiveness and love—prevent him from easing Jeanine's terrible pain? "But it's awful!" I said. The nurses were listening, and so was the dark-skinned man guiding a huge vacuum in the hallway. "Her gut's an open wound! What difference does it make?"

Helms walked away, avoiding the door to Jeanine's room. Seeing him not bother to check in on her, I felt a flash of moral superiority and thought of the traveler in The Good Samaritan story in the Bible who refused to stop and help a suffering person. Jesus condemned the passerby for not seeing in the broken body a life like his own.

As I bring back that moment, I see the noble clergywoman spill the dish of candy at the nurses' station with an elbow—probably an unconscious expression of anger—and stoop to pick up the scattered corn, a woman minister on her knees.

Then I stood in the doorway of Jeanine's room and couldn't walk in. I didn't want to be there any more than Helms did. I didn't want to see that pain, listen to the moaning or smell the sickness.

Remembering Jesus' words, "I was sick and you visited me," I felt coins of guilt jangling, but I snatched my red jacket without taking a breath and left Jeanine to her hapless nurses and Christian doctor. Unlike the Silver Wolf—in the story by Martin Bell I'd used in a sermon—who stood by a tiny carcass, I did not stay.

I took the stairs in clumsy boots, hurrying downward. Though I'd vowed to be a presence at the bedside of suffering, I didn't have the will to keep my promise and return to the third floor, the moral high ground. I stepped into the winter cold trying to shake off the image of myself standing in the doorway. The clergywoman up there didn't match my vision of a Spirit Woman who served and comforted people in pain.

The trip to California took me away from white rooms. I needed the respite, a chance to be with our shocked family and forget promises not kept. At the end of the flight, John and I headed north in a rental car from Fresno in central California, enjoying a temperate climate after having left a winter freeze in Northern Arizona—like being returned to living color after black and white. The crude industrial commerce in this agricultural belt, trucks and cars by the thousands, didn't bother me. I chose to see only the acres of tilled land and ranks of healthy fruit trees. California was home.

My parents had retired to a mountain town on a tributary of the Kaweah River at the entrance of Sequoia National Park where the small community of Three Rivers presided over ranches and forest like Prescott, but this was a mountain village nestled among giant redwood trees. More snow had fallen here than in Prescott, and I felt far from Arizona.

Leaving John to rest the next day, I drove back to Fresno to pick up Margaret and her baby, Katherine. Though I was glad my daughter was joining us for her grandfather's memorial service, I felt unsure about what she might say or do at the family gathering. She'd never liked my father much, saying he "tried to be the boss of me." We all tried to be the boss of Margaret, and she never allowed it.

"Baby Kate looks wonderful." I held the baby for a moment before we started back to Three Rivers. "You're looking good too,

Marg. I'm glad you wanted to come."

"Nothing's going on at home." She watched the ranks of olive and nut trees on the side of the highway. "Miss my video job."

"Remember our drives up to Berkeley? I thought I'd go crazy with you blasting the radio and having to stop all the time."

She laughed and patted the baby. "Yeah," she said. "I miss Daisy—and the kids in Berkeley. You like your church?"

"I do. I've learned to give shorter sermons and get along with all sorts of people. Are you feeling okay?"

"Yeah. Kate's good. I like church sometimes. I'd like to see yours."

Thinking this was not the time to speak of the Dewey murder to my daughter— though she'd love the story—I said, "Tell me about your video job." Margaret never held a job before other than delivering pizza.

"It was so cool. I learned the computer. The owner—this Chinese guy—was a real chicken. He was afraid to collect from people when they owed him, so he let me demand the money." She knew her toughness frightened me a little. "People get scared when you threaten them." We laughed.

The mountain road circled Lake Kaweah. "The lake's way down!" Margaret said.

"I know. So sad. Another California drought."

"I loved the 'Strawberry Float,' Grandpa's houseboat. Really neat."

"So he wasn't so bad."

"Gimme a break, Mom." She sounded like Sally. If it hadn't been for the two of them I'd be Spirit-Woman-With-No-Clue. "I visited Dad in the hospital," she added. "Took Kate along. Had to bust in with the baby. Did you know that?"

No. I hadn't known.

The next afternoon, avoiding icy patches on the parking lot, we headed for the redwood doors of the Three Rivers Presbyterian Church, a modest sanctuary surrounded by stately trees. Mother—an agnostic who'd affiliated with the Presbyterians only to be neighborly—ushered us inside to a front pew. She'd not weep in this public gathering. "I've written this service," she whispered, "so the preacher doesn't get carried away."

After music from the church choir, a group my baritone father had joined, Mother stepped into the pulpit and told about his youth as an immigrant farmer—sole support of his mother and six sisters after his father deserted them—and successful retailer. Her speech made us laugh. Like me, Mother enjoyed entertaining a crowd. Then she allowed the minister a word of prayer and we adjourned.

At my parents' home, aunts, uncles, cousins, my sister, and her children mingled and wandered. Margaret followed Mother into the kitchen drinking a Coke and minding a baby. She whispered something to her grandmother, and I left them there surrounded by enough bustle that sorrow couldn't penetrate the afternoon.

In the hallway I touched my son's arm. "Joe, wait a minute." He stopped, a piece of cake on a paper plate in his hand. "I wondered what you thought of the service. Sit down with me a second." We sat at a wobbly card table in the guest room while the rest of the family roamed the house carrying food and admiring the home that some of them had never visited before. "I'm curious about your take on the memorial service."

"I liked it." Joe pushed the cake around his plate with his fork. "That's a neat church, with the redwood, but I think Catholic churches are better." We could hear feminine chatter from the kitchen.

"Something in you likes smells and bells, I think. It's genetic."

Joe's Portuguese ancestry was probably steeped in Catholicism. I'd seen in him a childhood fascination with medieval art at the San Diego Art Museum, especially the paintings featuring Madonna and baby, but I didn't remind him of that. The small paintings of maternal love may have attracted him because he never knew his birth mother. The day we talked of adoption when he was very small was the last time he asked about his birth mother.

Four-year-old Joey climbed up onto the soft flowered loveseat and teased the new puppy, Daisy, with his faded security blanket, well chewed and faded.

"Is Daisy adopted?" he asked.

"Yes. We've got a lot of adopted people around here." I picked up the spaniel and sat next to Joey. "Remember the day we brought baby Margaret home from the adoption place? You were only two."

Joey blinked, his green eyes concerned. "Did I go?" His black hair, worn long—1970s style—framed his skeptical face.

"Sure. You had to be with us when we met her. You're her big brother." I gave him a kiss, wondering if there would be any more questions. Daisy wriggled free and tumbled down from the loveseat.

"Was Margaret adopted too?" Joey asked, sniffing. I nodded and wiped his nose. "Why did my mother make me adopted?"

"Your mother loved you. Only she couldn't take care of you. Babies are a lot of work, you know." I smiled but my son didn't smile back.

"Did that mother look like me?"

"Yes, and—"

"Can I nail some boards?"

"Sure. The hammer and wood are down in the garage."

We went down the outside stairs, Joey holding my hand, and I noticed the modest homes of fishermen across the street. Their boats bobbed in the San Diego harbor, and I wished Joey could know his Portuguese seagoing ancestors. We entered the dark garage, out of sunlight momentarily, and I sensed the darkness surrounding Joey's unknown parentage. The adoption agency had removed the switches to the overhead lights, refusing identifying information—a decision I regard as cruel.

"I think it's good to be adopted," Joey said on our return with the materials. "It gives you a place to live and everything." He paused. "Where does my other mother live?" We set up a work space for him outside.

"I don't know because the adoption people think it's better if we stay apart while you're growing up."

"I wish I could make her a picture."

"Yes. I do too."

I thought of my Native American baby upstairs. She'd not know her heritage either. I wanted her to know a mother who reflected back a version of her features, her skin, her eyes. People needed to see the land they came from too. San Diego was not Joey's Hawaiian birthplace, nor was it my daughter's Indian country.

One afternoon, on a visit to Balboa Park, Joey and I stopped at the fish pond, staring down at the golden-orange streaks in the shallow waters. He knew those carp. "There's that spotted one. He's the fastest."

Then we climbed the echoing stairs of the Fine Arts Museum. In the small Renaissance Room we took in each diminutive painting. Some were renderings of the Virgin Mary and her baby; others were scenes depicting the crucifixion of Jesus. Joey studied the small dense oils.

"Who are the people with the lights behind their heads?"

"They're saints. That means they love God and are very good."

"Tell me about that baby again." He pointed to a stern-looking upright Jesus on his mother's knee. The child held a scepter.

"That's Jesus and his mother, Mary. Lots of people think he's the finest man who ever lived, so he has that light around his head—called a halo." I glanced at the museum guard, hoping he admired my gifted son.

"That stick. What's he doing with that stick?"

"It's a golden stick. Means he's a king, sort of."

Then Joey stopped in front of a bloody crucifixion scene. "I want to know about this one again." He took my hand.

"I know. That's the day Jesus was killed. They carried his body to a cave, called a tomb. You can see that everyone around is very sad."

"Is his skull still rolling around in the tomb?"

"No. That was a long time ago, and people tell stories about what happened to his bones."

"Was he adopted?"

Joe, all grown now, tasted the cake, and I admired his suit and tie, his conservative appearance. "Mom. Forget about the genes. I don't care about that stuff." And he didn't. Joe never asked again about his parentage. "It's just that Protestants do things so plain, you could say."

"I suppose. But our simplicity has its beauty." We looked out the window at the mountainside. "I can see you on that mountain when you were a teenager. I watched you, a speck on the side of it climbing by yourself, remember?"

"I just think the older churches, the statues and candles, seem kind of, you know, holy. At school they held chapel service in an old church. I liked it." The San Gabriel Mission Archangel with its icons and incense had enchanted me too.

"You have to admit, though, Grandma's stories about Grandpa were touching and funny," I said. "You wouldn't find that informality in a cathedral."

"No. But you'd find stuff to look at that helps you feel better." He gave his attention to the cake, curly dark hair bent over the plate. Recently he'd asked me to send him a book of classic prayers after Carl was hospitalized, but today we'd not mention Carl Ludlow, confined to a nursing home.

Mother came in, her gait unsteady, the only sign of grief she couldn't hide. "Margaret's got a good sense of humor, Elaine. Don't know why you worry about her so much." She joined Joe and me at the table and put down a cup of coffee that she ignored.

"Worrying's what I do, Mom. It's genetic." I glanced at Joe, making sure he caught my word. "I get it from Grandma Aurelia. She visits me from another reality, you know." No one said anything. "I think she was a worrier too. You okay?"

"No time for self-pity," Mother said. "Aunt Hermina's ready to leave. You'd better say good-bye."

My sister poked her blonde head into the room. "Good cake, Mom. Let's get out your slides. The kids would love to see themselves, and—" Her voice broke.

"I'll get them," Joe said. "I think there's one of me catching a fish in the Kaweah."

After I told Margaret about the murder in Dewey, she asked me how I could stand being around death so much, and I tried to explain that to be present with a family or patient answered a powerful curiosity I had about what death meant, how we manage through the losses and accept our own dying. I confessed that sometimes I couldn't maintain a compassionate presence, like the time I'd turned away from Jeanine and her agony, but I didn't tell Margaret that story.

Back in Arizona, after three days in California, Advent was underway. We lighted a candle each week in a wreath placed on the altar. It marked the four Sundays of the season leading to Christmas. The brief ceremony of a few words and a circlet of candlelight seemed to lift the darkness of murder in our neighborhood and my father's death. We were on our way to the season of light, Christmas.

At work on a sermon about miracles, I considered the stories about when Jesus walked on water, cured the blind man with a bit of spittle, and fed five thousand people with a single basket of bread and fish. Traditional Christians believed every one of those stories, certain they proved Jesus was the Son of God. My belief was that the more extreme tales are beautiful fables. Beautiful fables. Oh dear. Janet and Jim Godfrey wouldn't like that. For them, the Bible was accurate history written by the hand of God.

Reading about miracles led me to thoughts of John's illness. Like so many stricken people, he hoped he wasn't being punished by God for his failures, thinking they were reasons for his serious illness. I reassured him that God didn't dole out punishments, and John tried to believe me, but the worry continued. My patience thinned as he weakened and needed more attention. At times the Spirit Woman wished his death would come. What would people say if they knew these thoughts? We both needed a miracle.

During a recent Bible study class we'd been talking about the miracle of the birth of Jesus to a virgin. After a prayer for Ardith, who'd been diagnosed with cancer, I began the discussion by explaining that the Christmas story was not strictly true, that it was lifted from pre-Christian mythology. The wise men, shepherds, and a star—and the Virgin—were probably inserted into the Jesus story to raise him to the status of a god. The twelve people seated around the table leaned toward me listening.

"The manger story is a compilation of old pagan myths pre-dating Jesus' birth," I repeated. "But that should not take away its beauty and importance to us. We can still celebrate the birth with the star and manger and—"

"I don't care about that stuff. I believe it really happened," Janet-of-the-stout-broom interrupted.

"Oh. Yes. Your reading of these stories is more literal than mine. Does it bother you that I speak about other sources for the

Christmas story?"

"Of course not. I think it's interesting," she said, her face flushed. "It's just that I believe Jesus was born in a manger and Mary was a virgin. I'm not alone."

Sarah smiled. "No, you're not alone. You can believe what you want. This class is for people who want history. Don't worry about it." That made me smile too. "I'm not alone," a perfect statement of faith. My own doubts about Jesus seemed pale beside Janet's certainties.

Janet represented many—if not most—Christians' thinking. She thought my ideas interesting but she believed every word of the Bible stories anyway because she chose to. I was not dealing with students here but with believers who listened politely but maintained beliefs in miracles they'd held since they were children. Reason, scholarship, and research didn't change many of my listeners. We were speaking different languages. The fascinating part is that the group loved to join me each week and listen to what I had to teach. I can't say I really understand that.

Glad for a new heater in the office, I pulled my red chenille sweater around me and typed sermon notes about my favorite miracle story in Luke of Jesus' encounter with his disciples after he'd been murdered:

> The story of Jesus on the road to Emmaus is one of the most beautiful miracles in the Bible—full of honesty, doubt, and stumbling. In it the disciples meet Jesus face to face after his death. Thinking he's an interested stranger, they include him in conversation about the empty tomb. I can picture Jesus nodding and smiling while they tell their story. Not until Jesus shared bread with them do they recognize him, a man alive whom they knew had been murdered. "Then their eyes were opened," Luke says. *Then their eyes were opened.*

The vision at Emmaus reminded me of Tina's vision of a shining tree of heaven, though the disciples were not afraid, like Tina. They were surprised. *Then their eyes were opened.* They offered bread and their eyes were opened. In keeping with that idea, I asked the women of the church to prepare small loaves of homemade bread for me to bring to people who visited our church for the first time. Nourishing, tasty bread seemed better than preacher's words.

Sunday afternoon I drove through the December cold to visit Ardith in her home. Over coffee and cinnamon coffee cake, I let her know we missed her in Bible study class and asked about her situation. Ardith's red hair, a bonny Irish color, framed a deeply worried face. She tried to smile as she explained her cancer diagnosis—an advanced form of the disease—and said she hadn't the energy to face people but she'd come back to class as soon as she could. My memory of that conversation includes a calico cat that joined us in the small living room.

"I'm so sorry. I know your friends in the Bible class want to help." She looked pensive but didn't tell me her thoughts, so I read the comforting biblical passage "Fear not, for I am with you…"

Before I finished, she blurted, "My daughter's going to be upset. She's in New York and really can't come out. I'm not sure what to do." I didn't know Ardith had a daughter. "Oh, she's wonderful. Colleen has a real great job. I'm not sure what she does. She's always busy. Not married yet." The cat stretched, yawned, and wandered away.

"Could she come for a short visit?" I asked and enjoyed another generous bite of cake. Preaching left me starving for sweets.

"I'm not so sure. I hate to ask." Ardith watched me eat, and I glanced through a window with a view of a tiny windswept front yard with one pine tree.

"Okay, let me see," I began, still chewing. "Your first duty is to call her, and then we'll get the machinery going at the church to help out. I'll come to your next doctor's appointment with you. Good to have another pair of ears, don't you think?" Ardith nodded and took a handkerchief like my grandmother would have used and blew her nose. Outside, the wind caused the pine tree to sway, needles scattering, and I felt a palpable loneliness in the room.

Within days a team of church members brought food, cleaned the house, took out the trash and cared for the cat. Ardith got weaker, and we worried about how she'd manage as the disease progressed.

Her daughter continued to be an absent figure.

When no word came from New York, a retired couple in the church, the Goodmans, decided to move Ardith into their home for her last months. Within days, Pat and Jay had a dying houseguest. The church members accepted the Goodman's decision with amazement. So did I. It wasn't usual for such a commitment to actually happen before your eyes. Goodman indeed.

Then Pat contacted Ardith's daughter by telephone. She worked a miracle that I imagine went something like this: "Colleen, I'm sure you know your mother is very sick. I'm afraid she's dying. She has a house here that needs your capable attention. I know you'll want to make plans to visit as soon as possible."

The next week I ventured through snowy streets to the Goodman's home to lend encouragement. "Be a non-anxious presence," I reminded myself. That was ministry, I learned, to stand composed beside the hurt and afraid.

Pat met me at the door drying her hands on a dishtowel. Her neat salt-and-pepper hair cut short around her face, she smiled a welcome. I noticed the required jewelry, earrings at all times. Hers today were discs of pearl.

"I've come to see your new boarder. How's it going?"

"Come on in. We're about finished getting organized. Ardith will be glad to see you. Jay's playing golf."

In the living room, Ardith waited in a wheelchair facing us. I could smell baking and imagined bran muffins with raisins. "You look settled in," I said. "You've sure found a perfect spot."

"Yes," Ardith said and reached out her arms to me. She felt thinner, but her face was calm. "Jay has been an angel," she said, guessing my unspoken question about Jay's acceptance of the new arrangement. "Can't believe anyone would do this."

The pale green room had a window facing a quiet avenue of country club homes. Over the fireplace hung an antique ornamental clock, perhaps one of Jim Godfrey's restorations. I loved our fireplaces in the desert. They smelled of wood ash, like the one in my seminary apartment.

"I know what you mean." Pat returned my gaze and folded her

competent hands. Then a bird squawked from a cage in the kitchen, and she left the room as if called.

"I'm so glad you came, Pastor," Ardith said. "I wanted to tell you that Colleen flew out last week to sell the house. She looked so well-dressed and all. She had the business taken care of in no time."

Pat returned to stand next to the wheelchair. Right away I remembered the image in a story I used in a sermon about a Silver Wolf standing witness at the death of Barrington Bunny: *The great Silver Wolf came to stand beside...*

"Elaine, I have to tell you I'm glad Council voted not to give Doctor Haasen a raise," Pat said, startling me. "He's making me nervous. Those ideas about speaking with the dead and all."

"He talked to the choir about that?"

"Yes!" Ardith said. "Pat told me he said he could communicate with spirits and that he knew the future."

"Could you follow it?" I asked. "Sometimes he goes into ideas I can't understand."

Pat smoothed her apron and gazed down at Ardith, deciding to settle matters: "Sounded pretty New Age to me."

"We have to allow people their beliefs," I said. "We don't have all the answers, of course, so we really can't condemn Timothy out of hand." Schoolteacher talk again.

Pat ignored the remark. "I appreciated that sermon on miracles. I'd like a copy if you have any for us."

"Of course," I said, flattered.

Ardith smiled. "When I think of what the Goodmans have done..." She wiped her eyes. "It's a miracle." She explained the routines of care, adding, "The hospice doctor comes out here to the house. Can you believe it?"

"Yes," Pat added, tucking the blanket around Ardith's knees. "They're in and out all the time. The little nurse who comes twice a week to take vitals and check on medications is a wonder. She's the tiniest little thing and still she helps with the bath."

"I think she has a Spanish accent," Ardith added.

"No. It's French," Pat said. "We'd like a prayer, Reverend."

The three of us waited until I could say what I felt about the charity I'd seen in the Goodman home. I hoped that Janet was right—that we were not alone: "God of the miracles of kindness, we ask for courage as we face change. In the name of Christ Jesus we ask for the healing of pain and for calm in the midst of worry. Bring us stillness that we may cover the sorrows of our hearts with folded hands."

Pat showed me the room off a hallway they'd prepared for Ardith. A hospital bed stood in front of a window shaded by a thick old pine. I wondered when we'd need a hospital bed in our house.

Ardith died at the Goodman's, helped along by hospice. The dying was not a simple process and demanded much of the couple in charge. They remain for me heroic examples of the power of love and faith—and the value of congregations. Their commitment to Ardith is all the evidence I need to convince me that the Christian church has a place in our world, imperfect as the church can be.

When I think now of the time a golfing couple in a country club offered to care for a dying woman, religious words come—Grace. Mercy. Compassion. No other terms are adequate.

*Wouldn't it be wonderful if we could stay aware of how precious those near to us really are! We know it, but we keep forgetting, at least I do. Luckily we have the baby Jesus returning every year to remind us. This Christmas business is God's gift—the lesson that we are loved and, in turn, called to love each other. We must learn that lesson before death and loss teach us in their way.*

Called to Love

TWELVE

Driving the steep mountain road had its scary moments, especially with patches of snow along the roadside. But I needed this trip. I'd stay alone at a bed and breakfast inn in the mountain town of Jerome, and I was intoxicated with anticipation, even more than on that January day five years ago when we drove into Northern Arizona searching for Dewey. Time away from church and home animated every drop of bravery in my heart.

I was on a study leave before Christmas overwhelmed church life. John stayed at home monitored by church members so I could retreat for five days. A mystery novel, *Original Sin* by P.D. James, rested beside me on the car seat waiting to be read in a cozy setting in the mountains. James writes of crimes relating to vicars and churches, perfect reading for a minister with a love of the dramatic.

The getaway was supposed to restore my energy, feed my spirit, and inspire a sermon to preach the Sunday I returned. I'd been thinking about the account in Matthew when Jesus says he brings a sword: "I have not come to bring peace on earth," he said, telling his disciples that if they followed him they were asking for trouble. The sword of Jesus. Not an easy topic for those who love the pacifist Jesus. Before writing a sermon, though, I'd lose myself on a fictional British landscape and the murders thereon.

The air got colder and the sky changed to stark ice-blue. At a sharp turn I couldn't avoid the sight of a gash cut into the mountainside. Stripped of trees, the exposed earth was metallic gray from mineral tailings, an "abomination of desolation" as the Bible says. This land was exploited by silver, gold, and copper mining. Jerome was built on its successes. I had to look away, just as I looked away from the sad eyes around me.

Closer to Jerome, buildings of the town appeared beside the road. An old church, and what may have once been city hall, clung to the side of the narrow pass. Several houses were cantilevered over Verde Valley on my right. Past the fire station was the turnoff to a gold mine with a clutter of signs to tempt tourists. Every structure seemed to balance on a perilous cliff above the world.

The town itself didn't look like a tourist destination even though Jerome was preserved as a national historic landmark. Modest shops, galleries and dilapidated buildings lined the dirty sidewalks. Cars were parked haphazardly on the street. Some structures, roped off by renovators, looked abandoned. Sounds of rock music exploded from a corner bar where a swarm of motorcycles guarded the entrance. Stetson man with the gun was probably inside. Now, five years later, his menace seemed only mildly titillating.

I drove watchfully, looking for the inn where I'd made a reservation. A few blocks past the business district, a two-story wooden house stood next to a dress shop—my destination, "Jerome Inn, Historic Bed and Breakfast." A yellow pennant with a daffodil design fluttered from the balcony over the street and strings of colored Christmas lights dangled from the railing.

The middle-aged innkeeper welcomed me inside what was really her home. She escorted me upstairs to my quarters, a bedroom and spacious sitting room furnished with a couch and a table under a window. Dusty Christmas arrangements provided an attempt at holiday décor on a mammoth antique sideboard standing next to the far wall. The piece could have been from old mining days when Jerome was thriving.

"You'll have the whole place to yourself every day," my landlady said, patting her hair, a wild auburn heap. "I teach down the mountain in Sedona and have to get going early. I'll leave coffee and breakfast fixings in the kitchen when I go." She belonged in Sedona's quirky atmosphere where psychics and soothsayers flourished, the proper place for ladies with wild red hair.

"Thanks," I said softly, respectful of the historic atmosphere. "Be nice if it were haunted."

"Stuff around here goes way back. Bathroom through that door." She gestured with a painted fingernail. "We're not particularly haunted, but the town has its ghosts. Anything special you need?"

An ideal place to read a murder mystery, I thought, hugging my book. "No. Can't think of a thing."

"The cat won't bother you," she said. "You'll have lots of privacy, and the only noise from down below is from tourists walking by and the occasional motorcycle."

A cat. Perfect. "I'm used to that," I said. "I just want time alone. May I use the telephone in the morning? I have to call my husband at least two times while I'm here these four nights."

"Phone's on the kitchen table downstairs."

My hostess left quickly, glad to be done with duties. I unpacked everything—including my blue bathrobe—hid the Christmas decorations and inspected the drawers of the sideboard. The flowered shelf-paper layered with dust and dead bugs must have been placed in the nineteenth century when ladies in ample skirts and aprons worked in this room. I could see the shadows thrown by their candles. I could hear their gossip about deaths in childbirth, about the excessive drinking of the miners.

At the table by the window I made up an agenda for my five days: check out the shops, buy a candle to hide the musty smell, and search for food. I'd read the James novel without stopping until I finished and do the sermon afterward. A glorious plan. No husband or church member could disrupt in a place forgotten by everyone except bikers and redheads. I put down my pen along with all of life's cares.

Too soon it was time to think about Jesus and the sword. I started some notes:

> Jesus won the allegiance of his disciples by demonstrating an amazing kindness, a resistance to evil, and a genius for healing—but some of his words sound militant: "I have not come to bring peace, but a *sword*." Commitment to Jesus demanded breaking with a comfortable life.

The candle flickered as I jotted down more thoughts about the call to be brave: "Jesus doesn't understate how hard it is to follow him. 'If you join me you will suffer,' he implies." The irony of a cautious minister preaching bravery didn't escape me.

Suddenly I heard the creaky sound of footfalls. Jesus was coming up the stairs! I waited. Then he changed his mind and stopped. Thank God. I didn't want Jesus telling me to be strong and do my Christian duty. My husband was dying!

To the clink of my guilt coins, I blew out the candle and went to bed.

Friday morning after breakfast in a kitchen with scuffed black-and-white linoleum and an ancient refrigerator, I called John and told him when to expect me home. He and a friend had visited the ruins by Lynx Lake yesterday, he said, an abandoned place with broken walls and rock drawings to photograph. He seemed content.

Upstairs in my haunted retreat, still wearing a bathrobe and raggedy mukluks, Spirit Woman finished her coffee at the window table. Perched above the town's streets, she could look back on her years at the church, see herself standing at the pulpit or walking by fields dotted with antelope, pondering the mysteries of God and congregation. The view gave her new perspectives on her encounters with hot-fudge sundaes, glowing ghostly trees, perplexing doctors, people suffering from loss—and snow.

Her intentions had been to teach modern theology, deepen moral commitment, and develop a progressive Christian church. She'd not managed to fulfill those earnest ideals. Reality had interfered with such high-mindedness. She was *called to love* and questioned whether she could continue to accept that responsibility. It seemed not only overwhelming in its idealism but also exhausting—to keep a pleasant face, to listen in a loving way, to speak words she didn't believe.

I sighed a self-indulgent sigh worthy of Timothy Haasen, pulled up my wooly slippers, and turned to the sermon, knowing my words spoken in the pulpit often shored up my faltering views of the Christian church and my role in it.

> In order to bring in a more humane and just society, there are enormous hazards. People like Jesus, who risk pain and death for ideals, astound me. Chinese students, who would normally be doing their calculus, are in hiding from family and neighbors because of their bravery on Tiananmen Square. I wonder what I would have said if a child of mine were about to tear down the Berlin Wall. Heroic acts, standing up for principles, take a certitude and bravery that leave me breathless…

I thought of the bulletin board at the church—empty of cartoons— we'd arranged on Memorial weekend the previous May to honor our members who'd served in the military. One photo showed Diana's husband who'd parachuted behind enemy lines in World War II. In another, Muriel grinned in wrinkled fatigues. Vernon had been trapped in a cave on Iwo Jima with no food. I'd be preaching courage to heroes.

> Some of us must confront massive, unfair, and evil systems; others extend the cup of cold water to the thirsty. Who knows what call will come, where we will be needed?…We are challenged by Jesus to correct wrongs, speak truth to power, and extend the cup.

When it was time to return to Dewey, I gathered up my sermon draft, stuffed it in my soft-sided briefcase, and arranged the Christmas decorations as they'd been before. John would be waiting for me dressed in his usual beige. Bless his heart, I thought, sounding like the Christian Science woman in our neighborhood when I was a child. I'd never gone to her Sunday school, but that heart-blessing lady said her magical words even to me.

Sandra bustled around the church decorating for the Christmas season, setting candles, placing altar decorations, fastening garlands while her tape recorder played popular Christmas tunes. She was a blue bee—blue eyes and a denim jumper—buzzing back and forth from closet to altar to wall fixture.

Her commentary provided a buzzing counterpoint to the Christmas music. "Did you see Peter Jennings last night?" she asked. "Well. That war in Rwanda—awful. Blood everywhere."

"No. I didn't get it," I said over the music. "John watches CNN all the—" She disappeared into a closet before I could finish my sentence. She'd already reported on many topics—controversial welfare programs, Indian archaeology, the election of Mandela—but she rarely stopped moving long enough to hear anything I said.

"Reverend, what do you think about these silver stars?" she called out. "I mean, are they going to look right with the brass? I'm not sure I should combine the gold color and the silver. Take a look here and tell me what you think."

I stepped into the sanctuary. "Okay. Let's see, I—"

"The lighting does soften all of it. I mean, well, I suppose you can't tell I've mixed the fake and the real—but I don't want to offend."

"I know what—"

"I love the old look, like an English chapel. So glad Bernice let me decorate this year and Fred's got over that heart thing," she added, touching her chest. "Thanks for your help!"

"It looks beautiful."

I retreated to my office, and Sandra hummed past my door to the sound of "Silver Bells" as she draped and arranged. I was glad that Timothy, who had zero tolerance for popular carols, was not in the building.

Inside a quieter place, I read again the note I'd got in my Christmas card from a woman minister serving a small church in Connecticut, the Rev. Dorothy Slater.

*I've had a call from a mother—the usual glitch in the nativity pageant for Sunday morning—turns out her son, the innkeeper, has to leave at 10:30 a.m. (church starts at 10) for a wrestling match. She wonders if there's something I could do to "relocate" the pageant so Steve can leave at 10:30. I mean this ISN'T why I spent three years in seminary. No one calls the great male ministers and tells them the INKEEPER has to go wrestle!*

*So there you are, my dear.*

Slater was the smartest—and the funniest—minister I knew, and she had no luck finding a church deserving of her. She belonged in a thriving big church with a literate congregation who could appreciate her wit and learning. Her note was a reminder of how impossible it was to create a haven of compassion in the real world, and it belonged under the glass on my desk next to Auden's "We pray to become." Slater eventually chose to leave ministry when her opportunities dried up, a loss to the Christian church.

After Sandra left, I walked through the sanctuary. Along the walls she'd hung pine boughs with touches of gold ribbon. The altar was set with clay images of mother and child—done by one of our members—in a wisp of straw and silver stars. Everything looked touched by a loving hand.

At home that afternoon, while John napped, I took a mug of tea outside to the table on the deck where two lizards, feasting on flies and spiders, made their home on the windowsill. They posed motionless, holding up their tiny alert heads as if danger lurked in the shadows. At certain angles they could be dinosaurs. The snowy hills provided a fitting backdrop for the tiny reptiles and for my wintry mood.

On our recent trip to the Mayo Clinic, John and I met with a hematologist who'd cautioned us that John had a heightened susceptibility to germs. He was ordered to lower his sugar intake, stay away from crowds, and avoid the company of sick people. He refused a stem cell transplant—replacing his immune system with healthy bone marrow—sparing himself a procedure that had little chance of changing anything. The cold air burned my nose, and I felt unable to prepare for John's death. I couldn't imagine his absence.

News of Sally was discouraging. Her health had deteriorated until she had to be placed in a nursing home, a horrifying thought. She was permanently in a wheelchair, and her daughter had been sent to live with Sally's sister. At age fifty, Sally was stripped of home, of daughter, of her life! I sent her spiritless letters because of what had happened when I visited her in the nursing home.

The care facility where Sally was confined had no frills like landscaping or cunning pets. The smells were predictable, and the lonely figures seated in the hallway were what I expected. When I walked into Sally's room—shared with another patient—I found it pleasant enough, considering it was a placement funded by welfare, but it was Sally's home now, and the entire situation seemed grotesque.

Sitting in a raised bed beside a window, Sally smiled when she saw me. With no makeup, her face was dead white beneath her freckles. A stuffed cat snuggled next to her, a gift from her daughter, she said.

"Could we go to the Mall in Fashion Valley?" she asked. "I'd love to get out of here."

"Of course. I have all day to take you anywhere that sounds good." We'd escape and have our usual conversations, talk about the books we loved.

After hefting the wheelchair into the trunk and getting an orderly's help to manage Sally's body, we drove to an upscale shopping mall with high-end stores. She was excited, already enjoying the excursion. Pleased to have brought her pleasure, I pushed her wheelchair into one of the department stores where we approached the jewelry counter. I decided not to ask if she'd ever retrieved her mother's pieces from the pawn shop. It seemed an unkind question.

The clerk was delighted to have customers in her deserted corner display, and Sally made informed comments about the jewelry she asked to examine closely: an ornate pin, several rings on a gray velvet cloth. Then she whispered that she wanted to be alone, so I wandered to the other end of the cases leaving her to fondle the jewelry while the clerk busied herself elsewhere.

When the sparkling items on the counter slipped into Sally's purse, she gestured for me to return. I wheeled her away, astonished by what I'd just seen.

"Did you take…?" I asked, stunned.

"Just a few things," Sally said, smiling up at me. "It's so easy when you're in a chair."

By the time Sally had stolen several pairs of slacks, I had trouble breathing. My eyesight seemed to fail. How could this be? I wanted to sit down. I wanted to cry. I wanted my friend back, my personal counselor who sewed with Quilters at church, who loved her daughter, and had faith in mine.

I remember nothing about getting Sally into the car, only churning thoughts about calling the police, about returning the goods, about contacting the store and confessing. I did none of that. For one who carried so much guilt in her pockets it's surprising that I had so little concern for the clerk selling jewelry or for the store's other losses. I took my friend to McDonald's and bought her two chocolate milkshakes.

A note arrived from Sally a few weeks after I returned to Arizona but I've forgotten its words. I know I sent a perfunctory answer, unable to respond with any more sympathy than her stuffed cat. This was the third time I'd walked away from a person confined in a hospital room. I don't like to think of God's take on the matter.

Watching the little dinosaurs do their push-ups and snap at the flies hitting the window, I wished for the folded hands, spoken of in our book of worship, to cover my guilt over abandoning Sally. I later learned that my glittering, funny friend had died, having overdosed purposely on meds, I believe. I wish I'd been able to say good-bye, to tell her how often I remember her words, how much I loved her.

I stared at the tiny distant homes dotting the Blue Hills, a good place to bird watch, Marjorie said. I could still see her with the enormous binoculars dangling around her skinny neck. Shades were pulled at her home across the street, and I suspected her husband drank alone in the late afternoons after his golf game.

I dropped the leaves from the teabag over the railing of the deck and pulled gloves out of my pocket as the sky darkened to steel. The snow began to fall in slanted streaks and then slowed to heavier flakes. John was inside making a holiday toddy. That sounded like a good idea.

"Can't you ask Sandra to stop interrupting?" someone whispered to me. We church members were seated in the sanctuary around long tables arrayed with Christmas decorations as we waited for the start of our potluck dinner. A lighted pine tree stood in the corner near the pulpit. "She brings up the most useless arguments, and she talks too much!"

Sandra. Sandra. Sandra. I resented having to deal with her. "No. I can't do it," I said softly, annoyed with the suggestion. I wasn't the church bouncer. Out loud, I added as pleasantly as I could, "I'd like to get out of here before midnight too, but all members can have their say, as you know." A memory of another Christmas long ago made me irritable.

We worried that Sandra would use up time at the business meeting after dinner and bore us with opinions recited too loudly and laced with too many personal anecdotes. Maybe she wouldn't come this afternoon. Then Stan opened the door and Sandra carried her hot dish to the kitchen. She paraded to a full table and squeezed in, making a space for Stan. "We'll just sit here at the end." Every church probably has a Sandra, I thought, feeling martyred.

Our moderator, Jack, welcomed everyone and asked me to say a prayer before we lined up to serve ourselves from the potluck tables.

After the meal, when plates were returned to the kitchen and decaf was poured, Jack began the official annual meeting of the Faith United Church. "We'll take time to discuss ideas for next year," he said, looking at notes, "after a report from the building committee. The treasurer has suggested—"

"You know, this church has meant so much to me and Stan," Sandra interrupted. "I mean, I thought we could purchase that land over by the junior high. We need to grow!"

Property? We've just burned the mortgage!

"Sandra," Jack said, "I have a full agenda here." A lean friendly man of conservative opinions, Jack was a patient and fair leader who supported our giving to worthy projects worldwide. I hoped he'd move this meeting along and I could go home to fireside and husband.

"Oh, that's fine," Sandra went on. "Stan used to say—back in California—that our church was the very spine of our lives." She smiled at her husband. "Stan was moderator, you know, and we had a building program too. I really prefer this small congregation. It makes all the difference to know everyone, and—"

My face betrayed my annoyance as I rose to say, "You've got a point there, Sandra." I forced a smile. "But I think we'd better get on with the business this evening so we can keep this church functioning." My Christmas wish—air-conditioning.

Jack picked up the momentum. "Yes, we'll hear the minutes from Tina and then get to the Building Committee report. Our pledges are up, I understand, especially with the sixteen new members for this year. Tina?"

Tina's streaked brown hair gleamed in the Christmas light as she read her minutes. Her hunched bearing, crone-like, made her seem all-wise, and we listened in respectful quiet. After that, Sandra's outbursts seemed more outrageous as she grabbed chances to talk about her dream of a land purchase. We tried to maintain a Christian attitude, but after a while we wanted to strangle the loud voice at the end of the row.

While the meeting progressed—funny and exasperating and productive all at once—I stared at the Christmas tree in the front of the church. Decorated with white Christian symbols, made of yarn and called *chrismons* by the ladies who'd crocheted them, the tree reminded me of a Christmas past when, like Scrooge, I had a shock that changed my life.

This Christmas potluck brought it all back. The remains of food on my plate—pasta salad, tuna rice casserole, and orange Jell-O—could be my cooking in the seventies when I was married to Carl and living in San Diego. Memories from those days dulled everything, even the lighted tree and my butterscotch pie.

I hurried around the kitchen cleaning up after dinner. The room smelled of ham, too much ham. Carl hadn't shown up for the meal, and I worried he'd forgotten his promise to stay with the children while I went to a parents' meeting at the co-operative preschool. I readied my papers, put on my sweater, and peered out the window.

Carl was at his San Diego bar, his latest business venture. I'd never visited him there but could imagine the bar's atmosphere with sounds of folk ballads and creative people laughing. He'd be wearing his winter outfit, a torn T-shirt and shorts, as he hauled cases of beer into his charming little place full of San Diego characters.

I ushered the children into the family room where costume pieces lay heaped on the floor, Lego toys were scattered about, and a multi-colored Big Wheel motorcycle was parked in the center, as if to carry the driver off to Charlie's chocolate factory. Where was Carl?

While I listened for his car, toddler Margaret approached me with a large denim laundry bag. I helped her climb inside and pulled the string at the top. She peeked out through the opening, a sprout of hair and one eye looking out. Five-year-old Joey came running in dressed in a green Robin Hood hat and cowboy scarf. A flowing green satin skirt open in the front revealed his bobbing penis. He sang a made-up song about living in a forest. With Margaret's one eye peering at him, the picture was funny, but I wasn't amused. I glanced at the clock. No sounds of a car, so I pulled off my sweater, furious and hurt that Carl ignored my plans.

Margaret—out of her bag now—grabbed a red wig off the floor and put it on her head, transforming herself to a stocky little Lucille Ball.

The play the children then devised comes as I like to remember it, a scene from my unconscious.

"I want to do mommies and daddies," Joey said. He started to clear a space and pushed the Big Wheel into a yellow bean bag chair.

"You see, the mommy is very sick. She's got these—" Joey explained.

"I be the daddy," Margaret insisted.

"Girls can't be daddies."

"I can!" The production commenced on her terms, and Joey lay on the floor, a mommy with a migraine.

At thirty minutes past the arranged time, I wanted to leave the children alone and go to my meeting. Not possible. I'd drive to the bar and put the children in Carl's hands. I removed the red wig from Margaret's head, gathered my materials, and ushered both children to my car. I might not be welcomed at the bar, but I didn't care. I had right on my side.

We arrived in an unfamiliar part of town, a shabby area empty of humanity. A blast of winter air pushed on us telling me to get back in the car, but—carrying Margaret and holding Joey by the hand—I headed for the door, energized by righteousness. Startled by the sign, "Jerry's Hole" at the entrance, I ignored what the sign might mean and went inside with the children. I had no regrets for spoiling Carl's fun.

It was too dark to see anything at first, but I could hear recorded music of a woman singing what I remember as "Killing Me Softly." This was not a jolly place for surfers and folk-music fans as I thought. It was more like a cave. A beer smell made my nose itch. A feeling of unease hit me. The atmosphere seemed erotic, as if lovers met here. The three of us hesitated in the doorway, and no one acknowledged us foreigners, a tall mommy with a little girl in her arms and a small boy at her side. Refugees just off the boat.

Couples on the dance floor emerged out of the smoky haze like ghosts meant to scare us. They were not ghosts. They were gay couples, and the realization shook me. I wanted to return to the safety of ignorance, but the children were clinging, holding me in place, and I had to face the fact that Carl had created a gay bar for his gay life.

I was close to forty! Why didn't I know? I hated myself for being so stupid, a child mother holding her toy children. As I think now about our children in that dark bar, I wonder about their perceptions of the scene.

We moved around the men on the dance floor toward my husband sitting at the bar, his large bulk dominating the room and his cigarette smoke hanging visible in the darkness above him. He wasn't wearing the shorts and torn T-shirt I'd imagined. Instead, his Hawaiian shirt, a bloom of blazing color, made him an overweight tourist to the islands. I walked toward him, determined to complete my errand. Bottles and glasses sparkled in the dim light. The curly-headed man behind the counter retreated.

Loud enough to clash with the music and be heard over it, I said, "Did you forget your promise to sit with the kids tonight?" I could hear anger in my voice and knew it was aimed at both him and me, a fury that scared me.

Carl turned around. He stared as if he didn't recognize me then stabbed out his cigarette, grabbed Joey, walked outside to his car—a chocolate-colored convertible parked at the curb—and placed Joey inside and drove away. For all I knew, they were off to Honolulu.

I followed with Margaret, heading toward home. My mind raced with thoughts about absences at night and lack of affection from my husband. Jerry's Hole? How could I not know?

Our white house rested on a perch above the Pacific, a huge seabird. Inside we could hear Julie Andrews singing "The hills are alive with the sound of music"—an offensive contrast to my life at the moment—coming from the television in the family room where Joey sat in front of the screen. Margaret joined him, silent.

In the kitchen doorway, I stopped, frozen by the sight of my husband glaring at me like a ferocious animal. He'd stolen my anger, taken the rage for himself. His energy seemed to permeate very detail of the room, including the painted dancers on my mother's Austrian wall plates and the carrot drawing on the face of the cupboards. The kitchen pulsed in a frenzied gallery of malice.

Carl jerked the hot electric coffeepot from the outlet and raised it above his head, aiming at me. I couldn't move, couldn't accept that he wanted to hurt me. I said nothing to stop him, having no idea how to protect myself. In the next instant the lid from the pot crashed to the floor and the boiling liquid poured down Carl's gaily-colored back. Every drop fell on him in slow motion, a lengthening, languid stream.

I felt relief. It was not me. Carl cried out and dropped to one knee, heaving for air like a man ending a race. He took hold of the counter and slowly lifted himself to his feet. The overhead lighting glared. The coffee smelled. Carl moaned. I went from a blur of fear and self-pity to stupefied amazement, barely able to process what happened.

"I'll take you to the doctor." Have I done this to you? Made you a gay man?

"No!" he cried, as if he'd heard my question. "I'll—handle—it," he said, his chest heaving.

The children appeared beside me and I touched their heads. "Daddy's hurt himself. It's okay," I said. "I need to clean up here, so you both stay out of the kitchen for now." Neither child asked anything or protested. They moved in tandem back to Julie Andrews, the Austrian hills and "a song they have sung for a thousand years."

Revelations have come to me often in kitchens: Joe told me he wanted to leave and go live with his father, John confessed to a love affair, Sally gave me sisterly advice, Janet swept the church kitchen and stonewalled, and then my husband collapsed in a kitchen after my intrusion into his private life. We women have been rooted in kitchens for a thousand years.

It took a time of reading, thinking, and therapy for me to accept that Carl and I needed to divorce. He protested ending the marriage and argued that he would keep his gay life away from home, but I persisted, knowing handsome gay husband would do well on his own. I dropped my wifely persona, started divorce proceedings, found a teaching job and bought a small house. My friends moved me in while I hummed the "Hokey Pokey."

Sitting at the church dinner in Arizona, memory of the crises with Carl vibrated with a screaming noise. No wonder people drank. Without that confrontation in a kitchen I'd never have examined my life enough to know I wanted to explore religion. Of course the sanctuary of the Christian church, its outstretched hand of grace, appealed to me. It was a refuge from the reality of bombs and hotrods and deceptions.

I gazed at the Christmas tree with its handmade snowflakes, feeling glad I'd come to this church where Sandra, like our own Tinkerbell, distracted us from darkness with stories, crazy plans, and what I now saw as an exuberant joy. She accepted the brass and the silver—the grumpy and the holy—in this church with an energy that changed and awakened us, especially me. I saw her in a new light—a Christmas light you could say—her earrings twinkling, her smile broad. Over the pull of depressing memory, I thought of how our church life nurtured me with Mrs. Ogg's music, the beauty of scripture and sanctuary, and the noisy clamor of "these people" like Sandra. How had I missed that?

Forgive us our trespasses.

Christmastime brought several things to an end: annoyance with Sandra, another church year, and my full commitment to ministry. The role of Christian minister demanded acceptance of a story I didn't believe. I could, like Auden, pray to become the person Jesus asks us to be but couldn't accept that he came into the world as messiah and redeemer. I'd been hiding too much from the congregation. My dedication to the religious life fluttered to the floor around me.

Christmas Eve morning dawned frosty but clear. No sign of storm. Dressed in my blue bathrobe, I stood at the living room window admiring rooftops touched with snow. I looked forward to the evening service at the church. I wanted the music and poetry to reach even the most jaded. No one except Lew knew of my secret plans for the occasion.

Below me the various greens in the pinions and juniper contrasted with the soft grays of the native brush. Three mammoth boulders in our yard—smoothed by the wind to a soft tan color—rested substantial, as eternal as the trinity of Father, Son, and Holy Ghost I couldn't accept. With the black-headed junco birds at the feeder, the scene fluttered with movement. Our bronze wind chime, its bells shaped like waves and fish, clanged bong bong, sounding the Pacific Ocean I'd left behind when I'd moved from playland to storms and solid darkness. Here in Northern Arizona I confronted real weather and felt like a grown-up.

On a low table, a small decorated fir tree smelled of forest green. John cursed while trying to position it but took care to show off each ornament to advantage. He always cursed at Christmas trees.

I'd miss that.

To the sounds of the shower, I checked the thermostat on the wall and started breakfast. As soon as the coffee was done, John came in, his greyhound body neatly dressed in a maroon velour shirt that gave him some bulk. He plugged in the string of lights. I filled our mugs.

"Want a fire?" John asked.

"Up to you." I glanced at the woodpile next to the fireplace. "Want me to do it?"

"No. I'll do it. After breakfast." John faced outside so he could see the birds between glances at *The Arizona Republic*. "My transfusion is scheduled the day after Christmas," he said, turning the pages. "Hate those things."

"You seem so much stronger afterward." I served our plates.

"Spooks me—the thought of having someone else's blood in my veins."

"Oh? It feels like you're being taken over?"

"Yeah. Like I'm losing myself. I hate it." He drank his coffee and set the mug on the table as if it was too heavy to hold.

"Sorry. You've sure been through a lot."

"Are you going over to the church today?" He wasn't reading the paper.

"Goodness no. The place has to sit empty for the day. I'll go over at six tonight to get ready. That's soon enough."

"I like the Christmas Eve service, but I think I'll skip this one tonight. Can't seem to work up energy by evening."

"I know," I said, sorry John would miss the dramatic scene I'd arranged. His absences from church events were getting more frequent.

The candlelight service would lighten winter dark and soften the feel of the cold. It didn't matter that the Jesus I'd studied wasn't really born in a stable. The story offered hope. *Christmas is God's gift.*

Everything at the church was ready for Christmas Eve worship. In front of the altar, decorated with two candelabra of nine candles each, Lew had set a rustic wooden cradle, spilling straw, to represent a manger.

People arrived early, including neighbors who were not members but considered Faith United their church. They contributed to our building fund, came to our rummage sales, planned their weddings and memorial services with us, and now filed into the church with an air of ownership. Millie and Curtis greeted at the door and handed everyone a small white candle. Mrs. Ogg, seated at her harp, began a medley of Christmas carols. At the sound of beginnings, I had the jitters of a stage director about to launch a massive production.

Becky and Dana burst in high with Christmas excitement, ready to do the scripture readings with me. Dressed in clean shirts, jeans, and big shoes, they added a homely touch to the candlelit delicacy of the atmosphere. In my office we practiced the Bible readings from an updated translation of the King James Bible. The girls were as anxious as I was.

At the appointed time on a cold winter night in the high desert of Arizona we three, another homely trinity, walked down the center aisle behind the choir singing "Hark! The Herald Angels Sing." A tall woman minister in black robe, red stole, and gold earrings—accompanied by two impish girls in clumpy shoes—moved toward the altar with its eighteen flickering candles.

Seated facing the congregation I noticed Johnie Fain wearing a winter fur. The Barringers looked as extraordinary as ever in glamorous clothes. Next to them was Tina of the heavenly tree. Stan Mattson beamed from the choir loft, along with sober Janet and a composed Virginia. In a sparkling Christmas shawl, Bernice sat with Fred. No sign of Marjorie McLellan's grieving husband, or John. Lew, standing alone in the back, counted the congregation, as always.

My thoughts went to the next days when I'd be taking months off to be with John. Leaving my church obligations to care for him was the Christian thing to do. What would people say if I kept office hours while my husband was at home weakening by the day? I had to do this duty but I didn't look forward to full-time caretaking.

I heard the rattle of guilt for my puny Christian soul as I stepped into the pulpit and read from Mary's "Magnificat" in Luke:

My soul magnifies the Lord,
And my spirit rejoices in God my Savior,

> For he has regarded the low estate of his
> handmaiden…
> He has scattered the proud in the imagination of
> their hearts,
> And has exalted those of low degree…

The choir sang "O Holy Night," including a contralto solo from Annette accompanied by hand-held chimes. Then Becky, standing at the lectern with her sister, began the nativity story:

> And in those days a decree went out from Caesar
> Augustus that all the world should be enrolled,
> each to his own city. And Joseph also went up from
> Galilee, from the city of Nazareth, to Judea, to the
> city of David, which is called Bethlehem…

When she came to the words "and she gave birth to her firstborn," a young woman in a long skirt with a filmy blue drape over her dark hair came down the center aisle holding her infant child. Everyone stopped breathing, including me. The Madonna stepped up into the chancel, placed the baby in the rustic cradle, and sat beside it. Neighbors, children, believers, skeptics, and the faithful members of Faith United Church watched the hypnotic figure of Mary gazing down into the face of her baby.

Mrs. Ogg—with no advance notice—began playing the Coventry Carol "Lullay, thou little tiny child" while I admired my staging of this surprise vision. When the song ended, I nodded at Dana, and she continued the reading her sister began:

> …But Mary kept all these things pondering them
> in her heart. And the shepherds returned, glorifying
> and praising God for all they had heard and seen…

After my Christmas prayer, Mrs. Ogg played "Silent Night" on the organ. We lit the hand-held candles with flames from the altar candles while Lew dimmed the overhead sanctuary lights and we sang all verses of the old German hymn. At the final words, "Jesus lord at thy birth" everyone carried their tiny candles outside into the night, except Lew and me. He and I tidied up and extinguished the eighteen altar candles, leaving us as shadows in the dark sanctuary.

*Great God of all mystery, if in the presence of death our thoughts are startled and our words flutter about like frightened birds, bring us stillness that we may cover the sorrow of our hearts with folded hands…*

"For the Time of Dying"
Book of Worship,
United Church of Christ

## THIRTEEN

In February we were told that John had only a short time left to live. "I can't imagine what you must be feeling," I said on the drive home from the doctor's office in Prescott. Black hills in the distance appeared ominous in front of us.

"I'm not surprised, just stunned, I guess," John said. "It doesn't scare me most of the time."

We didn't speak for a while, and the Chrysler clattered along. It felt wrong to be at the wheel when John always had done the driving.

"Doc said it would be painless if it's a hemorrhage," John said.

"I know. He said we should get hospice right away."

"Yeah, but I get to interview them. Can't stand those bleeding-heart types."

"They've got a social worker now, a man who comes by to talk. I think you'll like him."

I'd been on a leave of absence from the church since Christmas, managing John's needs and taking care of our home. Spring was on its way again with flowering fruit trees and the sound of a mower on the golf course—the same season when John had come to live with me in Dewey. The thought that he would die in the spring gave a roundness to our lives, a cycle of rebirth and death I preached about. Looking back, I doubt I had poetic thoughts about cycles of rebirth. Only in retrospect do images of the "roundness of spring" come.

I turned up the driveway and into the garage. "Better get this car checked," John said as he walked up the stairs ahead of me. His khaki pants hung loosely, and his head tilted to one side. I felt diminished to the size of a sapling beside a windblown pine.

We now had an oxygen tank in the laundry room, the tube snaking through the house, following John like a transparent worm. Television kept us distracted from the silence, particularly *Law and Order*. I thought the justice that prevailed at the end of those programs affirmed the existence of God. I doubt if John felt so theological.

John still watched the progress of the struggles in the Middle East. He identified with fighters, like the giant Goliath he'd once portrayed in a children's play back in San Diego. I was a single mom then, teaching at the high school. Before seminary. Before we met. He was a unique figure when I first saw him, a loner with a melancholy face.

The Barbie minister, Carole Keim, had persuaded me to direct *David and Goliath*, a musical extravaganza to be presented during a service at the church across the street from my house in San Diego.

On entering the sanctuary with Margaret the first afternoon of rehearsals, I stopped to breathe in the atmosphere because the thick-walled white interior, lit by wrought-iron hanging lamps, had a Southwestern religious feeling that settled the spirit. How lucky Carole was to work in that enchanted space.

Margaret and I headed for the little actors and big adults milling in the front of the sanctuary. My eleven-year-old daughter, cast as a soldier in the Israelite army chorus, joined the youngsters chattering and hiding between the dark pews while I walked down the center aisle toward the cross.

Reverend Carole Keim stood talking to a bald man in casual clothes. He looked pale among the tan children and older than the parents on the sidelines. Goliath. He'd be a perfect contrast with the little red-headed David, a nine-year-old girl who'd already introduced herself—"I'm Gillian"—and scampered away.

In the chancel alcove, with altar, pulpit, and choir loft, I studied how the space could be used for a chorus of children and the two performers I'd already noticed. Reverend Keim gestured for me to join her, so I stepped down the three-carpeted steps toward her and the bald man who grew taller as I approached.

"This is John Greensmith, Elaine. He's our Goliath!" Carole said before she dashed off, a sheaf of papers in her hand.

"I knew you were the giant. I'm happy to meet you."

"I'm not sure I'm happy about anything," the giant answered in a deep priestly voice, appropriate to this sanctuary.

"Not to worry. It can be painless. I can make you look good."

"No you can't." He glanced away.

"Just say your lines and don't bump into the cross," I said with all the cheer I could muster.

"I don't bump into crosses," he said, not missing a beat. "I carry them."

I took a harder look at this gloomy man. Large blue eyes dominated his face, and his smooth head gave him a Kojak appearance—a little threatening and very attractive. "How did Reverend Keim get you to do this?"

"I have no idea. She played on my goodwill I guess."

I liked the irony in Greensmith's manner and paid more attention, pretending to assess his talent. You couldn't miss his sad blue eyes.

In the following performance, John read his lines from the back of his shield and the congregation tittered. Margaret had a grand time being one of the soldiers in her paper helmet, a girl with a warrior temperament.

"You were a splendid Goliath," I told John later that month as we walked a path through a green quad at Pomona College where

Greensmith and I were delegates to a state-wide church conference held at the college that summer. Under leafy sycamores, we licked our ice cream cones like children in a forest paradise. I assumed John was a vanilla sort of person, but he chose chocolate. I had the vanilla.

"You've a comic talent."

"I come by it naturally," he said. "My father and grandfather were ministers."

"Great heavens! A preacher's kid. You poor thing." I liked walking next to this imposing figure, a man inches taller than I. He had a sober face and a gentle modesty. Compared to my former husband, Carl—given to flowing colorful caftans, bursts of song, and outrageous plans—John seemed composed, dignified. "Did your father make pious demands on you?"

"He tried, but I had a flawless sister." His voice had the deep tones of the actor James Earl Jones. "She pleased my father so much he ignored me." Slowing his pace he regarded his cone as if it might tell him something.

"I've a perfect sister too. She's tough as nails—farms in Michigan where she's raising five kids. We're complete opposites." I tossed my napkin into a trash container, sorry the ice cream was gone.

We approached a familiar garden behind the music building. Through wrought iron gates, I saw a statue of Pan, sleek and wistful, in the center of a circle of flowers. I remembered him from years before. "This is where I went to college, and it brings memories of being so innocent," I said, longing to be eighteen again instead of a divorced single mother teaching in inner-city San Diego.

"I don't think I was ever innocent. I'm a photographer, sports mostly now, but I also love crime—big surprise. I'm one of those guys who hangs out of helicopters and clings to rooftops to get the shot. I'm pretty damn good."

Impressed by the daring romantic image, I waited for more. When he didn't continue, I said, "John, I passed by your dorm room yesterday—the door was open— and I saw you looking, well, miserable. Sorry I snooped, but is something wrong? Don't you feel well?"

"Oh, depends on your definition of *well*. I tend to collapse when discouraged—which is too often I guess."

"What's the matter? Are you discouraged now?"

"It's a lot of things. I've lost faith in God, which lends an absurdity to my coming to this conference, and I've just been through a horrible divorce. Want to hear more?"

"Not at the moment. Let's just—"

He talked on anyway, partly to himself, "One of my sons hasn't forgiven me for the break-up of my marriage. I was an unfaithful husband." I wanted no more news, but he kept talking. "I'm not the great success I'd planned to be when I was in the Navy staring off into the Pacific." He stopped and finished his ice cream. "I loved that war, number two that is. I mean I loved the adventure, the uniform and all. I was eighteen."

"Did you see combat?" *An unfaithful husband?*

"No, but I wanted to. We all wanted to be heroes. I can't shake this sense of failure. It doesn't make for jolly company. The woman I fell in love with left me, so I failed there too. Can't seem to get over it."

"Sounds like you've had an exciting life."

He paused. "I still get royalties on my Elvis shots."

"Elvis? Shades of the fifties! Are you a fan?"

"I'm not a fan of anything."

That was the beginning. In time, John ceased mourning over his losses and we began a relationship. After I finished two years of seminary, we married, and I thought I'd at last found true love. As for the matter of an unfaithful husband, I didn't worry. Our marriage would be different.

John's death approached just as I found my footing in the Wild West and discarded fears of fat men with guns and fears of failing as a minister. I've saved these words by Apollinaire from that time:

> "Come to the edge," he said.
> They said, "We are afraid"
> "Come to the edge," he said.
> They came. He pushed them.

And we fell into the necessities of time and disease.

A frail but courageous Goliath, John never descended into

a depression or retreated from me during those weeks. There was a serenity about him, and his sarcasm had disappeared. Our conversation was about daily things. We established an unspoken accord in our words, in our silences. He took the lead and I followed. I'd lost control—of the future, of the day's events, of my feelings.

Keeping house, as Mother called it, was my role, and I soon grew weary of being always loving and helpful, a perpetual saint. The Benedictines may find holiness in tedious tasks, but I couldn't. I preferred showing off my talents preaching and teaching, or gazing out of my office window where God might appear. At the new K-Mart pharmacy I bought John's medications and lingered over the appliances and cheap clothes, dreading to return home where I was confronted by guilt—enough coins to keep me supplied until old age—for wanting the dying process to hurry, for not having enough compassion.

Church members helped vary our days, and I was grateful for their attention. John was up and dressed every day, ready to greet them as they carried flowers from their gardens—roses, tulips, yellow hyacinth—and their visits brought the outdoors inside. We talked of the weather, changes at church, their anticipation of fresh fruit from their trees. No topic was trivial as we enjoyed the treats they brought with them.

Visits from hospice volunteers helped break the tedium too. They enlisted the French nurse who'd attended Ardith at the Goodman's, but John protested that the nurse was too small. He wanted a tougher one. The second nurse was a stout older woman with a serious face, very acceptable. The social worker met John's standards as well. They spoke together like old friends. We were in competent hands.

One evening, at his desk next to the fireplace, John began to compose a letter to the congregation, his broad back in a beige shirt bending over his project. He turned and asked me, as I faced outdoors watching the sunset, what he should write. The sky was an Arizona wonder; then the colors disappeared and it was just the two of us in a fading room.

"Be yourself," I said, "and don't forget to be funny."

"Sometimes I think you love me only for my rapier wit."

"You got that right."

"Saying good-bye is hard," he said, holding the framed school photo of his twelve-year-old grandson, Justin. "I'll miss this guy." The boy had John's stillness, his ironic humor, his tall frame and blue eyes. It was as if John was saying good-bye to himself. He shook his head, tears filling his eyes.

"I know." I stood over him and put my arms around his shoulders, feeling his warmth, the thinness of his body, and a persistent, powerful heartbeat.

After a week or so, John rested on the couch in front of the television frowning at the glass of green vegetable juice in his hand, a celery-smelling concoction. He drank part of the mixture and then headed for the bathroom where he vomited. I helped him into bed. His debility frightened me and I called hospice. They reached Charlotte, a neighborhood hospice volunteer and church member, who arrived and called the hospice nurse who came right away and immediately telephoned the doctor. The nurse asked if John wanted to see the doctor at his office. We relayed his answer, a ringing "Bullshit," and we laughed.

Three days later, Charlotte sat with John while I napped until she awakened me. "He's going." I lay next to him and curled around his body while she stood back from us in the doorway waiting like the Silver Wolf in the snow, witness to the death of a lop-eared rabbit. John quivered briefly, made throaty sounds, and settled into death. Silenced, I felt vanished with him. After some moments I got up and looked at Charlotte.

When the mortuary people left with John's body, and after medicines were cleared away and family called, I sent Charlotte home and waited in the stillness. John was gone. Dazed and unfocused, I didn't collapse into tears. My grief had a desert dryness, an unhinged feeling. I wandered: to John's green chair, to our bed, but mostly to the windows where I could watch. The wide skies had the same blue; the clouds continued to dominate over the mountains. The birds visited the feeders; the trees and flowers bloomed. I had to make sense of that.

People came to the house, letting me know they cared. Lew

repaired our shower curtain, and I felt as grateful to him as if he'd remodeled the whole house. Clergy colleagues dropped in and offered prayer. Church members brought food. One white-haired lady brought a "better than sex" cake, a gift I'll not forget. Because I had no circle of close friends in Arizona, I had no visits from confidants, but the house filled with attentive people.

Family began to arrive. Mother had died by then, but Margaret and Joe, along with John's sister, his three adult sons and young grandson, came to attend John's memorial service. Margaret felt deeply the loss of her stepfather. He'd visited her in rehab, stood with me through her run-ins with the police, kept faith in her. His photos of her baby are among her treasures.

Mrs. Ogg's music and the prayers of my colleagues at his memorial service, along with the surrounding faces, comforted me as if they'd placed their hands on my heart. I like to think God's mercy was mediated to me in that rush of love from everyone.

John's written message to the congregation was handed out to everyone at the service:

> Thank you for being here. I'm sorry I can't be with you, but I've been called away. As the epitaph on the tombstone of a well-known hypochondriac stated, "See, I told you I was sick!"
>
> I don't have the proper words to express my love for my dear wife, Elaine. She was always a loving, caring, and cheerful companion. Elaine is one of those rare persons God lets us experience. I was blessed to have her in my life...
>
> I also want to extend my love to my grandson, Justin, who has been a continual joy to me. We seemed to have had a very special bond...To my extended family at Faith United, thank you for your love, concern, and support.
>
> So that's it. It was a good life in so many ways. I would have liked to stay longer, but that was not up to me. I leave you with my love.

Given his dark moods and his disappointments in himself, John could have shaken a grim fist at everyone, including God and me, but he didn't. I know the full story of our marriage was more complicated than this simple tribute, but we'd managed despite everything, and we managed in full view of a congregation.

After everyone left, Rosemary of the lovely tea service spirited me off to Scottsdale in southern Arizona to go shopping. I felt dizzy as we wandered the stores, reminding me of Mother's unsteadiness after my father's death. I bought an ugly jacket and came home cheered. The Stricklands treated me at a nice restaurant, and it was a pleasure to be cared for. The Goodmans offered a meal at the country club where our table overlooked the new green of the golf links.

Though I wasn't able to look at John's photographs at first, after a while I took the large black-and-white portfolio of horses, movie stars, and prizefighters on a pilgrimage to people he'd designated. One mounted, poster-sized image went to the owner of the shop who'd done some excellent developing work for him. One to the couple who'd driven him to the doctor. One to the handyman who'd done repairs when John became too weak. Delivering them felt important.

I sensed a welcome freedom. The frightening edge was gone. I felt lighter, as if I could move more easily, sing with new energy. At Faith United Church, it was a blessing to have my work, but I also explored other activities. Three women clergy had by that time been hired by churches in our area, and we became friends. Letting my hair grow longer I appeared as the fairy godmother in *The Velveteen Rabbit* at the Prescott community theater. I went Western line-dancing in a Whisky Row saloon, wishing Marjorie McLellan could see me in a fringed shirt.

My huge teacher's desk was now in a room I converted to an office. John's two sons hauled it to a spot under a window before they returned to California. I piled the desk with word-processor, pens, notes, and photos, intending to write a memoir, a story of children and church and John and Carl and me. My sister returned my letters to her, so I had those narratives along with journals I'd kept.

I wrote a poem while I leaned against a tree in the White Mountains of Arizona:

The writing life—so untouched and private—
pulls me to myself in this unmoving place of green.

This tree wants me to be

Authorial.
Centered.
Regal.

But I hear the golden river moving, spilling out,
And it giggles a bit at pen and words,
And solid serious trees.

The giggling river expressed my embarrassment and fears about putting real feelings on paper, but in time I began to reread the old letters and look at photos, getting encouragement from my sister to lean against a supportive tree and write. I didn't start, though, until I gave in to another push.

I was painting my front door a fresh green and discovered a dead mouse, in bright green at the bottom of my paint bucket. It was a message from the universe. Dead and green. Ends and beginnings. It was time to tell the truth and resign. My focus upon a religious quest had diminished as much as John's deep voice had faded. My pose at the pulpit was hypocritical.

I'd served a rich five years but the role of compassionate minister who listened and looked into the faces of the troubled and lonely exhausted me. My will was failing and wanted rest from trying. Without a depth of Christian faith to give me energy to serve, the tasks were too draining. By the end of the year, weariness in the role told me my commitment was over. The mouse had expired.

So I gave in to a shove from something that didn't feel at all like that rental Buick from five years ago and chose to move into an unknown I hoped was green with new life. A year after John's death, I wrote to my sister telling her that by the time she got my letter…

I will have submitted my resignation. I am retiring
in June. There is no way I can keep doing this,
though I love these people and the preaching and

teaching. My real problem is, of course, the limiting boundaries of the Christian mind-set, or theology, or whatever. I feel dishonest.

I'm genuinely frightened about being free, which is what I want. I am just getting used to being alone, and now this decision! What kind of craziness is this, I ask in bad moments. However, I know better...

I woke up this morning to forsythia! And plum blossoms! They popped overnight, after unseasonal warmth and lots of rain...I'm thinking about getting a used dog—one that can't live in the home he has. I'll be visiting him this weekend...

Update on Margaret: She is working steadily, and her new husband got a raise. Her ex continues to be quite weird, but she's dealing with that less violently. She makes birthday cakes, takes my granddaughter, Katherine, to speech therapy, and collects tropical fish. It makes you believe in God.

# END WORDS

I was not an easy fit for Christian ministry from the beginning. I'd set down my class register at the high school and gone to seminary thinking I'd gain spiritual strength and become an authentic person representing Jesus. But I was not like the other ministerial candidates, and what awaited me in Berkeley were students who came from church backgrounds, believing families—kindly folk who I thought were rather dull. I assumed I'd be a more enlightened minister than they were, but I wasn't. I was faking it a lot of the time while they were serving churches with unconditional belief. My hope is that my time at Faith United Church had meaning for the members and was nurturing for them. I know it was for me.

John's image returns to me often—blue sad eyes, beige windbreaker, a deep voice. I wish we'd found a greyhound dog for him. I wish a lot of things. Memories of him come when I hear references to the Gulf War or see a bald man in aviator sunglasses. In a photograph of us, John's thin body leans toward me, and I'm leaning too—on his humor, his creative soul, his grace in the face of death.

Mrs. Ogg, my blessed archangel, died a few years after my ministry ended. She was a Catholic and an active member of All Saints Church, a fitting name. While our church was going about our business in Dewey, Mrs. Ogg founded a day camp for Girl Scouts, painted china, taught piano, and raised three children in Prescott. Our other musician, Timothy Haasen, a disguised character, left Faith United shortly after I did.

Carl Ludlow, my first husband, died in a hospital in San Diego a few months after John died. Our son, Joe, keeps the memory of his father by displaying his art collection, using his dishes and preserving his Mercedes. I remember Carl's exuberant personality, his complex character, and know he was the most confounding human being I've ever known. He certainly suffered more than coffee burns. If the times had been accepting of gays, his life and mine would have been so different. I know first-hand what secrecy did to us, and my failure to help the Dewey congregation discuss opening our church to gays weighs heavily on me.

Margaret now has two daughters. She's a hairdresser and a vibrant, funny person who loves to update me with news of her exploits as an almost-respectable married woman. The mystery of her birth heritage was solved when she turned thirty-five, a few months after I finished the first draft of this memoir. She found the Comanche woman who is her birth mother, a woman with the same wide face and tawny skin. Her meeting with a Native American family, mother, brother, and grandmother, has brought her peace. She no longer feels she lives in a cloud, she says.

Rosemary Barringer died young. A brain tumor took her. LaVerne McLachlan died not long after from the effects of Alzheimer's disease, and her husband, Lew, died a few years later. His death deeply affected me, and I wept uncontrollably. The church wrapped its arms around the McLachlan family, but we were unable to honor Rosemary in a memorial because Grant had a service for her in California. Sandra Mattson died after a struggle with cancer, her bravery astounding. Johnie Fain is gone too, as are Cal Appleton, Fred Miller, and Stan Mattson.

Becky and Dana have become young adults, of course; one of them married early, the ceremony held in my living room on the common carpet. The mysteries surrounding others mentioned in this memoir—Bernice's daughter's fate, Cal's wife's disappearance, Sarah's past history—have not been solved by time or disclosures. I didn't pursue answers. It was not my business.

I take my skepticism about Christian dogma with me into retirement. I've not changed my views about Jesus, who, I believe, was a fine Mediterranean teacher and healer, but I cannot accept that he was sent by God to die for the sins of the world. Those disagreements with Christian doctrine have continued to estrange me from church life since I retired from ministry, even though I feel certain that God is with us as we join together to do more than we could alone. Only small gatherings can meet my needs now.

Critics of organized religion continue to say the church should be dismantled. In John Updike's novel *A Month of Sundays*, I remember reading that the church should let its "adamantine walls explode, releasing us to the soft desert air." I've heard that sort of comment for years, but I don't agree. Progressive churches need to stay the course and confront biblical literalists who challenge rationality, argue for creationism, protest sex education and a diverse society that openly includes gays. I'm aware, of course, that I'm advocating for courage I never could summon.

I did not leave northern Arizona. The land of the rising phoenix has become as necessary to me as music in a minor key. I've stayed here to watch—from down below—the graceful hawks dip and turn. Here is where I've met myself on the dusty roads and in my office, sneezing. I find bits of the sacred here and reminders to look around the corners and into the storms.

I've tried in this memoir to open the doors of one small church where a group of people stayed together and helped each other *become*. Our spiritual center was in that effort, I think, and in the choices we made to value each other and our church. I like to think that God brooded over us like the mother eagle at Lynx Creek. At times now, when the bustle ceases, I can hear Mrs. Ogg playing beloved melodies on her golden harp. Those sounds are enough.

Prescott, Arizona 2011